Rebecca Bender is a true leader in the fight against trafficking. She provides a voice to the voiceless. She is an inspiration and an expert who is changing the world with action.

Ashton Kutcher, cofounder of Thorn

I firmly believe every person on the planet has been created to live in complete freedom, not just physical freedom but emotional and spiritual freedom. In *In Pursuit of Love*, Rebecca's journey of transformation and healing will encourage you with the truth that redemption is possible—even in our darkest moments.

Christine Caine, founder of A21 and Propel Women

Rebecca is a powerful example of transformation, resilience, and courage. *In Pursuit of Love* will bring you to tears as she talks about her harrowing journey of escaping sex trafficking and how she now puts her life on the line to help others find their freedom. This book will open your eyes to one of the biggest epidemics of our time, and Rebecca will inspire you with her strength and unshakable faith.

DeVon Franklin, producer and bestselling author

In Pursuit of Love is a raw story of redemption, healing, and the relentless love of God. It is a powerful book from Rebecca Bender, who—through the love of Jesus—is bringing hope to so many.

Bill Johnson, Bethel Church, Redding, California, author of *The Way of Life* and *Raising Giant-Killers*

Rebecca not only learned to embrace the loving power of God's transformative power but is on a quest to see others break out of the captivity of sex trafficking. But her book isn't just for people who want to end trafficking; it is a beautiful story of God's pursuit of someone who looks unchangeable and will leave you with so much hope.

Shawn Bolz, author of *Through the Eyes of Love* and *Breakthrough*, host of *Translating God* on TBN and *Exploring the Prophetic* podcast

This story will rock your world! We have to put an end to violence against women, and Rebecca has taken the time to explore her own heart in hopes of breaking stereotypes in ours. Light and love will prevail even in the darkest times—Rebecca's story is proof.

Rosanna Arquette, actor, activist, and producer

Insider information into the underground world of modern-day slavery is paramount to recognizing the warning signs and helping victims escape. Rebecca's bravery teaches each of us something about what it means to have the courage to help others.

John Douglas, the FBI's architect for criminal personality profiling and the inspiration for the Netflix series *Mindhunter*

Rebecca is a force to be reckoned with, but more than that, she inspires us to let God's power renew and restore the worst of circumstances.

Tommy Barnett, global pastor, Dream City Church, Phoenix, Los Angeles Dream Center

Rebecca's riveting story takes us through a dark world of exploitation to redemption. She inspires us to believe in deliverance—for others and for ourselves.

Ambassador Swanee Hunt, founder and chair of Demand Abolition

Rebecca vulnerably shows us what God can do when he truly plucks us from the pit of hell and sets our feet on a solid rock. It is a compelling and gripping journey that will radically shift your heart and open your eyes as to how our young people are being sold a lie of false empowerment. Her story inspires us not to let our past hold us back from all God has for us.

Caitlin Zick, codirector of Moral Revolution, author of *Look at You, Girl*

Rebecca is an absolutely incredible woman of faith who is shaking the grounds of normalcy within society. She gives us the raw truth of what is currently happening around us that people often turn a blind eye to. *In Pursuit of Love*, each page distinctively shows us that God pursues us in the depths of our despair and reminds us that he wants a relationship with each one of us, right where we're at.

Will Hart, CEO of Iris Global

In Pursuit of Love is a book you won't be able to put down! It captures Rebecca's story of brokenness, heartbreak, freedom, and redemption. Her story is one that needs to be heard because it reminds us that God will use *all* things for his glory!

Christa Smith, international speaker, codirector of Pointblank International

IN PURSUIT OF *love*

IN PURSUIT OF *love*

One Woman's Journey from Trafficked to Triumphant

A True Story

REBECCA BENDER

 ZONDERVAN®

ZONDERVAN

In Pursuit of Love
Copyright © 2020 by Rebecca Bender

Requests for information should be addressed to:
Zondervan, 3900 Sparks Dr. SE, Grand Rapids, Michigan 49546

Zondervan titles may be purchased in bulk for educational, business, fundraising, or promotional use. For information, please email SpecialMarkets@Zondervan.com.

ISBN 978-0-310-35685-1 (softcover)

ISBN 978-0-310-35687-5 (audio)

ISBN 978-0-310-35686-8 (ebook)

Published in association with The Blythe Daniel Agency, Inc., P.O. Box 64197, Colorado Springs, CO 80962.

Cover design: Brock Book Design Co.
Author photo: April Haberman / Photophire
Cover photos: Odyssey Stock / Stocksy / © PicsFive / Depositphotos
Interior design: Denise Froehlich

Printed in the United States of America

19 20 21 22 23 24   LSC   10 9 8 7 6 5 4 3 2 1

To my talented, feisty, independent, incredible daughters,
Deshae, Ila, Evie, and Stella. You were born for greatness,
and someday you too will have a story to tell.

To my incredible husband, Matt. My whole life
I've been searching for you. I am blessed to have
found a man who embodies true love. Thank
you for supporting me on this journey.

CONTENTS

AUTHOR NOTE

Trauma and time are peculiar things—they hide memories in deep neurological caves. Sometimes the only thing that draws them out is the bait of our senses: taste, touch, hearing, sight, smell. I've taken years to process my trauma and my healing by seeking after inner-healing sessions and various trauma therapies. I've revisited Las Vegas and sat in the parking lot of my daughter's elementary school, memories of our morning rituals flooding my mind. I've sought the *why*, in hopes of explaining what happened. *Why* didn't I run? *Why* did I stay? *Why* did I go left instead of right? *Why* didn't I call home?

I've done my best to remember the facts as accurately as possible, but time and trauma blur details. Did we meet that one person at a birthday party or a dinner reception? Did that incident happen during the second arrest or the third, in 2002 or 2004? Was the traumatic event at this hotel or that one? Though maybe later I'll recall or learn more, trust that I've done my best as of today.

During the indictment, my trafficker told me he took a twelve-month plea deal. For years, when I shared my story, I said he was sentenced to twelve months in prison. When validating my story with the federal government more recently, I learned that he actually had been sentenced to twenty-four months. He lied. And I believed the lie.

I have purposely left out stories that would have made this book too long or provided too much explicit content. Telling a thirty-something-year-old's story in a few thousand words isn't easy, and not every detail made the final cut.

This is real life. Things are messy, and we're simply remembering the best we can. But the story remains the same whether I made a person a blond, brunette, or redhead. And whether an event took place in the Venetian or the Bellagio doesn't change the importance of what happened.

Rebecca Bender, October 2018

PROLOGUE

The phone rang. I sat up in bed and looked at the digital clock on the nightstand. The vibrant red of 6:00 a.m. glared at me. I turned to look at Kevin, who was already getting up, pulling on his sweatpants with one hand, and holding his phone out on speaker in the other.

"They're here." My wife-in-law Brandi was trying to be calm, but her voice quivered with fear. "The feds are in the driveway."

I was suddenly wide awake.

"Hide the money in the curtain hems," Kevin told her mechanically. "Flush the SIM card. And keep your mouth shut."

Through the phone I could hear a pounding on Brandi's door and a muffled voice. "Brandi Dudley, this is Federal Agent Mark Parsons. We have a warrant for your arrest."

Kevin paced back and forth at the end of the bed, making me anxious despite his cool and collected voice. "We'll call the lawyer as soon as his office opens. Stay strong."

"No worries," Brandi said. "I love you." Then she was gone.

He hung up and turned to me with an intensely focused look. "Get the kids," he ordered. "The feds will come here next."

I jumped out of bed.

When I was little, I wanted to be an artist when I grew up. Then a kindergarten teacher. By middle school I had become a class clown, putting on plays in the classroom and spending weekends practicing *Saturday Night Live* skits with my cousin. After taking an ROTC elective class in high school, I entertained the thought of becoming a sniper but was accepted into Oregon State University with the more realistic goal of studying architecture.

I never dreamed of being a prostitute. This wasn't the life I was promised when my "boyfriend" told me he loved me and wanted me and my baby to move with him to Vegas.

As an only child growing up in the eighties, I had been taught about "stranger danger," but I was never taught how to tell whether you were dating a con artist or how to tell when you were being brainwashed. No one explained how a pimp enforced his indoctrination through fear, sleep deprivation, or social ostracism when you didn't comply with his rules, or, if you did, how you'd be rewarded with shopping sprees, new cars, and lavish vacations. No one mentioned the risks of federal prison, complex PTSD, and an addiction to money.

Would Brandi talk? Would she snitch on our "organized crime family," which the feds had charged with four million dollars of tax evasion? What about the other wives? Would they talk? Would they sacrifice me? Would they tell on Kevin? I couldn't be certain, but what I did know was that being indicted for federal crimes was not the snake oil I had been sold.

"Come with me and I'll leave you in despair," says no boyfriend ever.

CHAPTER 1 **vice night**

Then I passed by and saw you kicking about in your blood,
and as you lay there in your blood I said to you, "Live!"

September 2006

I zipped into the handicapped spot closest to the parking garage elevator and hooked the fake blue handicap placard around my rearview mirror. My brick-red Christian Dior pumps and matching pencil skirt weren't ideal for the long-distance trek from the upper decks of the parking garage into the lobby of the Paris Las Vegas Hotel and Casino.

Of all my working spots, this was far from my favorite one on the track. Though the Paris was better than the dingy, smoke-infested Tropicana, high-dollar clients stayed in the palatial suites of the Wynn, Venetian, or Bellagio. The Paris ranked about a seven out of ten on the Las Vegas working girl's scale. An average trick in the Paris would probably spend around $500 on a call girl. But I had become accustomed to much higher-paying buyers.

As I checked my makeup in the rearview mirror, my mind buzzed with stories of girls getting robbed late at night in garages. I puckered my lips, applied another layer of Ruby Rouge, and dialed the escort service. Maddy answered.

"Hey, it's Kelby. I'm here," I said.

Maddy's bubbly personality won over most of the customers at Girls To You, one among dozens of Vegas escort services. The most lucrative phone girls could "hear" money, but not Maddy. She was friendly, and everyone liked her, but booking the biggest calls wasn't her strength.

"Okay, Kelb." She practically sang my name. "23145 Johnson. $150 pick-up." Her giving my fake name a nickname cracked me up, though it was a common practice among the phone girls.

"Thanks," I said, feigning gratitude. All of us, even the phone girls, wanted the biggest, best call of the night.

Vegas escort services stay legal by claiming to send a dancer to a hotel room for $150. Anything the girl and the john discuss is between two consenting adults, allowing the booking agency to claim no knowledge of having hired such a girl if she ends up in a bust. The company gets the $150 pick-up, the phone girl gets a 20 percent tip, and the working girl keeps the rest.

Of course, the phone girls wanted to send the best of us to draw a larger tip. If one of us started tips at $600, then the phone girl racked up $100 simply by answering the phone. We'd give $150 to the service, $100 to the phone girl, and $500 to the pimp. Fifteen hundred dollars for "full service" (the nice way to say sex) was always the goal, even if the john had to put it on a credit card. I usually took anything between $500 and $1500. I hated negotiating, but what I hated more was pissing off the buyer and risking getting hurt.

When I stepped out of my air-conditioned car into the parking garage, a wall of heat hit me. Though it was ten o'clock at night, stifling temperatures oozed from the concrete jungle. A rim of sweat lined my forehead as the elevator bell dinged and the doors slid open.

My already aching feet were grateful for the dated brownish-orange floral carpet that lined the casino's halls. As I walked,

I studied Toni Braxton's airbrushed cheekbones on the posters advertising the hotel's current shows, *Rock-and-Roll Relived* and *Toni Braxton*.

An escalator swept me down another floor to the shopping area. Under a painted blue sky, Parisian-style streetlamps held signs that beckoned guests toward the casino, hotel, parking, and boutiques, where customers could buy crystal at Swarovski or the latest designer scent at Perfume de Paris.

I grabbed the escalator rail, white-knuckled, and steadied my high heels to brave the bumpy cobblestones. Years of experience proved helpful in maneuvering over the uneven ground. I breezed past two dueling pianos arranged like jigsaw pieces, where two smiling men pounded out requests pulled from the fishbowl perched atop their Yamahas. Inside a bar, a boisterous crowd sang off-key while swinging mugs of beer in tempo with an eighties ballad.

I inhaled the savory decadence that wafted from the crepe kiosk. The white-aproned chef poured the batter on the buttered crepe stone as I walked by; the smell of sautéed mushrooms and onions teased my taste buds. He gracefully scooped the dinner crepe into a perfect triple fold and plated it with a dash of parsley. I promised my rumbling stomach we'd pay him a visit on the way out. Just past the crepe man, I squinted at the bright lights of the casino. As I approached, the sky-blue ceiling soared and the air around me seemed to lift with it. Painted birds flew through clouds as the slot machines chinked and gamblers barked at the craps table.

The intoxicating smell of money—the scent of Vegas—saturated the Parisian air. I inhaled its alluring scent.

To avoid the drunk, gambling oglers and the casino security guards, I took the route that would draw the least attention. I beelined through the gift shop and landed at the elevator corridor. On a regular basis, rookie girls would fall prey to the cameras and be abruptly escorted to the exit doors.

"23145," I repeated while scanning the corridor options: floors 1–15, 16–35, and 36–42. I headed to the second option and selected the twenty-third floor. When the elevator dinged, I stepped into the immaculate hallway, complete with dazzling white crown molding. I wasn't expecting this from the often-outdated Paris. A shiny marble floor led to a central foyer, where a huge white square pillar stood. Large mirrors flanked the pillar, and underneath sat dark wood benches topped with light-blue satin cushions.

Three hallways led to the rooms: 100–145, 200–245, and 300–345. The luxurious combination of marble, blue satin, and the location of room 145 at the end of the hall brought me to one delightful conclusion: I was heading to a suite with a high-dollar view. I reveled in the familiar smell of luxury and anticipated a heftier tip.

Not bad, Maddy. Not bad at all.

I knocked on the door of room 145. A forty-something man with a dirty-blond ponytail opened the door. His muscles bulged beneath his flannel shirt as he smiled at me and gestured me inside.

"I'm Mitch," he said.

"My name's Kelby." I extended my manicured hand.

"Kelby?" He shook my hand slowly and scanned me from head to toe.

"Yep. Kelly with a B." I smiled, quickly assessing the room: a rental car key on the nightstand, luggage without a baggage claim sticker, an ice chest loaded with a few beers perched on the dresser, and an old guitar amp on a table near the window.

I sat on the end of the bed and straightened my pinched feet, grateful to sit down.

"So, where you from?"

"Missouri," he replied with a thick Manhattan accent.

"Oh yeah? Sounds like you're from the East Coast." I flirted.

"Originally from there but moved to Missouri a couple years ago." He cracked open a cold beer and tipped it toward me, inviting me to join him.

I shook my head to decline. "Did you drive here from Missouri?" I said pointing to his car keys. "That's quite the drive."

"No." He laughed. "I flew in and picked up the rental at the airport. I have a ton of work to do while I'm here."

Who brings an ice chest on a plane? I thought. But I played it cool, forcing a calm appearance despite my increasing suspicion that he wasn't an average buyer.

"What kind of work do you do?"

"Uh . . ." His eyes scanned the room. "Well, I um . . . I am doing some . . . I'm here for a . . . tool tradeshow." He looked up at me. "I make this tool that helps the back of slot machines when something drops down inside, like if a mechanic drops a screw. I use this amp to demonstrate at the tradeshow." He pointed to the heavy piece of equipment on the table.

How did he get that thing on the plane? Why couldn't he simply use an old slot machine? Something wasn't right.

"So how much is this going to cost?" he said, trying to change the subject.

"Well, the service sent me to your room for $150. This will get you a strip tease for up to an hour. Anything you tip above that goes directly to me, and your tip will determine your entertainment." We were careful to commit to "up to" an hour so if they didn't tip, we could leave after one song of dancing. Most men were too preoccupied to catch our disclaimer.

"How much for sex? $500? Will $500 get me laid?" he blurted.

Sensing his nerves, I tried to play along. "Sweetheart." I

smiled, tipped my chin, and batted my eyes. "Prostitution is illegal." This guy wasn't taking my hint. "Let's slow down." I patted the bed, luring him to sit next to me. "So, why did you move from Missouri? That's a long way from New York."

He sat down and rested his hand on my leg, trying to relax. He jiggled his left leg.

"My brother and I started our business there."

"Really? You relocated from New York to Missouri for business? Why didn't you move somewhere with less business tax, like Nevada? I mean, Missouri has like a 30 percent self-employment tax, no?"

He raised his eyebrows, and a look of surprise crossed his face.

I stood and walked over to the amp. He followed. "What's the name of the tool you invented?"

"Huh?"

We were standing twelve inches from one another. He'd heard me perfectly.

"The tool," I repeated. "What did you name it?"

"A s-s-s-solder," he stuttered.

A wave of dread rushed through me. *What the . . . ? A solder? How stupid does he think I am?*

"Five hundred bucks?" he asked again, grasping at straws.

"Can I see your ID, *Mitch*?" My request was my only weapon against undercover vice cops. Your typical john will gladly show ID. But vice cops won't carry fake IDs to match their fake room names. It's far too expensive to make one for every sting.

"What do you need to see my ID for?" he asked. The color rapidly drained from his face, and my flirtatiousness fled.

"Maybe because I'm a young girl in the room of a strange man who looks like he can bench four hundred pounds."

He took a drink of his beer but made no move toward his wallet. I adjusted my skirt and put my purse over my shoulder.

"I think you're looking for something I don't provide," I said, moving cautiously but quickly toward the door. "Prostitution is illegal, sweetie. I'm a dancer."

The last time I had made that statement, I was arrested for entertaining in an establishment without a license. Vice would get you any way they could. I braced myself and reached for the door. Stepping into the hallway, I breathed relief as the door closed behind me.

I pulled my phone from my purse and dialed the agency to have the phone girls issue an alert. Before anyone answered, the door to the adjacent room cracked open.

"Hey!" A man with a five o'clock shadow peeked out the gap in the door. "Keep it down out there," he whispered, even though I hadn't said a word. "We have kids!"

"Then go to Disneyland!" I countered.

I speed-walked toward the elevator and hit redial on my phone. Suddenly, a hand grabbed my shoulder.

"Las Vegas Police Department. You're under arrest."

"Really?" I whined. "I didn't even solicit you!" I turned around to face Mitch. But instead of the beer-drinking mechanic from Missouri, I stood eye-to-eye with the one who supposedly had sleeping children in his room.

"Disturbing the peace." He beamed.

My blood boiled. *Is that why he asked me to keep it down, so he could put it in his report that he had tried to quiet me?*

"Do you always talk to hotel guests like that?" The officer's words dripped with sarcasm as he grabbed my purse and phone. He yanked me by the arm and led me back to his hotel room.

"My attorney is going to have a heyday with this!" I ranted. He pulled my hands behind my back and zip-tied me like a rodeo cowboy wrangling a wild hog.

"Oooh, I'm scared." He wiggled his stubby fingers in my face.

Instead of children inside the room, various officers sat around listening on devices, awaiting their next bust. In the reflection of the bathroom mirror, I saw a cluster of working girls. A sign that read "Happy Vice Night" hung over a bouquet of balloons in the entry hall. I was taken aback by their amusement in our arrests. As I stood there taking in the scene, my surprise morphed into anger.

Forced to join the girls, I took my place against the wall next to the toilet paper holder. We were crammed into every niche and corner like some overcrowded subway car. Girls stood in the shower, in the bathtub, next to the counter, all in zip ties. My anger ebbed into empathy. These girls looked more than frustrated and annoyed. They were afraid.

Officer Sarcastic crouched in front of the sink with a pen and paper. After dumping the contents of my purse, he studied my driver's license and scribbled down my name, height, and weight on his form. He yelled for a brown paper bag from the other officers and wrote my name on that as well.

"Hey, Bill!" he shouted. "Take a look at this name. Rebecca Saffer. Does it sound familiar?" He handed off my license.

"Yeah, it does. I think we got a memo on her." He adjusted his headset. "We'll take a look when we get back. We've got another one on her way." He headed back into the main room.

A memo? What was that about? I thought I might know. *I need to tell my man. This could be serious.*

After inventorying my belongings, Sarcastic tossed my purse contents and the form into the bag and dumped it by several other bags. He glared at each of us crammed into the bathroom. "Not one word. If you tip this girl off, I'll add charges to your case." He turned and waited in the bathroom doorway.

Between the crackle of static, we strained to hear the radio transmitting the next victim's introduction to the Missouri businessman. She quickly incriminated herself by offering her sexual services for $500.

The businessman escorted her into the hotel room without any chase. "Surprise!" the men cheered and laughed. Sarcastic took her from the businessman and put her hands behind her back, reading her rights. She pursed her lips as her zip ties were applied. She wore tight jeans with a purple sleeveless shirt. The color popped against her skin. Her long straight hair was midnight black. With one brief head-to-toe glance at her, I knew she was new to the Game.

Sizing people up not only saved me from dangerous situations but helped me land the high-dollar tricks. I could pick out a high roller in a casino solely by his shoes. Wealthy men from Dallas wore subtle gator cowboy boots with their suits. Men from Atlanta wore penny loafer/docker-style shoes but always in a darker brown hue. From across the craps table, I could spot the telltale sign of wealth: the watch. A Rolex, Franck Muller, or Cartier was a dead giveaway.

The girl in the purple shirt looked rough. With her hands behind her back, she cocked one hip, fierce and furious.

"I don't know what I did!" She rolled her eyes at the officer and whipped her head side to side with attitude.

"What do you mean?" Officer Sarcastic bent over, annoyed by her ability to play dumb. He rested his hands on his knees so he could look her in the eye. He spoke slowly. "You. Said. You'd. Have. Sex. For $500! Prostitution is illegal. Now take your charge and shut up!" He straightened up and rolled his eyes at the other officers.

She leaned in for round two. "I want to call my attorney. I'm allowed one phone call." The rest of us girls giggled and exchanged knowing looks. *First arrest,* I thought.

"This ain't *Law & Order*, sweetheart. Your attorney ain't

going to rush down here at 11:00 p.m. for you." The officer still had his back to her.

As much as I hated to admit it, he was right. In this town, seven to ten girls a night went to jail. You'd do your night in jail, get released in the morning, and receive a court date. *Then* you'd call your attorney, whom you were well acquainted with if you'd been doing this awhile. He'd show up at court and plea your charge down to a $500 fine and a mandatory online class to learn more than you ever wanted to know about STDs. The more arrests on your record, the greater the fine, and eventually you'd be banned from the Strip.

After several arrests, I was all too familiar with how things worked.

Officer Sarcastic yanked her money out of her purse and counted under his breath as he shuffled dollar bills.

"Fourteen dollars?" He held up a fistful of ones, waving them proudly to all of us. "You're a broke hoe." His eyes scoured her. He pulled her cell phone out and thumbed through the contacts while scowling.

He glanced up and tilted his head. "Daddy?" He scowled at her. "How about I call your pimp and let him know his girl chose me?" he said, perhaps trying to sound like her man.

"He ain't gonna believe you." She stared him down hard.

"Oh, so you do have a pimp?" He stood up, eyes wide.

"I didn't say that!" she quipped.

"You are a stupid duck, you know that?" Mockery dripped from his every word as his eyes narrowed. "When you get home, I hope your pimp slaps the s— out of you."

My stomach lurched. This clueless newbie didn't deserve the hatred Sarcastic spewed. None of us did.

"Just shut up and sit down like the rest of these girls. Take some lessons from the veterans." He grabbed her arm and shoved her down into the bathtub, hands still zip-tied behind her back. "Now be quiet!" he snarled. He swept across us all with one final shame-on-you glance, then slammed the bathroom door.

Seconds later, the whispering began. Hoping to soften his blows, we offered advice.

"Girl! He could make your charges worse," one whispered. "Be cool!"

"Stop talking so much. You're going to get your man in trouble," another advised.

"You'll get out tomorrow, so stop trippin'."

We'd been crammed in the small room for only twenty minutes, but it felt like an hour. Eventually the bathroom door flung open, and Sarcastic announced, "Time to load up. Everyone in a single-file line by the door." He motioned to the front hallway.

The hotel room door was propped open, and officers were picking up the brown paper bags that contained our personal belongings. All the officers helped, checking our zip ties, picking up bags, and pushing us into line. They led us to the elevator, which took us downstairs. The officers marched us through the casino to a side door, like criminals busted for a casino heist. The tourists' stares were humiliating, yet the shock and drama had become my norm. They gawked and snapped photos with their camera phones. A real-life Vegas bust wasn't something they saw every day.

The officers led us through the back door to a deserted alleyway. The hot air reeked of rotten buffet leftovers. It seemed there was little difference between us—a bundle of zip-tied girls—and the twist-tied trash bags that had passed through these same doors. We were both going to a sort of wasteland to be forgotten by those who had dumped us there.

Instead of a dumpster, a paddy wagon flanked by two

uniformed officers awaited our arrival. One by one, each girl climbed into the back of the wagon, navigating the awkward step in our professional attire. The steep climb seemed daunting in my pencil skirt and heels, especially with my hands pinned behind my back. I took each step sideways, with the professional grace acquired from years of managing stairs, escalators, and uneven pavement in heels.

My eyes met one of the officer's eyes. Immediately, shame formed a hard rock in the pit of my stomach. Over the past month, we had exchanged pleasantries most nights around nine o'clock while sipping dark roast at the Starbucks near my house.

"Wow. You?" He shook his head and half smiled, half frowned at me. His confused expression felt like a slap of disappointment from a betrayed friend. I hung my head and stared at my feet as I sat down.

"I never would have guessed." His statement was a first this evening—I hungered for someone to acknowledge my decency. I was glad I knew him, even if the bust had shattered his nice-girl perceptions of me.

A vice officer jumped in the back of the wagon and buckled our seatbelts. He loaded our brown paper bags in front and stepped out, then slammed the armored door. The windowless vehicle was a prison on wheels. It weaved and bumped, stopped and started, giving no clues to where we were going. A redhead looked me up and down, checking out my shoes. I returned the favor, noticing her slightly too large, blingy diamond stud earrings. *Probably cubic zirconia,* I thought.

The designer bags, jewelry, and shoes made us feel cared for. That's what we wanted—for someone, anyone, to care. And to get the h— out of this wagon full of hoes sizing each other up, wondering whether we were better or worse off than the next girl.

The silence was fleeting. Within minutes, the stories began

flying. Each girl tried to one-up the other, explaining how her bust went down, claiming she'd never agree to sleep with anyone for only a couple hundred dollars. Before long, the conversation shifted to our "families."

"You got a man?"

"How many wife-in-laws in your family? Are you bottom?"

For every ten working girls in Las Vegas, I'd guess nine had pimps. But to us, they weren't our pimps but our men—our "husbands," or so they'd call themselves. The way we saw it, our husbands consistently proved they were more than pimps. They went to great lengths to convince us they were our lifeline—our heartbeat—and if we even considered severing our sacred bond, life as we knew it would end.

Our in-laws were like "wives" or "sisters." The "bottom" was the "wife" who had been around the longest. She was typically the most trusted and respected, both in the family and by the pimp.

I am pretty sure each girl in that wagon believed she had the same privileges as a traditionally married woman. Our God-given desire for intimacy and belonging ran so deep that we willingly settled for and even grew to love the counterfeit family. At the time, it never occurred to me that there was something better than the fake family bond formed among the zip-tied sisterhood in the back of a paddy wagon.

I sat quietly. I had been taught to follow strict orders. Talking about my family, my "folks," was considered "out of pocket." No girl wanted to be out of pocket. Not if she wanted to stay in her man's good graces.

In my house, even letting another working girl say her man's name in front of you was considered out of pocket. Letting her talk to you about her man was even more offensive. If a girl did this, my wife-in-laws made it clear that it was my responsibility to shut her up by telling her off or fighting her. Tolerating this kind of talk would only end in my pimp beating me. But this wasn't the venue for a fight.

My silence unsettled the other girls, who eyed me curiously. "You got folks?" one asked. Now, talking about *my* man to other broads was not out of pocket. I would gladly tell a girl about my family all day if she'd listen. Talking up the family was a recruiting tactic demanded of us. Then maybe she'd leave with me and we could teach her how to make some real money.

"Yeah, I got a man." I stuck out my chin and crossed my legs to make sure they noticed my designer shoes. "I have three sisters too."

"Sisters?" one asked. Her dark brows came together, and she leaned forward a little.

"Yeah. Sisters," I began. "In my family, we call our wife-in-laws sisters. We're all really close. Ain't no drama in our home."

The girls craned their necks until every pair of mascara-caked eyes were fixed on me. I could tell the concept of sisters living together as a family was foreign to them. Many pimps kept their girls separate, which caused them to compete for his time and attention. The rivalry between some wife-in-laws was so fierce that they couldn't work for the same escort service and often got caught up in street fights with each other. Pimps preferred the competition because it produced more income. Girls who earned more money earned more of "daddy's" attention.

My sisters and I never called our man "daddy." The term disgusted him. In my own deluded mind, I believed this meant he had a conscience.

"You bottom?" one asked me.

"No, our bottom has been with my man eighteen years. She's retired now and has her own retail business." I divulged just enough to keep them wondering and hoping that their own retirement plans would also come true.

The wishful look on their faces was familiar. I knew that look. I'd been there. Most working girls dreamed of marrying their pimp. But in the Game, hope breeds eternal misery. The belief that "my situation is different from everyone else's" kept every one of us with our pimp, even on the dark days when we watched the older women get kicked out on the street with nothing or dumped penniless at another pimp's house.

But still, even tainted hope is hope, and the human heart hangs on to whatever it has. *It will never happen to me,* I reasoned. *My man loves me. We are different.* I too clung to these lies, as I had since the beginning.

CHAPTER 2 **the romeo effect**

But the serpent said to the woman,
"You will not surely die."

February 1999

P ositive. The pregnancy test revealed two distinct pink lines.
I sat there frozen on my boyfriend's mom's toilet, my cut-off
jean shorts around my ankles. *Do two lines mean yes or no?* I
mustered the courage to read the directions again, my hands
shaking so much that I had to take deep breaths to focus on the
small print. The instructions confirmed my fear.

What was I going to tell my parents? My grandma? I had
planned to stay at my cousin's on the East Coast only through
the summer, but then I met my boyfriend. I was there to work,
experience the world, and get out of Grants Pass, a sleepy lumber
town in Oregon, before setting off to college. My dorm room at
Oregon State University had been assigned and was ready and
waiting. I was going to be an Oregon State Beaver—orange and
black.

But now, pregnant at seventeen! I had graduated high school
a year early, a varsity athlete with a promising future. The last
thing I wanted was to go back to small-town Oregon to become
a single teen mom while all my friends went off to college.

What if I don't have to? What if my boyfriend wants to make our little family work?

Jonathan was getting ready to try out for the new semipro Baltimore basketball team, and he had a real chance at landing a spot. Between his athletic talent and my desire to go to school, I figured I could apply to a university near his home.

When I told him the news, his face lit up and hope filled my heart. I pictured a future together. A baby, a beautiful baby, would be mine—*ours*. I *wanted* her or him. At that moment, a small shift occurred in my heart, making room for a yearning, gnawing, raw love fiercer than any I'd ever known.

I called my dad.

"Hey, Dad, so . . ." I had no reason to beat around the bush. "I'm pregnant. I'm not going to come back to Oregon. I'm going to apply to a college here instead."

Dad said nothing. He was silent. He wasn't much for words in any case, but after the collapse of my parents' marriage when I was only nine, then losing his job to alcoholism, he'd lost the right to judge, which was precisely why I had called him first. My mom wasn't perfect either, but I was looking for the grace and understanding I knew he'd give me after having his own tough times.

"Tell Nannie for me. Gotta run." I hung up quickly.

"Jonathan Wise, you are considered a habitual, subsequent offender, and you are hereby sentenced to seven to fifteen years in maximum security prison." The judge's gavel fell with a loud whack, shattering my dreams of a healthy family. At five months pregnant, I was barely showing, but expecting our little girl. And now her daddy was a convicted felon, again.

After the sentencing, I slumped into the front seat of his mother's gray Nissan Sentra.

"I told him not to mess with Antwon," Miss Tessa muttered while digging through her purse for her car keys. "That boy is always up to no good."

It was hard to tell whether she was more angry or saddened by her son's incarceration. Probably both. Jonathan's blunder wasn't only a blow for us and our baby. It crushed his hopes for a basketball career. In an instant, the countless hours of drills, hammering three-pointers, and running suicides were made worthless.

Miss Tessa and I drove home from court in silence. She parked her Nissan in the driveway, but neither of us moved to get out of the car.

"I think you should go home." Miss Tessa's quiet words broke the stillness. Tears fell down my cheeks. I knew she was right, but for some reason I couldn't move my legs. I knew once I stepped out of this moment, I would be forced to begin making choices *alone*. Choices I didn't want to make.

But it was time.

As an only child, I had spent a lot of time alone when my mom had to work a couple of jobs to make ends meet. I partied on the weekends with friends, got good grades, and played sports. I was not a quiet, nerdy overachiever. I was a party girl with a lot of friends and no one to teach me boundaries. I sought love and attention by saying yes to anyone and anything.

My high school boyfriend, three years older than me, had shattered my heart into a million pieces. I had made him my everything for nearly four years when he told me he had been cheating on me . . . and had married the other woman. Between him and Jonathan, I felt my heart harden. I didn't care anymore. I vowed not to let men get the better of me again. I could no longer be vulnerable.

"If you were my daughter"—she stared straight ahead—"I'd want you home."

Mom and Ken, my stepdad, picked me up from the airport in Medford, Oregon. They had come to terms with my news months prior and now welcomed seeing their only child pregnant with their first grandbaby. My mom had a "Welcome Home, Rebecca" sign and flowers. My aunts and cousins were there too. They were all excited to have me home, taking pictures and touching my growing belly. I was terrified of the future but happy to be home and to have excitement surrounding the arrival of my baby. My family made it special, as they always did. They always took time to celebrate what was important.

Right away Mom helped me settle in. We crammed a twin bed and crib into my parents' only spare room, which the baby and I would share. We painted a stripe around the middle of the blue walls, and my three-year-old cousin's pink, white, and yellow handprints formed an adorable border.

I enrolled at the community college, determined to carve out a life for us. I tapped the same ambition that allowed me to graduate a year early on the honor roll, all while cheerleading, running track, and playing goalie for the varsity soccer team. I may have been the only one of my friends with divorced parents, but I refused to be labeled an "at-risk youth."

The same friends who voted me into the prom court and crowned me Harvest Ball Queen embraced me again, driving two hours from the OSU and U of O campuses to attend my baby shower. I soaked up their kindness and longed to be a part of their adventures as university students. I mentally filed these same hopes into a "someday" file next to the fantasy family photo of me, my husband, two kids, and a dog. But I was on a different path. I closed that file and chose to open a new one.

She came two weeks early. Deshae Wise. She was the most

beautiful thing I'd ever laid eyes on. Her caramel skin and big brown eyes were beyond beautiful; she was perfect. She slept through the night and laughed and giggled when she was hungry or tired. She even nursed well.

I couldn't have dreamed it being easier. I enrolled her with a sitter close to our house and started classes at the local community college. My parents bought me a 1991 white Ford Probe. Nothing fancy, but it was something. My new adventure was falling into place. *If I work hard at this, I will make something out of our life together. I can do this,* I thought. I silently vowed to give my daughter everything I didn't have when my parents divorced. The divorce had made finances difficult for us.

After my first semester at the local community college, my friends moved out of the university dorms and into a townhouse in Eugene, home of the Ducks. They invited me to move into their extra room. This was exactly what I had been waiting for! I could finally break out of the small-town world where everyone knew everyone's business and claim a world of opportunity for myself and my daughter. I could smell freedom in the air, and I was ready to inhale deeply.

Eugene was different from what I had imagined. Part of me loved it—new foods, new people, sporting events, parties. If only I could do it all! But I was a mother, a nineteen-year-old mother. Guys rarely, if ever, called me back for second dates. While my friends went out, I sat at home with Deshae. I missed the family support I had received at home. Juggling finding a job, finding daycare, enrolling in college, figuring out financial aid, and single parenting proved to be a lot to handle. By the summer of 2000, I was terribly lonely.

After I put Deshae to bed, voices would creep into my thoughts.

You are unwanted and unimportant. You are alone, and you always will be.

Money got tight, and my financial aid from home wasn't enough to make ends meet. As I struggled, my roommate got a job as a stripper. I wasn't about to judge; an aunt on my mom's side was a stripper.

My middle-class family was loving and fun, but we were plagued with dysfunction. On my dad's side were church planters, missionaries, preachers, and Jesus-loving folk born and bred in the church. As a worldly teen, I saw them as religious, modern-day Pharisees who lived a religious life without the adventure my spirit craved.

My mom's side was the opposite. After growing up in and escaping an abusive household, my maternal grandmother lived out of her car and did the best she could, working tirelessly to turn things around for her family but married a really bad guy. Eventually my mom, aunts, and uncle overcame their abusive childhoods and made families of their own. Loving, resourceful, kind, and optimistic, some of my mom's family did well for themselves, got their degrees, and moved into careers. But others struggled with drugs, alcohol, and abuse.

And here I was, having inherited the spiritual bloodline of both.

I knew my parents loved me, but after the divorce, Mom was busy working, with little to no time to invest in parenting. As a latchkey kid, I walked myself to and from school and soccer practice each day and often made my own dinner. Mom had one jerk of a boyfriend for a few years. Then when Ken and she were dating and early in their marriage, they traveled all the time.

My dad, chin-deep in alcohol, would either indulge and leave me in the car while he drank at the bar during my weekend visitations, or he would drop me off at Nannie's. I knew he was depressed and hurting, but little me didn't understand that.

Sometimes on Saturday mornings, I'd wake up to find him wrestling the rabbit ear antennas so we could watch a basketball game. I watched Dr. J, Patrick Ewing, and Spud Webb use their talent to make something of their lives. Then we'd head to the local diner for a tuna melt before going to see Nannie—the fervently praying grandma in my life. My aunt would bring my cousins over, and between recording fake news broadcasts, we'd go to Sunday school, Awana club, or vacation Bible school.

I had never set foot in a church before Nannie took me. It was as if I'd walked out of a smoke-filled backwoods pool hall. The buttoned-up, blue-haired ladies' crinkled faces let me know they could still smell the smoke on my clothes. Life with this side of my family may have seemed normal to others, but I preferred Mom's house, where I was left to my own devices.

Now I was here in Eugene, where "normal" meant I was still alone and longing for a picture-perfect family.

"You made how much this weekend?" I asked my stripper roommate one day.

"I make around $300 per night."

"Per night?!" I exclaimed. "Shoot, I could do that Fridays and Saturdays and still be able to enroll in school." I was curious. "What's it like?"

"It's not that bad. You basically have on a bathing suit. Then you're only naked for a second. You have to be twenty-one to sit on the floor, so since you're under age, you'd come out from the dressing room to dance the stage for your set when your name comes up. You'd only give a lap dance if someone asks from the stage. But no touching. And bouncers are right there to watch."

"That doesn't sound too bad," I said.

"It's not, and great money."

It didn't take long for me to join her.

I'd found the perfect solution. I could do this on the weekends and have all day to go to school and be a mom. I hadn't enrolled in fall classes yet but was sure dancing would be the answer to all my problems. After all, I was the opposite of a prude. After the devastation of losing my high school sweetheart and Jonathan, I'd have one-night stands with guys on purpose. Turning the tables on men gave me a false sense of empowerment. I was the one calling the shots. This made me feel desirable, beautiful, sexy, and strangely in control of choosing whether to engage emotionally. It was the perfect way to protect myself from further heartbreak.

One day that summer, on my way home to pick up Deshae, I went into the campus sports bar to grab my to-go order. I glanced over and noticed a friend from back home, Seth, chatting with a cute bald guy who wore great clothes.

I walked over to Seth and gave him a hug. "Hey," I said, then extended my hand to the bald guy. "I'm Rebecca."

"My name's Bryan," he said, flashing a huge smile.

"What's your hurry?" Seth asked, seeing my to-go bag. "Chill with us."

"Nah. I've gotta run back home before work." What I wanted to do was hang here and get to know Bryan. His smile lit up the place, and he struck me as more sophisticated than the typical U of O guys.

"Don't leave us." Bryan continued flirting with me. I felt flattered when he asked for my number. I gave it to him and watched him put it into his phone.

A few days later, while dancing at the Silver Dollar, I saw a guy in a hat sitting toward the back of the room. Our eyes met and he quickly looked away. Later that night, as I got ready to leave the bar, I felt a tap on my shoulder. I turned around to find that same guy standing in front of me.

"Bryan! I didn't know that was you!" I was flattered that he had come to the club and touched that he had looked away. *Out of respect?* I guessed.

"Whatcha doin' now?" he asked. "I'm heading to a house party. It's low-key. You should come." His smile made my heart race. My skin tingled all over.

I glanced up at the clock behind the bar. It was late, so Deshae and my sitter would already be asleep. "Sure. Why not?" I agreed. "I've got nothing to lose but sleep at this point." He took my hand, and my heart fluttered.

His luxury SUV was loaded. *This guy's not only funny and good looking. He's apparently good with money too,* I thought. As we got to know each other at the party, I learned that he was a record producer. He lit up with passion as he told me about his label and his life goals. He had tons more ambition than any guy I'd dated before.

Before long, our relationship fell into place. Everything was about "us" and "we"—including Deshae. On dates we'd go to the park or family pizza places with ball pits. He helped with the baby. Despite the promises I'd made myself, I allowed myself to picture our future together as I had with my high-school boyfriend, then with Jonathan.

Is this guy the one? I hoped. *Had I finally been given a silver spoon to replace the broken McDonald's spork?* Deshae was mesmerized by him. She was almost one year old and interacting more with those I let into her life.

Bryan's career as a record producer and music manager fascinated me. He lived two hours away in Portland but would make frequent trips down to Eugene. Sometimes we'd visit him and go to Chuck E. Cheese's. Other times I'd drive two hours in the opposite direction to drop Deshae off with my mom for the weekend, so I could join Bryan at concerts. Being a backstage insider and rubbing elbows with talented artists and agents was invigorating, a welcome departure from the daily grind of raising a baby by myself. Not wanting to appear as an overeager groupie, I gave him plenty of room to do what I assumed was important business. We would drink and occasionally use recreational drugs or go to other strip clubs afterward.

After a couple of months, he invited me to go on vacation to Las Vegas with him for a work trip. We stayed at Bally's, dined in expensive restaurants, and frequented the vibrant nightclubs, thanks to an ID I had borrowed from an older friend. The lights and energy of Vegas were exhilarating, nothing like Oregon. We'd buzz through nightclubs while Bryan took business calls. He'd drop me at our hotel room, telling me he had to go handle something, and would return the next day. We'd sit in the VIP area at the Luxor and dream about one of the bands he produced getting a gig there. My head spun with the possibilities of what all this could mean for me and Deshae. Bryan was my chance to build a more financially stable life than I had envisioned.

I felt like I'd stepped into a made-for-TV movie. *Could this actually be my life? Could I marry someone with such a drive to succeed?* Bryan briefly mentioned that he also occasionally "managed girls" on the side, to supplement some income until things with the record label picked up. I got the impression that the girls were backup dancers who danced at big events as a launch point into the industry, or something. "It's just business," he reassured me, giving only vague insight. My stomach tensed when he mentioned this side venture, but I trusted his instincts as a brilliant businessman and didn't want to do or say anything to upset this new future of ours.

On our last day in Vegas, Bryan's phone rang as we pulled into the airport. His voice perked up instantly, and even though I could only hear his side of the conversation, it was clear he had good news. He shoved his phone in his pocket and grabbed my hands.

"How does first class sound?" he asked. "She just made $3,700!" He was smiling ear to ear. He could have told me the sky was purple and I'd have believed him in that moment. I had no clue how the entertainment industry worked, but his passion and excitement energized me. More than anything, I wanted to be a part of something bigger than my hopelessness. I wanted to love and be loved. I wanted to get out of poverty, get out of my small town, and experience adventure.

After six months of dating, things quickly turned serious. One afternoon, Bryan asked me to move in with him. He had been out of town a lot, and I missed him and told him so. His invitation confirmed what I believed he felt about me. I agreed. While I was planning and packing one afternoon, he stopped by. Standing in the doorway with his hands in his pockets, I could tell he had something serious to talk about.

"I have to move to Vegas for my job. My groups are getting gigs there. But . . . I can't ask you to come. Vegas isn't the place to raise a family."

He thinks we're a family!

"I want to come!" I begged. "Lots of women follow their man. Many families live in Vegas," I assured him and myself.

His desire to raise a family with me made me want to be with him even more. I envisioned my life as a stay-at-home mom with my successful husband, the entertainment-industry executive.

We drove down to Grants Pass and told my parents. Their tentative body language, cold handshakes, and terse small talk betrayed their reservations about Bryan. Something seemed off to them. But I wasn't about to let their fears hold me back from my dreams. They reluctantly gave me their blessing. Bryan's brother, Tim, came and helped us pack the U-Haul truck. I was excited to see him, my future brother-in-law, because the four of us had hung out together many times before. Tim hitched up my car and drove it to Vegas. Deshae and I hopped on a plane a few days later.

January 2001

Bryan and Tim quickly unloaded the truck, then Bryan told me to get dressed up because he wanted to take me out. I put on my best club gear, grabbed my fake ID, and kissed Deshae as Tim held her and she waved bye-bye. I didn't think twice about leaving her in the care of beloved Uncle Tim, who was great with kids.

As we drove down the street—the wind in my hair, the music thumping—the lights and energy of Vegas charged the atmosphere and gave me an intoxicating high. But instead of heading toward the Strip, Bryan pulled down a dead-end street, turned the car around at the end, and parked along the curb. A deserted mall to our right had no lights, no signs. It was a ghost town.

Bryan turned to me and started talking about how much he'd spent on moving me to Las Vegas. I hated the thought of being a burden to the man I believed would be my husband. I did not want to be a drain on the business that was going to support us.

"Of course, whatever I can do to help," I assured him.

"That door"—he pointed—"right over there with the camera above it. It's an escort service. I'm gonna need you to sign up." He said this as if he were asking me to sign up for a cable subscription.

"Escort?" I asked. "Like . . . *prostitution?*" That was a line I knew better than to cross.

"It's just dancing," he said. "It's nothing like the movies make it out to be. You don't have to do anything more than you're comfortable with. This is how it works in Las Vegas—in order to send dancers to those nice hotel suites with basketball courts and bowling alleys." I looked out the car window and thought about all he'd done for me. He'd taken me out to so many nice dinners. He'd fallen in love with Deshae. Surely he knew what he was doing. But this felt wrong. My gut knew it was wrong.

"Babe," he prodded. "This is how it works here. It's different from Eugene. And I'll be there to make sure you're okay, because I love you."

"But escort sounds like prostitution. I don't—"

His hand struck my cheek with more shock than force. I was stunned.

"You're gonna go inside, and you're gonna get my money back." His kind demeanor had shifted.

In that moment, scenes from my childhood raced back to my mind. Sometimes, in the years before my mom broke up with her jerk boyfriend, he had hit her. But this, what I had with Bryan— this was a relationship.

Does he love me at all? Did any of our dates and park days with Deshae mean anything to him? I dared not speak these questions aloud for fear of being slapped again. *Maybe this is just how adults fight.*

Suddenly, like a splash of cold water in my face, I was struck by a sobering realization that filled me with panic. *I don't know where my daughter is. I don't know my new address by heart.*

I needed things to get back to how they were yesterday, when I was excited and in love, when the world and all its possibilities awaited me. I needed to earn the moving money back, get through this night, and get back in Bryan's good graces. Could that door be my way back in?

Plus, I love him. I trust him. It can't be much different from the dancing I'm already doing. Right?

I climbed out of the car and walked to the door. I pulled hard to open it. *Locked.* Bryan sat watching from the car window. A buzzing noise prompted me to try the door again. A cubicle partition prevented doorway peepers. Four women, two of whom were overweight, sat facing one another at desks that butted up against each other.

"Hi, I'm here to sign up." I swallowed hard and glanced around the room, wondering whether I would have to audition. They looked me up and down as one finished a phone call. They glanced at each other. Then the blond took a long drag from her cigarette and pulled a paper out of her desk drawer.

"Fill this out, and I need a copy of your ID. You're eighteen, right?" I supplied my name and Oregon contact info. She handed me a checklist of rules and told me to initial beside each one. I quickly glanced over the legal jargon.

"It's basically saying you're not going to solicit sex," she explained. "We don't hire those kinds of girls. Okay?"

I nodded. *Phew.* I knew I could trust him.

"What's your stage name?" she asked, pointing at the board. On the wall, a dry-erase board displayed columns labeled blond, brunette, redhead, Asian, and exotic, with names under each, like Candy, Bambi, Ivy—just like it was done at the strip club.

I asked if I could run back out to the car. They nodded.

I opened the door and leaned in. Bryan was on the phone. He told the caller to hold on. "Hey, what should my name be?"

"You should go with Kelby, like Kelly with a B," he suggested.

I went back inside and wrote my stage name and phone number under the brunette category.

"Great. Nice to meet you, Kelby. I'm Taylor. This is Maddy and Dani." She pointed around the room. "That's Lenora, the owner," she said, indicating a skinny smoker who looked like Yzma from *The Emperor's New Groove.* I smiled.

"We'll call you when we get something." Taylor waved me out.

My phone rang as soon as I climbed back into the car. The call was from a Vegas area code. I punched the speaker button to answer.

"Hello?" I said.

"You take locals?" Taylor asked.

I looked at Bryan and raised my eyebrows. He nodded. Taylor rattled off an address while Bryan grabbed a notebook and pen from his center console. He'd clearly had this planned. I had her repeat the info and wrote it down.

As we drove, he explained the routine. "You'll get there and get the drop—that's the service fee. That's how the company makes money. Then you work for a tip, and the phone girl will get 20 percent of whatever tip you make. The company gets the drop, the phone girl gets the tip." He reiterated. "Got it?"

I nodded.

"You want to start your tips at $600 so you can give the phone girl a hundred and you keep five. Got it?" I heard in his voice the same twinge of excitement that he had when he talked to his music clients. I felt less like his girlfriend and more like one of his many toys. Six hundred dollars seemed like a ridiculous amount for dancing. I took a deep breath and exhaled loudly.

As we drove to the first call, I felt numb. Numb to the chains that had just been placed on me. I was completely unaware that other women he controlled had been turning tricks to pay for my earlier spending sprees, fine dinners, and move to Vegas.

That night I became one of them.

He turned to me and grinned. "Welcome to the Game."

CHAPTER 3   **the slammer**

*Stand firm, then, and do not let yourselves
be burdened again by a yoke of slavery.*

September 2006

We emerged from the paddy wagon and sauntered into line
to wait for the jail door to open. The guards shuffled slowly
in the sultry night. Only the frenetic insects showed any sign of
urgency as they buzzed around the exterior light. I squinted as we
entered the main booking room, my eyes adjusting to the harsh
lighting. An open area was filled with rows of chairs, classroom-
style. Men sat in cuffs on one side, women on the other.

The men craned their necks, jeered, and whistled as we
came in. We formed a single-file line, our backs against the cool
concrete wall, and stared at the floor, trying to ignore the taunts
while an officer patted us down. The heavy chain belt around my
waist that was attached to my handcuffs seemed extreme. After
all, we weren't hardened criminals, just women in the Game.
One officer checked the fit to ensure I had the prescribed lim-
ited range of motion. Next we were herded to the back of the
room, where another officer emptied and documented the contents of our brown paper bags.

We were told to sit, starting in the back row on the right-hand side. We had to fill in each seat, leaving no free seats between us. The men were seated starting in the front row and on the left side. They turned around in their seats to gawk at us. The undercover vice officers who had arrested us were long gone. The new officers yelled at the men to stay facing forward.

It was about midnight. I'd learned that the next two hours of booking would go by faster than the remainder of the night in the holding tank. Our names were called one at a time to start our rounds through the different stations.

"Rebecca Saffer," the first lady yelled while standing with a clipboard at the front of the room. When I stood up, my $2,500 Cartier watch clinked against the cuffs, and I cringed, hoping it didn't scratch.

She huffed her disapproval, applied a blood pressure cuff to my upper arm, and squeezed the small rubber pump with a vengeance.

"Are you allergic to anything? Do you suffer from any ailment?" I shook my head as she continued down her list.

"Put out your arm." I extended my right arm, and she grabbed my wrist, wrapped a rubber band around my bicep, and pricked my vein with a needle. She filled a vial with my blood and labeled it with my name. I had learned that if the HIV test returned positive, we could be booked for attempted manslaughter.

Mugshots were next. I stood facing forward on a white line while the blinding flash went off without warning. I turned sideways. Another flash. I gave the officer my fiercest eyes and a Hollywood smile, as if auditioning for *America's Next Top Inmate*. He laughed.

Once we all had our "prick and pic," we would be moved through the rest of the stations.

Time flew. As I was watching each girl get called, questioned about her medical history, and tested for HIV, an officer appeared by my row of chairs.

"Rebecca." He looked right at me. "This the one?" he asked another officer. The second officer nodded.

"Yes?" I answered slowly. My stomach tightened.

"Come with me, please." He held a manila folder in his hands and gestured toward a private room. The other girls' whispers hissed in the background. A shot of cold ran down my spine. *What's going on?* The cloak of confidence I wore hid my trembling insides. When you've turned tricks for as long as I had, you get pretty used to wearing disguises.

"Go ahead and take a seat." His voice was surprisingly gentle. He sat and put the folder on the table. "So how long have you been in Vegas?"

I shifted in my seat and crinkled my brow. I didn't trust his quiet demeanor or the contents of the manila folder.

"You're in the Game, obviously. Do you have a pimp?"

I froze. Pimping and pandering carried a seven- to fifteen-year felony sentence. Prostitution would get a slap on the wrist, a fine, and a night in jail. Rumors swirled of girls who had been murdered, even doused with gasoline and burned, for telling on their man. My answer could mean life or death. I stayed quiet and stared down the officer, my eyes locked on his.

My heart raced. The answer that had quite literally been beaten into me for years was all that came to my mind. "Lawyer." I didn't allow my intense gaze to waver from his.

"I don't think you can call your attorney right now." He smirked and glanced at his watch.

"I didn't ask to call him," I shot back. "But any further questions you have can be directed toward him. Are we done here?"

I waited for him to stand. *Calm down. Getting mouthy will only make things harder.*

He escorted me back into the main room after I left a few more prodding questions unanswered. All the girls had had their pictures taken by then, and they stood in a line at a door. I took my place at the end of the line. We entered a small room that reminded me of a gym's locker area, with a shower drain in the middle and nonslip mats lying on top of concrete. One at a time, we each sat in the only chair in the room. A female officer gave us a thorough pat down and removed our handcuffs. She shook out our hair while we tucked our head between our knees, then opened our mouths as she looked inside for contraband.

During previous stints, I'd whispered to the cute, petite blond cop as she leaned over me, "I can make you more money." She never paid attention, even when I said, "I make your salary in a week."

But tonight, my disgust with this life was written on my face. It was her turn. "You're too pretty to do this," she whispered.

"No duh," I quipped back. "That's *why* I do this." I rolled my eyes, and when she dismissed me, I walked to the adjacent counter to get a uniform and a list of my belongings. Depending on what a girl wore in, she was assigned an orange Clark County Detention Center (CCDC) shirt or pants. They must have been too short stocked to ever give a female a complete uniform. It was one or the other: shirt or pants.

I pulled the ghastly orange shirt over my black V-neck. Other girls in extremely short skirts received pants. Our shoes and jewelry were confiscated and logged on a sheet. In exchange, we received brown plastic sandals resembling the ones from Dollar General.

"Can I get some socks, please?" I asked while signing my paper.

"None left," the lady behind the counter said without even looking up. She seemed annoyed that I asked, as if her words and the effort they required were wasted on the likes of me.

Grateful that there were no mirrors in the CCDC, I stood

in my orange shirt, red pencil skirt, and brown jail sandals in front of my reflection in the glass door. The officer pressed the intercom button, buzzing me through. In the next room, chairs were lined up as before, men on the left and women on the right. At the front of the room was a wall of telephones that we were allowed to use after we completed all the stations. The perimeter of the room was lined with cubicles.

As soon as I sat down, my name was called. At the first station, I gave my name, address, phone number, employer, and so on. I had been taught to give completely fictional information other than my name. The woman across the desk explained that unless someone paid my five-hundred-dollar bail, I would be released on my own recognizance, or "OR'd." I nodded, and she handed me a piece of paper with the details of my arrest, inmate number, and false contact info. I moved to the next cubicle as if I were speed dating.

The next officer went over a checklist of questions to identify the appropriate holding tank for me. "Are you involved in any gangs?"

"No."

"Do you identify as lesbian?"

"No."

"Do you feel like harming yourself or others?"

"No."

At the next station, a nurse pricked me again to test for tuberculosis, and we waited to see whether my skin would swell. As we waited, she reached over and examined my wrists.

"These bruises look like fingerprints." Her voice was flat, as if stating that my hair was brown or my uniform was orange. She looked at my puffy, purple eyes hidden under fading concealer. "Are you being hurt at home?" Her narrowed gaze settled on me.

I wasn't surprised she was digging, but then again, no one

else had noticed, or they didn't care enough to take the time to look.

"No." I smiled sweetly and shrugged. I shifted in my seat while giving silent thanks for the awful orange T-shirt that hid the purplish-blue marks left by my pimp's fist the previous day. My skirt hid another on my thigh.

My skin didn't react to the TB test, so I moved on to the fingerprinting station. An officer helped guide my fingers across a small touch pad on a machine that resembled an ATM. My prints instantly showed up on the monitor. Like a scene from a crime show, little red dots scanned the fingerprints on the screen, and when it found a match, my name appeared.

"Not your first arrest, huh?" His grin told me he seemed like a decent guy. More likely he wanted information from me. Something deep inside me longed for the hint of kindness I heard in his voice, but I knew better than to allow him in.

"Sixth?" I flashed a fake grin and prepared my left-hand fingers to be scanned. We went through the process a second time. Then he took my registration paper, checked my name, and confirmed it with the one on the screen.

"All right, you're all done. Go ahead and take a seat. You can use the phone now too."

"Thank you."

Cooperating with the authorities for the small things, such as crossing my arms across my chest while walking to each station, earned me a measure of respect, an occasional gesture of kindness, and brief interactions that made me feel human again.

I dialed my man's number. I knew it by heart. Kevin had us memorize all our numbers: phone numbers, credit card numbers, and bank account numbers all had to be memorized; we never put any of it in writing.

"You locked up?" he said after a few rings. He knew

something had happened because he hadn't heard from me in a while. I usually checked in every couple hours as instructed.

"Yeah," I said, trying to sound disappointed.

"Well, try to get some rest. I'll see you tomorrow." He paused. "You all right?"

"Yep, I'm fine." I did my best to sound cheerful so he wouldn't get upset.

"Okay, Poc. Call me later if you get bored." His sarcasm seeped through the phone.

"You know I will," I replied with a forced laugh.

I returned to my seat. Kevin gave all his girls nicknames once they'd proved themselves loyal. When he'd started calling me Poc (pronounced Poke), the endearment felt special, like I was part of something—a family. My dark hair and eyes, olive-toned skin, and high cheekbones, from a small amount of Choctaw heritage, reminded him of Pocahontas.

I shut my eyes against the loud jail noises and screaming fluorescent lights. Others sat around the telephones, joking about being locked up and swapping war stories about all the times they'd been in before. It was nearly impossible to sleep in this place.

My thoughts drifted to Deshae. At least I didn't have to worry about my daughter. Kevin had it handled. Every morning, our live-in nanny, Maria, got her ready for kindergarten. Because "Mommy works nights in a casino," Deshae was used to me being asleep while Maria got her breakfast, braided her hair, and walked her to the bus stop. With any luck, I'd be released before she got home from school, and she'd have no clue her mom had spent the night in the slammer.

I sighed. This wasn't the life I'd imagined for us.

I was starting to drift off to sleep when I was startled by an officer barking my name. The clock on the wall read 3:00 a.m.

as we formed a single-file line to walk to the holding tank. As we made our way there, we passed cells holding people for longer terms. Women with faces chiseled by what I could only imagine to be years of suffering sat solitarily on benches. Their vacant stares haunted me. Male gang members huddled together and leered at us while making crude gestures. Young white boys, probably tourists in for drunk driving, were still in their suits, trying to sober up.

How has this become my life? How did I get here?

A man strapped to a contraption like a wheelchair lowered to the ground was being pushed in our direction. Another officer walked backward, videotaping the transport. We paused against the wall, giving them room to pass. Though the man's hands and legs were strapped down, he violently jerked his body, trying to kick. The netted bag that had been placed over his head to shield officers from his spitting didn't stop him from ranting, "You stupid pigs!"

I have to get out of here.

My fellow cellmates and I reached our holding tank. All eight of us were locked up for prostitution-related charges, or in my case, disturbing the peace. One concrete bench spanned three walls. On the fourth, a toilet and a phone stood on either side of the door. A small, chest-high barrier blocked anyone from being able to see us do our business.

A handful of women were already in the cell. They were clearly not working girls. A skinny, homeless-looking white woman who appeared to be fifty or so sat in filthy socks and jeans in the corner. An overweight woman with cornrows, maybe in her midforties, propped herself up against the opposite wall. Her heavy eyes and slurred speech gave her up—she was most likely in for a DUI. A third woman, gaunt, with reddish-blond, wavy, chin-length hair was curled up in a ball under the bench, trying to sleep. She stank and shivered with cold sweats. *Heroin.*

Even with all the warm bodies crowded together, the cell was cold. I immediately grabbed toilet paper and claimed my prized seat in the corner, so I could lean my head against a wall to sleep, pretending to be in the window seat of a plane. I carefully wrapped my feet with toilet paper and slipped my sandals over the makeshift socks. Toilet paper is a hot commodity in jail. It can take hours for the guards to replenish it, which makes using the restroom even more unpleasant. I had learned to wrap my chilly feet right away, before the toilet paper was gone.

As I leaned my head against the grimy wall (my intake paper sufficed as a germ barrier), I heard the sound of gagging. The woman curled up under the bench, her body contorting with dry heaves, spat green bile on the floor. Her greasy strawberry-blond hair stuck to her sweaty, pale forehead. She clutched a wadded-up piece of dirty tissue, shaking, using it to wipe her mouth between heaves. Her skinny body shook violently as my cellmates and I pinched our noses and stared in disgust. The stench of rotten eggs and freshly laid linoleum wafted through the cell.

"You sick?" one of the girls asked. The junkie didn't respond or move. "I don't want to get sick." The whiny girl stood and pounded on the door's window, trying to alert a guard.

"She isn't sick." My voice cracked a little after hours of silence. "She's kicking." Eyes turned toward me as if noticing me for the first time. I'd kept to myself until now.

"So, we can't catch it?" one girl asked.

"No. She's dope sick—detoxing. She's a junkie." I wanted to tell the lady that God could set her free from drug addiction. He'd done it for me a few years earlier. But preaching the gospel in the jailhouse was too hypocritical for me, so I kept my mouth shut.

An officer appeared at the door. "Breakfast, ladies," he announced and then pounded on the window. "Everyone find a seat on the bench!" After we crammed onto the benches together, the cop opened the door, and a uniformed male inmate pushed in a cart stacked full of cafeteria trays. The cop recited instructions like a drill sergeant.

"Do not grab a tray until the door is shut and locked. When you are finished, you are to dump your food in the plastic bag and stack the trays on the cart. Do you understand?"

The cell smelled like a cafeteria now. Each cold plastic tray held a lifeless blob of oatmeal with no sugar, a small pint of milk, half an apple, a scoop of scrambled eggs, and a small piece of wheat toast. No butter, salt, or pepper. As women finished and sat their trays in a stack, the homeless lady grabbed any uneaten bread and hid it in her bra. I choked down the eggs, apple, and milk. Even though the food was cold and flavorless, I knew we wouldn't eat again for quite some time.

I repositioned my head against the paper on the wall, but it was too loud, cold, and bright to sleep. No matter how tightly I closed my eyes, I couldn't escape the twenty-four-hour glare of the fluorescent lights.

Minutes crept into hours, but I had no idea how much time had passed. With no clock in the holding tank, I lost my grasp on time. As each officer passed by the window, we'd jump, hoping it was time to be OR'd. Lunch came with the same drill as breakfast. I guessed it was nearing 11:00 a.m. and wondered how much longer I'd have to wait.

I collect-called Kevin again to pass the time. *He should be awake by now,* I thought as the phone rang.

"Hello?"

"Collect call from an inmate in the Clark County Detention Center," the automated recording informed him. "To accept, press one."

"Heeey, you!" Kevin sounded not only awake but super upbeat.

"Hey!" I said, trying to match his mood.

"You on vacation, I see." He teased.

"Oh yeah." I fake-laughed, remembering the beating he'd given me the day before. What I wanted to say was, "Nothing like a cold slab of concrete to make you feel like you're resting." I didn't dare. Instead, I silently thanked God that Kevin couldn't read my mind.

"Well, I'm heading to the gym over here with Boo." My wife-in-law's nickname sent a sharp pang of jealousy through my gut. I buried the hurt so that not even a hint was detectable in my response.

"Cool. All right, well, you guys have fun. Hope to be out soon and back before little mama gets home." I missed Deshae and was worried she'd wonder where I was.

"Yeah, she's good, though. Got off to school just fine."

"Okay, great. Well, love you." I responded cheerfully.

"Love you too, Poc." The line went dead.

Surprisingly, Kevin never got mad about us going to jail. "Just part of the Game," he'd say. It was the little things that set him off, like unmade beds, clothes left on the floor, and soup cans facing the wrong way in the pantry. He hated even the smallest hint of jealousy or sadness in my voice. I couldn't risk another day of abuse tipped off by sharing my true feelings or stating my honest opinion.

But as I returned to the concrete bench, I couldn't block out the memories of the day before.

I hurried around our bedroom, getting ready for the night. In the bathroom I looked in the mirror and reached for my concealer to cover up the dark circles that cradled my eyes from lack of sleep. My ringtone chimed in the other room. I fetched my cell and glanced at the caller ID. Girls To You, the escort service.

"Hey, Maddy," I answered politely.

"Hey, how quickly could you get to the Bellagio?"

"Thirty minutes?" I offered.

"That long?" she whined.

"I'll hurry, maybe twenty."

"Okay, thanks."

I scooped my makeup off the bathroom counter and into my bag, put it away under the sink, then smoothed my hair back into a low ponytail. I checked my outfit, kissed my sleeping daughter goodbye, and hustled to my car. I drove faster than I should have and arrived at the hotel just under the wire. Wasting Kevin's money on a $50 late fee from the escort service, or worse, losing the call, was entirely unacceptable.

After the call I got back into the car and checked my "back phone." Kevin called these disposable devices burner phones and instructed us to ditch them in a dumpster every month. These were the phones we used to call each other. Our regular cell phones through a carrier were for the escort service, family, and other typical contacts. Any photos taken together were also strictly forbidden. *No evidence.*

I glanced at the recent calls on my back phone. Ten missed calls from Kevin. I rang him right away.

"Get your a— home." Kevin's voice was strained and slow. My stomach seized. I swallowed the putrid taste of bile, then realized I hadn't taken a breath since I'd answered the phone. It was his voice. The one he typically used before he imploded about something, often something so random it seemed to come out of nowhere.

As I raced home, I sorted through every word I'd spoken to him and others over the last twenty-four hours. Did I say too much about my family to that girl the other night? Did she tell her man? Did he call mine, to warn him he had an out-of-pocket broad? Had I left the oven on when cooking dinner? Had I forgotten to take Maria home on her day off? My head throbbed, and I realized I was clenching my jaw. I tried to relax it, then I called my wife-in-law Brandi, who had become a true sister to me in the days when she first taught me the rules of the Game—Kevin's rules.

"He's mad and I don't know why." My heart raced. I bit my lip, hoping for some plan to help get me out of this mess. It seemed like I got beatings more frequently than the other girls. Almost daily.

"It will be okay, sweetie. Just remember to take responsibility for whatever he says you did, even if you didn't do it. Don't argue. You know how he hates excuses and backtalk. Just agree with him."

After I hung up, I did the only thing that came to mind. "In the name of Jesus, I bind the spirit of anger from Kevin." I said the words out loud. "I come against the spirit of rage and plead the blood of Jesus from the crown of his head to the soles of his feet." I'd learned this prayer a few years ago when I was admitted to a women's drug-treatment home. "I loosen a spirit of revelation and peace over my home, in the name of Jesus."

The prayer came out as naturally as it had long ago. I imagined Jesus next to me in the passenger seat and knew he would never leave me nor forsake me. A Scripture passed through my mind: "I am convinced that . . . neither height nor depth, nor anything else in all creation, will be able to separate us from the love of God that is in Christ Jesus our Lord" (Romans 8:38–39).

My mind and pulse were racing as I pulled into the garage. I tiptoed upstairs, trembling and trying not to wake Deshae. He sat on the edge of the bed, his head down, his elbows on his knees, rubbing his temples. I'd seen this stance a hundred times, and it never ended well.

I thought about running, but I'd never make it out with Deshae. My only hope was not to say or do anything to provoke him more. He looked me square in the eyes.

"You touch my s— again, b--ch?"

"I don't . . . I don't know what you mean." My voice sounded shaky. I *was* shaking.

He clenched his jaw.

I willed myself to relax. *Breathe. Don't freak out.*

"My face lotion, stupid!" The flash of hatred I recognized in his dark eyes sent panic racing through me.

"I don't know." Tears welled up, but I blinked them back.

"You expect me to believe that!" He flew off the bed, puffing his arms and chest out. Kevin wasn't tall, but he was strong. He could bench 350 pounds easy, and I only weighed 115.

Then it dawned on me.

"My makeup!" I said, briskly heading toward the bathroom. I grabbed my cosmetic bag from under the sink and rummaged through it while sitting on my knees. "I was in a hurry earlier and may have accidentally scooped it up with my makeup," I explained, still searching frantically through the bag. "Here it is! It was an accident."

I held the bottle high in the air, smiling with relief to have found his missing lotion. A heavy force knocked me off balance. The next thing I knew, my head slammed into the bathroom wall. The impact made my ears ring. My pulse throbbed behind my eyes. I collapsed in a heap.

"Get up," he said, finding an excuse to hurt me. "What have I told you about touching my things?" He gritted his teeth and leaned over my limp body.

Without even thinking, I covered my mouth with my hands to protect my teeth from being knocked out.

He towered over me, clenching his fists.

"I didn't mean to," I sobbed between words. "It was an accident. I found it. I'm sorry."

"You're lying. Stand up." He grabbed my arm and yanked me to my feet. "You knew all along where it was." He stepped back and smiled proudly as if he had figured out my grand lotion conspiracy.

"No, I swear I just remembered scooping all my makeup into my bag, because I was in a hurry earlier. Please, Pup," I begged.

He threw all his weight into his right arm and drove his fist into my midsection. I fell backward, the wind knocked out of me.

"Get up! You're faking. I barely hit you!" He grabbed my arms and yanked me to my feet again.

I gasped for air.

He dragged me out of the bathroom and pushed me onto the bed.

"I swear to God, Poc . . ." He drove all his weight into one pounding fist that landed like a sledgehammer on my thigh. I let out a shrill scream. I started crawling backward, but he grabbed me by one leg and pulled me toward him, hitting my ribs this time.

"Oh, you want to run from me?" He glared at me with hatred. I tried to take the hits, fearing that moving away would make it worse.

"Please, Pup. Please don't." I begged quietly so I wouldn't wake Deshae.

"If you don't stand up and take it, I'll hit you again." He raised his arm, ready to throw the next punch, a possessed look in his eye. "If you keep fighting back, I'll keep hitting. If you take it, I'll stop."

I mustered all my mental strength to survive, stood up by the side of the bed, and held my breath, bracing for the worst.

"Don't touch my stuff!" He turned, walked out of the bedroom, and stomped downstairs.

I stood there for what seemed like forever, fearing he might change his mind. I was terrified to move.

If he finds me checking my face in the bathroom, he'll hit me. If I start getting ready to go back to the casinos, he'll hit me. I stood still.

His car engine revved, and I heard the grind of the garage door opening. His Hummer's engine roared into the night. I finally exhaled. Like a deflated balloon, I drifted toward the bathroom, still shaking, to check the damage. My phone's ring tone made me jump.

It's him!

"Hey," I answered, trying to sound normal.

"Get your a— to work," he snipped.

"Okay," I said, faking my sweetest voice.

I was unprepared to see my reflection. Kevin's Hummer had only been out of the garage for two minutes, and already I had two purple eyes that must have formed when he slammed my head into the wall. I had no clue bruises could form so quickly. Shocked, I pulled out the special Dermablend concealer, which my sisters had taught me to keep around for these specific occasions. Professional makeup artists use it to cover tattoos. I changed my outfit, wincing as I peeled off my clothes.

I caught a glimpse of myself in the mirror and gasped. From my ribs to the top of my thighs, Kevin had left a trail of fist marks. It was as if he dipped his hand in purple paint and stamped my body with the exact outline of his knuckles up and down my side.

Waves of shame followed by sadness overcame me. "Jesus, where were you?" I cried. "Where were you in that room just now?" I crumpled to the floor like a burlap sack and sobbed until I had no tears left to cry.

CHAPTER 4 **no easy exits**

*Be alert and of sober mind. Your enemy the devil prowls
around like a roaring lion looking for someone to devour.*

January 2001

B ryan drove me to the local address from the phone girl, which
he had scratched on a notepad. It was a townhouse, and the
guy who answered the door was in his early twenties, with dark
brown, wavy hair. His college-quarterback physique and good
looks would have drawn the attention of any girl in her right
mind. He shattered stereotypes of fat, sweaty men unbuckling
their belt under their belly. If I'd met him during my bar-hopping
days, I'd have given him my number.

Maybe Bryan's right and this won't be like the movies, I hoped
as I entered.

I walked into his living room. He sat down and handed me
the escort service fee. I started with a simple strip tease, but he
grabbed my waist and pulled me in.

"Let's slow down a minute," I hinted, pushing away from
him. "How about we talk about my tip before we get carried
away here, 'kay?"

He reached for his wallet and handed me a wad of cash,

which I quickly counted. $320. I didn't know how to negotiate or what to do.

The entire ordeal couldn't have lasted longer than four minutes. Before I could think of a plan, he was finished with me. I didn't want to make him mad and get myself cornered or locked up in his house. More than anything, I just wanted it to be over.

I rushed out, crushed by the reality of what just happened. I slumped into the front seat of Bryan's car, and he punched the gas.

"How much did we make?" he said, holding out his hand.

He glanced over while I finished straightening my clothes.

"Three twenty." I handed him the wad of bills. His face and shoulders fell, and he shot an annoyed look my way.

"Don't worry. You'll do better next time," he promised. "You didn't have sex for this much, did you?" He looked back and forth between me and the road while maneuvering his car around the suburban maze. I shook my head, then turned toward the window and focused on the streetlights in the distance, willing myself to hold back the flow of emotion. A tear escaped, then another. I quickly wiped them away with the back of my hand, smearing my mascara.

This was nothing close to the dream life I'd imagined on the plane when Deshae and I flew over the dazzling Vegas skyline. Disappointment and embarrassment gripped me. I wanted a family and adventure, but not at this price. I felt stupid for not having understood the cost. *Varsity-Soccer-Playing, Honor-Roll Student Turns Prostitute*. The thought plastered itself across my mind like a front-page headline that all my friends and family would surely read. Shame crept into the depths of my heart and set up camp for an extended stay.

Despite my honor-roll brains, I couldn't figure out a way to physically leave Bryan. I loved him. I loved the idea of our family and future that he had painted while we were dating. I wanted the dangling carrot he held in front of me.

For months Bryan drove me around town on calls, promising I could drive once I was more familiar with the back roads of Vegas and how to navigate each parking garage. He told me what to charge the tricks, what to tip the phone girls, and how to look out for the police.

"I care about you, baby," he assured me each night as we set out for the Strip, leaving Deshae with Tim, our new nanny. "We're doing this for our future."

I wanted to believe him. I wanted to believe this gig was temporary, and I held tightly to the dream that he sold me. I wanted to believe that his driving me everywhere was a good thing. I didn't want to believe he was monitoring my every move and taking the money I gave him after every call, leaving me with no means to flee.

The more I followed the rules, the more "freedom" Bryan gave me. He eventually allowed me to drive my used Lexus to get to "dates" while I slept on the couch at home between calls from the escort service. Meanwhile, he told me he was managing his music clients and kept saying I could quit once his business took off.

Sometime after I turned twenty-one, I walked into the Mandalay Bay on a call from Taylor. I parked on the third floor as I was taught, took the elevator down to the ground floor, and entered at the back entrance of the hotel.

I was immediately engulfed in the pulse of nightclub music.

The dance club was busy as I crossed the dark, glossy stone floor in the open foyer. I was careful on the smooth surface in my four-inch Manolo Blahnik stilettos that Bryan had bought me for my birthday. In the center of the foyer, a massive water feature gave off a tropical, exotic aura—a welcome escape from

Vegas's dry desert air. The alluring, expansive atmosphere made my heart swell with anticipation. I took a deep breath, kept my eyes focused ahead, and strutted by drunk clubbers, whose cat-calls beckoned me and other female passersby. "Keep your eyes down at your feet or on a fixed point ahead," Bryan had taught me. "Never make eye contact with others."

He also trained me to stay on the perimeter of the room, which drew less attention than strutting through the center of the hotel, turning heads. I veered right to avoid the nightclub line, passed the water feature, and approached the hotel elevators. I preferred Mandalay calls because we greeted our clients in their room. At the Bellagio or the Wynn, it was harder for men to book a girl. Men risked being noticed on the casino floor because they had to escort us past the security guard while showing their room key. We used to keep an old hotel key on us to get past security, but they'd change colors so frequently that it wasn't worth the risk of getting thrown out.

A large Asian man greeted me at the room. Peter was a guy Taylor had booked for me a few months back. That time, he hadn't even wanted me to touch him. He watched from a chair in the corner as I pretended to be his victim, passed out on the bed with a sash laid flat over the top of my neck. It was a quick $500, and I figured this night would be more of the same.

I repeated the perverted role play as before, with my eyes closed. When I felt a heavy weight on top of me, I quickly opened my eyes. Peter was strangling me. I choked. I grabbed his arms, thinking this would go on for only a moment. His hands got tighter, and the crazy look in his eyes scared me. I fought to breathe, choking and gasping for air. I kicked and hit and pushed at him, trying to get away, but he wouldn't budge. As I struggled, his grasp only tightened.

As much as I wanted to, I couldn't scream. Trying to peel his fingers off my throat, I pleaded, "Pl . . . Pl . . ." But all I could get out was a breathy gurgle. My tears came hot and heavy. I began to lose strength; my hands and legs went limp. I couldn't fight anymore. My vision closed in, and little yellow stars appeared in my peripheral vision as I got lightheaded.

Soon my body shook and quivered.

This is it, I thought. *My baby's not going to have a mama.*

Suddenly, Peter let go.

Without hesitating, I gasped for air and jumped up, grabbing my clothes as I ran out of the room. I dressed in the elevator and tried to regain my composure as I rode down to the lobby and walked briskly to my car. I shut the door of my Lexus and burst into tears. I sobbed for several minutes while fumbling around in my purse for my phone. I punched Taylor's name on my speed dial.

"He's a weirdo," I said between sniffs, still shaking. "Don't send anyone. He tried to strangle me." I wiped my dripping nose with my forearm.

"Are you okay?" Taylor sounded concerned.

"No. I'm not."

She assured me she'd put him on a do-not-call list and notify the other services. I was pretty shaken, so I called Bryan.

"What'd you expect?" he said, unfazed. "It's like a policeman thinking he's never going to get shot. We make big money cuz we take big risks. You'll be good." The phone clicked off.

Bryan left our apartment one morning carrying his dirty laundry. *Strange,* I thought, *does he have another house?* I shuffled through the papers in his drawers and found the name of some woman, Trina Miller, on a piece of mail. I called the power company posing as Trina's sister. I claimed I was calling from the post office in a hurry to pay her bill. "Could I please have her house number? I don't need the street name," I convinced them.

Done.

I placed a few more calls to other utilities and did the same thing until, bit by bit, I pieced together her exact address. I put Deshae in the car and drove to the house, careful to park a good distance away. The garage was open, with Bryan's car parked inside. Until that moment, I'd still held out a tiny hint of hope that he actually loved me. I sat there with waves of anger and pity intermittently crashing over my heart, tears streaming down my face.

"Mommy, why you so sad?" Deshae asked. I glanced in the rearview mirror and faked a smile.

"Everything's okay, honey."

I looked back as Bryan and Trina were embracing. They kissed each other goodbye and got into their cars.

Later that night, I confronted him.

Bryan scoffed. "You think you're my only girl?" He told me I was stupid for not thinking he'd have other girls. He claimed he had told me on our first vacation to Vegas that he had other girls. I was upset, screaming and crying. He slapped me, pushed me against the kitchen counter, and left.

Slumping to the floor, I sat there and sobbed from the heartbreak. I swiped my hand across my mouth and noticed blood.

"What more can I do to make you love me? I've done everything for you!"

Desperate to be loved and approved of by a man who never seemed satisfied with me, I turned my thoughts toward ways to numb the ache. I saw no point in refusing drugs from tricks who offered them to me. The high helped me escape, making the Game a little less real for a while. But when I sobered up, the emptiness always gnawed at me, leaving a deep void that no drug, man, or expensive purchase could fill. Every last drop of hope was slowly being drained from my soul.

My occasional drug use soon grew into a full-blown addiction.

One day, as I left a call with another girl from the escort service, she asked me whether I wanted to get breakfast. My first friend! I'd never been so excited to eat at Denny's. We laughed and talked about our backgrounds and families. I got home around seven o'clock.

"Where have you been?" Bryan scowled, pacing back and forth.

"I was at breakfast with one of the girls from the service." I took off my earrings and let my hair down from a high ponytail. I walked over to sit on the couch, massaging my head. Before I could sit, he grabbed my forearms so hard I winced.

"Those girls don't want to be your friends," he barked in my face. "They are trying to knock you."

"What do you mean?" I asked, pulling away and rubbing my arms.

"They want to drive a wedge between us and take you home to their man." He took me in his arms and caressed my face, holding me gently and kissing me slowly. It had been a long time since I'd felt this close to him.

"Hey, look at me," he cooed softly. "Babe, we're going to get through this soon. Things will go back to normal. I'm sorry it's been rough." His eyes were soft, his voice tender and pure like when we'd first met. We enjoyed a long, slow kiss, and all the old sparks came back.

This is the Bryan I knew. This is the man I loved.

Unfortunately, Bryan's promises of a normal life proved hollow, and turning tricks all night began to take its toll. After only a year and a half in Vegas, I was down to barely ninety-five pounds. My tailbone and ribs were visible, and my hollowed face bore the stress and humility of living day-to-day in the Game. I relied heavily on cocaine, even stashing a plate of it under my passenger seat so I could use around the clock. I could no longer function without it.

When driving, I would play "the green-light game" with Deshae. I tried to sleep at red lights, waiting for her to yell, "Green light!" Using drugs consumed my thoughts. It allowed me not to feel, not to come to the realization that Bryan didn't love me. It also shut off other emotions.

Thoughts of escape or future goals fell away.

During this time, I was working with Kyra, another girl from the service. Whenever a group of men ordered two brunettes, the service would send us out together. Kyra was a free-spirited Native American with a Canadian accent. She was kind and sweet, an artistic type who didn't much care for the flashy, blingy, high-end cars and fashion of Vegas. She wore no makeup and dressed more eccentrically than typical Vegas girls.

After one of our calls, we walked to the parking garage.

She turned to me. "Kelb, can I talk with you for a sec?"

"Ummm . . ." I looked at my watch to stall. When Vegas was slow, other pimps hid out by cars in the parking garage to jump out and rob working girls of their cash. A flashy car late at night parked close to an elevator was a giveaway that it belonged to a working girl. I feared Bryan's warnings about other girls using me for their own men and wondered whether Kyra was luring me to her car so her man could rob me.

But that wasn't like Kyra. She always seemed kind and happy and natural, not all caught up like other fake Vegas girls.

"For a minute," I consented, glancing over my shoulder to check my surroundings.

"I don't know if you know God," she continued, "but I'm overwhelmed by the need to tell you that God loves you."

I was shocked. Her words pierced me. A powerful but gentle force came over me, and I felt as though my head was being pushed down to a bowing position. I hid my face in my hands and sobbed uncontrollably.

I felt Kyra's hand on my shoulder, "Don't be afraid," she urged. "God wants you to know he loves you, but this path you're on is going to kill you."

And with that, Kyra left.

Rattled by the encounter, I sat in my car, crying for quite some time. I thought maybe the drugs were making me react this way, but also I wondered whether there actually was some Power greater than myself, like my grandma used to talk about when I was little. And if there was, I wondered how I could find out what or who that Power was.

As Christmas approached, I took Deshae to preschool one morning. She bubbled over with excitement in the back seat, singing the Christmas carols she would perform later that day in her first-ever recital. After dropping her off, I went home and snorted a line of cocaine.

I awoke staring at the linoleum on our kitchen floor. I rolled over and looked up at the clock—4:00 p.m.!

"No! Deshae's recital!" I muttered under my breath. I pulled myself up off the floor and reached for my phone. *Why hasn't the school called? What if they've already called child services?*

Ten missed calls. I raced around in a panic, trying to find my purse and car keys.

I jumped in my car and raced to the school while placing a call to the principal. Even I didn't believe my lame excuse about work. When I arrived, I found Deshae sitting next to the principal in the office. I swallowed a wave of shame.

"Mommy, you missed my sing-songs." She rubbed her eyes, which were red from crying.

What kind of mother am I? How did my life get like this? The "escape route" I'd chosen from my miserable life was turning into a dead end. I was trapped. The timing could not have been worse for my sweet girl, who desperately needed me to be front and center in her life.

Days later, my mom came to visit us. Deshae was excited for Nana's first visit since we'd moved. We drove to the airport to pick her up. As we approached the welcome area, I held Deshae's hand. Mom rounded the corner and we waved.

"Look, sweetie! There's Nana!" Deshae ran to her. Mom's eyes shifted from my daughter to me, and I watched my mother's face morph from joy to despair. As she walked closer, tears pooled in her eyes.

She fell to her knees and scooped up my three-year-old in her arms. "You're coming home with Nana." Deshae looked first at me and then at my mom, a wordless question in her eyes.

"You're not getting her back until you turn your life around," Mom whispered as she hugged me goodbye.

My mom got back on the plane with my little girl in hand.

I tried hard to get clean but only sank deeper into my addiction. Deshae, my one reason to wake up each day, was safe—thank God—but her absence gave me an excuse to sink deeper into my hole. I saw no way out of my pitiful life. I didn't care whether I lived or died.

Soon after Mom took my daughter to Oregon, I jumped in my car and took off down I-95. Desperation filled my heart. I was ready to check out of the Game. Tears streamed down my face. "I can't do this. I can't believe this is where I've let myself get to." I spoke into the vacant passenger seat, as if someone were listening. "How can I be so dumb? Deshae will be better off without me. She'll love being with Nana. I can't do this. I would rather die than live this way."

My plan was to drive head-on into the first semitruck I saw, but as the mile markers ticked by, I saw none. Ten more minutes crept by, and not a single truck passed. *Where are all the trucks? They're usually all over this stretch of I-95 at this time of night.* I glanced at the clock. I'd been driving for an hour. *What if one doesn't come?*

I'd be in trouble if I stayed out much longer. I kept driving, torn between driving all night and going home be to be slapped around. Like everything else, I couldn't figure this out either. I turned my blinker on, took the next exit, and went home.

I continued to decline. Instead of working and getting paid, I'd party with any trick who had cocaine. Bryan ranted about how I was using up all his money and tried to control my drug habit, giving me only a certain amount each night. He'd played the compassion card and insisted I go to rehab months earlier, but after two weeks, I would be back again. I just couldn't kick it.

CHAPTER 5 **home from jail**

So let God work his will in you. Yell a loud no to the
Devil and watch him scamper. Say a quiet yes to God
and he'll be there in no time. Quit dabbling in sin.
Purify your inner life. Quit playing the field. Hit bottom,
and cry your eyes out. The fun and games are over. Get
serious, really serious. Get down on your knees before
the Master; it's the only way you'll get on your feet.

September 2006

"Sandra Comer, Tisha Berry, Shalonda Price, Rebecca Saffer."
Yes! I got up from the concrete bench, my body stiff
and sore. I was thankful to be in the first group to be released,
because it was late, and I'd already missed getting Deshae from
school. I hoped to make it home in time for dinner.

The doors opened, and we snaked single-file through the
labyrinth of hallways until we reached a bench along a wall.
As before, we sat and waited for our name to be called. At the
window, we received our court date and belongings. We sat back
down and put on our clothes, shoes, and jewelry.

"Do not turn on your phones until you have exited the building," the officer barked.

After being escorted to the back door, we threw our orange

CCDC uniforms and jail sandals into a large gray laundry bin. One at a time, we exited the jail.

The afternoon sun was blinding. I slipped on my Gucci sunglasses and stepped out from the cold jail into the sweltering desert heat. I let the warmth sink in and breathed fresh air—it was a welcome change. The exhilaration of being free chased off any fatigue from my sleepless night. I turned on my phone and started walking. All the others stood there on their phones, waiting for "Daddy" to come get them.

I bought a cold lemonade from a corner store. The man at the counter looked me up and down with narrowed eyes. He made sure not to touch my hand when I paid my two bucks. I started walking the three blocks to the Golden Nugget hotel. I'd catch a cab there and return to my car at the Paris. The tart lemonade was full of flavor and refreshing after the tasteless jail food. I tried to enjoy it while enduring the embarrassing glances cast by flip-flopped tourists strolling the Old Vegas Strip.

I felt dirty and grimy from being locked up all night and exhausted as the thrill of being released wore off. People gawked at my attire, clearly not daytime wear. The locals on that side of town, however, were used to seeing "the parade" at this time of day. Their stares and whispers reminded me that I wasn't a part of their world anymore. I could hardly remember it. Me and my folks in Vegas were my new normal—they were the only family and friends I thought I needed.

A black Cadillac Escalade with twenty-two-inch rims crawled by, blasting the song from the film *Hustle & Flow*, "It's Hard Out Here for a Pimp." I knew better than to turn and look. That would be considered "reckless eyeballing," another out-of-pocket move.

The side-view mirror gave me a glimpse of one of the girls from the holding tank. She stared back, smirking as if she had it better than me. Something burned through me, and I wanted to scream at her and everyone else.

You're no better than me! None of you are better than me!

I wanted to sit down, pull my knees in, and cry. Instead, I swallowed my thoughts into the dark pit of my aching soul. In Vegas, you must keep going. You never show your cards. I'd gotten good at stuffing emotions, and my feet weren't the only part of me with calluses. My heart had them too. I took a deep breath and kept moving. I would stand up and take it. That's what my man had taught me—to take it or get a worse beating, to take a deep breath and push the hurt away.

At the Golden Nugget, I went to the taxi line. A cab patiently waiting behind the Taxis Wait Here sign pulled up quickly. The taxi reeked of cigarettes.

"Paris hotel, please."

As we drove, I tried to make small talk, asking where he was from, whether he had kids, and so on. I honestly didn't care at all, but when I was nice and flirty, the cab drivers were more inclined to drive me into the parking garage where my car was located, even though taxis are not allowed in parking garages. Typically, I would be dropped off in front of the hotel, where I'd have to walk past more gaping tourists and security guards to get back to my car. Like a vampire, I looked for ways to avoid the daylight.

This time it worked. He took me straight to my car. I got out and grabbed some money from my glove box. I handed the cab driver a twenty.

"Keep the change." I winked at him and slammed the cab door shut.

My car smelled like strawberry air freshener from being detailed a few days prior. I took off my high heels and threw them onto the passenger floorboards. I stretched my feet and toes as I started my car, a midnight blue Mercedes CLS 500. I shot onto Paris Drive, then to Audrie Street, like a rock launched from a slingshot. I took the back roads to avoid the Strip. The powerful feeling of this $80,000 car seemed to soften the pain of reality. But I knew it was a fleeting surge of ecstasy.

I drove my Mercedes through the gated Aliante community thirty miles north of the Strip. The homes looked like mini castles, nothing like the trailer park I lived in through elementary school or the standard middle-class homes of Grants Pass.

As I walked into the house from the garage, Deshae came running and almost knocked me over. The nearly five-thousand-square-foot home boasted a grand foyer, dual staircases, two master bedrooms, a theatre, an in-ground heated pool, and travertine floors that extended out of the house and into the front courtyard.

"How was your day at school, sweetie?" I asked. I scooped her up and gave her a bear hug. She squeezed my neck tightly as I carried her upstairs.

"I missed you, Mama." Her sing-songy voice was one of my favorite sounds on earth. She was my greatest joy in life, and her resiliency left me dumbfounded.

"I missed you too. I'm going to shower, and then we'll hang out before dinner, okay?" I kissed her cheek and set her down.

"*Hola*, Maria," I yelled toward the hallway. "*¿Primero lavo antes cocinar, está bien?*" My high-school Spanish was choppy, but it worked.

We'd hired our housekeeper-nanny through a classified ad Kevin had me run in a Spanish newspaper. She spoke no English, which was exactly what he wanted. "It keeps things simpler," he'd told me. "That way she's not always listening to our conversations, plus you think *she's* gonna call the police?" He required her to wear a uniform—scrubs from a local medical supply store. And she had to follow his strict cleaning regimen, which included making the beds a certain way and keeping the houseplants watered just so—he checked their soil with a shish kebab stick to see how deep the water had gone into the soil. I wasn't sure if he was just picky or purposefully swapping out nannies every few months. Maria was the fourth nanny we had been through, and she seemed to be working the best.

"Hey, Poca!" Kevin's fourteen-year-old son, Little Kev, smiled at me as he darted upstairs, taking every other step. He was a handsome boy with great athletic talent and good manners. Little Kev, or "Dada" as Kevin liked to call him, never questioned the house dynamic or what his father did for a living. Instead, he embraced our family and called all us girls "auntie" as his dad had instructed.

I had three wife-in-laws with Kevin: Brandi, April, and Tori. Kevin had two other homes in Dallas, where April and Tori primarily resided. Brandi and I lived in Vegas, but we all made occasional trips back and forth. Little Kev had lived with all us girls, visiting his mom during the summers and sometimes holidays. She felt that a young man needed to live with his father. My three sisters had known Dada longer than I had, but I trusted Kevin's decision to let him live with us at the Big House, as we called it, so that it could be the home for the kids. With Maria's help, it was easiest for Deshae and Dada to stay here.

"How was football practice?" I asked.

"Great! Guess who's starting the game on Friday?" Little Kev beamed.

"Nice job, Dada!" I raised my hand for a fist bump.

"You gonna make it to my game?" He batted his long, dark eyelashes and flashed a beaming bright smile that no girl could resist. I knew my attendance was ultimately up to Kevin, but I answered anyway.

"Yep, I'm pretty sure I am. I'm excited to watch you play."

He returned my fist bump with a secret handshake and bounded off to Deshae's room. Being the oldest of several siblings on his mother's side made him good with other kids. He and Deshae rarely fought, and agreeable Little Kev was always willing to play her girly games.

Kevin sat at his computer desk in our bedroom as he often did, researching new business ideas or new equipment that he thought we needed for his multiple businesses—the moneymaking ventures that he promised would eventually get all four of us wives out of the Game.

"Hey, babe." He looked up with a smile. *Whew. He's in a good mood.* "You tired?"

"Yeah, but I'm fine." I smiled back, relieved. Coming home, I could never be sure what to expect from Kevin. My homecoming anxiety was always high. "Going to go take a shower. I'm nasty from being in that place!"

"Cool, what's for dinner?"

"Whatever you'd like." I shut the bedroom door and peeled off the sweaty clothes that had been stuck to my skin for days.

"Italian chicken with mashed potatoes?" His little-boy eyes begged me like a four-year-old begging for M&M's in the grocery checkout. "Tori is in town, so we'll all eat together."

"Oh, great!" I said, doing my best to act excited. The truth was, I desperately wanted to spend the night off at home with Kevin and the kids. This news burst my bubble, but I didn't dare let on. Our man hated drama. Get along or face the consequences. House rules.

After I showered, Kevin showed me his latest get-rich scheme. His entrepreneurial spirit was one of the things I loved about Kevin. He was a dreamer and always had some idea up his sleeve that would get everyone in the family out of the Life. That was my dream too, and it resonated deeply!

This time it was an expensive sublimation printer that would increase our profitability. As he talked, he pulled me onto his lap and caressed my arm.

"You're not only gorgeous, Poc, you're smart," he cooed. "You're my business partner. I can throw anything at you, and you always know how to roll with it. It's like you're inside my head. You can see the end of the business plan even before I tell it to you. I need you, Poc! I need you by my side," he continued. "You know, once we figure out this business stuff, maybe you and me can have a baby. Once we get this all figured out, it will come together for us. You can stay home then and be with the kids. No more turning tricks. But I need you in this with me so we can get there. Are you in?"

"I'm in," I said, beaming. My hope resurfaced as we researched and discussed all the future plans he had for his next business idea.

Kevin had forced other wives to have abortions, but maybe I *was* special. Maybe he would let me have the baby and family I always dreamed of.

Scenes of the many times he'd beaten me crossed my mind. But he beat me the most because I hadn't yet learned his likes and dislikes, like Brandi and the other girls had. I only needed a bit more time, then the beatings would stop. I was sure of it.

CHAPTER 6 rock bottom

Jesus said to them, "Truly I tell you, the tax
collectors and the prostitutes are entering
the kingdom of God ahead of you."

December 2002

After my failed suicide attempt, my misery produced a deep-seated self-hatred. I needed to get out. But this time, instead of thinking I'd end my life on the highway, I made another plan.

That winter, I was living in a small apartment that Bryan would frequently visit—though he'd been coming around less often because he was disappointed in me. I couldn't even make my pimp happy anymore. He was simply one more guy I couldn't hold on to, one more relationship I wasn't enough for. As I slipped deeper into addiction, Bryan came to despise me. He would drop by to pick up all the money I'd made, sometimes surprising me at two or three in the morning. He'd show up without notice at hotels where I worked, making me feel as if he was following me or keeping a check on me through the service. He had a sense of what I made; if he found me putting any money aside (known as "stacking" it), I'd be in trouble. Like the time I came out from the MGM to see him standing at my car. I went to the passenger's side and asked what he was doing. He started throwing the food he had in the to-go bag at me over the car, calling me all sorts of names. I kept thinking, "I have $1,300 in the glovebox, just grab it and run." So, in a panic, I did. I learned that day that no matter where I went, he knew where to find me.

I had no real friends to turn to. Those I did have were in pretty bad shape themselves, like my drug buddy Amy, who would come over when Bryan was away. Not long after my mom took Deshae, Amy and I decided to go big or go home by pooling our cocaine stash. This wasn't one more night of partying—at least not for me. I'd hit another low without Deshae to lift my eyes to the hope of a brighter future.

Between snorts, we heard a loud pounding at the front door. I ran to the peephole.

"Crap! It's Damien," I said.

Even through the distorted lens, it was obvious that Amy's man was furious. He kicked the door over and over.

Amy came to my side, slid the chain lock open, and twisted the deadbolt. The door swung open with such force it nearly peeled off its hinges.

"You b--ch!" Damien snarled. "What do you think you're doing snorting up my money?" He grabbed Amy and dragged her into the bathroom.

My heart raced, and a pit formed in my stomach as I remembered the hot curling iron I'd left plugged in. Damien's threats of torture were excruciating. I covered my ears and rocked back and forth on the couch. Amy screamed, "Please don't! I'll stop. I'm sorry, Damien . . . Please, don't!" Her begging continued between sobs and the audible hits she was taking.

My body shook from head to toe. If I ran to help Amy, I'd risk getting burned—or worse. If I called Bryan for help, he'd surely beat the crap out of me or kick me out to be homeless. I was trapped. Again.

I hate my life.

Damien cursed his way through the living room and stormed out the door without closing it. I shut and locked the door. I bent over and rested my head in my quivering hands on my knees.

"I just want to go home, Jesus," I sobbed. I reached out for the bag of cocaine and laid down line after line, snorting each one. "If You're there, God . . . if You're real, just take me home . . ."

My nose gushed blood. My vision fogged, and I felt as if I were being thrust from my living room into these weird scenes where I was interacting with Jesus. It was as if Jesus himself were ducking behind corners in my apartment. I turned to the left, then the right, but instead of seeing his face, all I could see was his back.

"Amy!" I screamed, shaking and covered in blood. "Amy! I can't see Jesus. He keeps ducking into another room, and I can't see his face!" Then everything went black.

At some point that night or the next morning, I awoke to bright lights and the sound of an incessant beeping. I blinked several times, trying to focus. A doctor stood near my bed, checking my chart.

"We're going to do a CT scan. Do you remember your name?" he asked.

"I don't need that," I murmured and messed with the IV in my arm.

"We need to see whether your brain is hemorrhaging. You've overdosed."

The doctor left the room.

I've got to get out of here. I struggled with the tubes again. My head pounded, and my tongue stuck to the roof of my mouth.

A nurse came into the room with a clipboard. "Where do you think you're going? You're in no state to leave."

"But I have to. You don't understand. I have to go." I searched the room for my clothes and found them in the corner in a plastic bag. My body craved another hit, plus I was terrified to disappoint Bryan by being gone if he did finally decide to come over.

She shuffled papers on the clipboard, then handed it to me. I read the form on top: "Against Medical Advice."

"What does this mean?" I asked.

"It means that if you walk out of here and die, we are not held liable. We believe your brain is hemorrhaging," she said stone-faced.

I signed the form, threw my clothes on, and walked out.

I have no recollection of what happened after I walked out of the hospital. When I came to, I coughed and struggled to swallow. The hot air was suffocating, and my throat felt like sandpaper.

When I forced my eyes open, I saw that I was in the back seat of an empty car in a parking lot I didn't recognize. I immediately jumped out. I grabbed my phone from my purse and powered it on. It was the morning of the third day since I had blacked out. I called Amy. She came and picked me up. The parking lot was about twenty blocks from the hospital, and to this day I have no recollection of how I got there. Did I drive? Did I get a ride? A cab?

I knew I needed professional help if I wanted to get my life together and my little girl back. Bryan was furious about the hospital incident and kept his distance, spending time with his other girls. Yet somehow he convinced me that it was my drug use that caused all the prostitution, and that he wanted me to go to rehab because *he loved me*. I called my mom and got a list of women's rehabs in the Pacific Northwest that she'd compiled for me: Last on the list was Victory Outreach, a Christian women's home.

"Those Christians don't have a clue what real life on the streets is like," I told her as she read the phone numbers to me. I hung up and began calling the numbers on the list.

No vacancy.

No vacancy.

No vacancy.

It was as if they had all teamed up against me. I learned that most treatment centers fill up right before Christmas. Apparently, there is no shortage of addicts and homeless people searching for a "room at the inn" for the holidays.

I swiftly came to the last treatment center on my list: Victory Outreach. I called, and a young lady answered.

"Hi," I said. "I was wondering if you have any beds available?"

"No, sorry," she replied quickly.

Overwhelmed by all the closed doors, I started bawling. "Listen," I sniffed, "I'm a prostitute and a drug addict, and I'm in Las Vegas, and my mom has my daughter. I need to get her back . . . please, I'm begging you . . . can you *please* help me?"

"Hold on," she quipped.

Great, I thought. *I probably shocked the poor Christian girl.* I blew my nose and sat patiently for a few minutes until I heard an older woman's voice.

"Hello, this is sister Debbie. How can I help you?"

"Hi. I live in Las Vegas, but my mom lives in Oregon. She has my daughter, and I need to get clean before I can get her back. I'm a drug addict and a prostitute, and I was hoping you have a bed available."

"Well, sister, God must really want you here. I'll tell you what. I have one bed left, but I can hold it for only twenty-four hours. Can you be here by tomorrow?"

"Yes, I can," I blurted without thinking. She explained that I would have to commit to a one-year program. I agreed, privately planning to leave as soon as I was clean.

The only problem was, I had zero dollars to my name. I called and got the cost of a plane ticket: $342. I cleaned up in a flash and dialed the escort service to request a call, knowing full well that calls were scarce during the holidays. Most men spend that season with their families, not with working girls in Vegas.

After a long wait, a call came in. I walked out of that hotel room with $350 in my pocket. The next morning, I drove directly to the airport. I bought the first ticket to Portland, Oregon.I had already called Mom to let her know when I was arriving and where she could take me. I left a message to my drug dealer and a terse voicemail for Bryan.

"I'm done. I'm going home."

As I boarded the plane, I wondered what this place would make of me. Would the sheltered Christians be disgusted by my past? Would they judge me? Would they make me feel like the girls in Grandma's Sunday school class did, staring and keeping their distance as if divorce were contagious?

I stared out the plane window at the miniature casinos. How bad could this Victory Outreach place be? I'd survived worse things than detox.

Mom, Ken, Deshae, and I squeezed into their Toyota Tacoma at the Portland airport parking lot. I was talking a mile a minute, happy to see everyone, but the waves of dread crashing over me made the cramped thirty-minute drive to Battle Ground, Washington, feel like hours. The name of the city was fitting, though I had zero understanding of the significant spiritual battleground I was about to enter.

At first sight, Victory Outreach wasn't what I'd expected. I later learned that the ministry was renting out the U-shaped building, formerly a nursing home, to operate their rehab home for men and women.

I stepped out of the truck grateful that I still had a few cigarettes left. I lit one and sucked in the menthol deeply. The drag calmed my nerves. Deshae and Mom were grateful to stretch their legs after their five-hour drive from home. I leaned back and exhaled smoke into the crisp, chilly air. The clear sky was rare for this part of the rain-ridden Pacific Northwest.

A man came out of the house attached to one side of the building. A wide smile lit up his weathered olive complexion, and a tattoo peeked out from his shirt collar. He walked with a confident skip in his step. His look reminded me of an old school gang member. He extended his hand to me.

"You must be sister Rebecca from Las Vegas," he said with a gravelly voice. His thick accent gave away his Latino roots.

I nodded, taking my last drag, and shook his hand weakly.

"I'm Pastor Joe, the home director. It's nice to have you," he said. Strangely, I believed he meant it, likely because he hadn't heard my whole story.

"You ready for Jesus to change your life, sister?" He half smiled and laughed.

I smiled back in agreement. I was ready, and Pastor Joe struck me as someone I could open up to without the fear of shocking him. *Maybe homeboy is a'right.*

Inside, Pastor Joe took me to an intake room where a tall African American woman greeted us. She stood as we entered.

"I'm sister Monica," she said, smiling warmly. "Nice to meet you."

I felt an instant connection to this woman, who was the assistant head staff. *I can do this. I'll do thirty days, get clean, and get Deshae back.*

We filled out a bunch of forms, and they searched my clothes to make sure I had no weapons or drugs, then we toured the building. The first room in the long hallway was known as the "detox room." I would spend three days detoxing without having to adhere to the daily routine. After that, it'd be one week of blackout—no phone calls or visits. It was supposed to help me adjust to the new daily schedule. The "women's side" was a hallway that housed up to eighteen women in nine bedrooms, each with two twin beds. There was a half bathroom between each pair of rooms and one shower at the end of the hall. We were restricted to five-minute showers on a closely monitored schedule and would be disciplined for going over time.

After the tour ended, my family and I circled up for prayer with Pastor Joe, who walked me through the "Sinner's Prayer." I was too strung out to appreciate its spiritual significance, but I knew I was beginning a new journey. Whatever was ahead couldn't be worse than what I'd been through. I would dig my heels in and stay for Deshae.

CHAPTER 7 **delivered**

Charm is deceptive, and beauty is fleeting;
   but a woman who fears the LORD is to be praised.

January 2003

C ocaine detox is not as extreme as heroin withdrawal. I experienced fatigue, restlessness, nausea, and strong cravings. But after a few days with more sleep than I was used to and regular meals, the cravings began to lessen. I relied on the buzz from my nicotine patch and nicotine gum, since smoking was not allowed.

I adjusted to the new routines, which were mostly a welcome distraction from all my cravings. Much like military boot camp, we woke at five o'clock and had to keep our rooms clean and our beds made. We'd groggily walk into our small living room area and pour cups of coffee (with sugar and powdered milk if some kind soul had donated them). The building was old and musty, with moldy window seals and peeling linoleum. The living space was filled with an odd combination of garage sale furniture. A "Read the Bible in a Year" plan torn from the back of *Our Daily Bread* was taped to the wall. We'd find the date and read the Scripture while waiting for sister Monica to finish room checks.

One morning, not long after detox, I turned to our required

daily reading. Tingles swept across my entire body as I read the words of Exodus 3:6 (NLT 2000): "When Moses heard this, he hid his face in his hands because he was afraid to look at God." And then in Exodus 14:13: "Don't be afraid. Just stand where you are and watch the LORD rescue you."

Those were *his* words. The words my friend Kyra had spoken to me in her sweet voice: *Do not be afraid.*

Sitting on the dumpy couch in the Victory Outreach living room that morning, I stared back at the words in Exodus.

"He hid his face in his hands because he was afraid to look at God . . . Do not be afraid."

Did that really happen? Could God have actually sent a working girl to deliver a word to me? Moses was afraid to look at God. I'd been unable to look at Kyra, hiding my face in my hands. *Is it possible that this book, written thousands of years ago, has the same words that Kyra spoke to me that day?*

Something stirred in me, and the Bible didn't seem quite so boring anymore.

Every morning after Bible reading, we'd go into the dining area, where we'd pray for one hour. At first I didn't know what to make of this. *An entire hour? What the heck could we pray about for a whole hour? Bless the food, keep it movin'!*

Sister Monica showed us what to do. As worship music filled the dining room, she prayed out loud. She started by praying for the women's home, then for our pastors, the home directors, the city, the government, each woman, the lost, the brokenhearted. By this time, the Spirit of God was flowing out of sister Monica, and she wept and prayed for her family, her children, her marriage and thanked God for her deliverance and the renewal of her mind and heart.

I was mesmerized. I'd never heard or seen this kind of prayer. I listened to the music, soaking up the peace I felt in these still moments of the early morning. I looked out the window to the earliest whispers of light before sunrise. I yawned and stretched my arms above my head. I wasn't used to being up early unless I was coming home from a call.

I closed my eyes and lifted my hands.

A strange sensation crept over me, and my body quivered. It felt exactly the same as the night Peter tried to strangle me, right before he stopped. Memories of that night came racing back. It startled me, and I opened my eyes.

Why am I remembering this now? I thought I had buried that terror in the back of my mind.

A silent thought, much like my own but altogether different and set apart, came suddenly, piercing my heart: "That is the feeling of life, not death. It was me who released his hands from your neck."

I fell to my knees and wept tears of gratitude.

"Well then, my life is yours to use as you wish," I prayed silently. "If it weren't for you, I wouldn't be here. Why did you save *me*? You not only helped me escape; you saved my life. What do you have for me, God?"

A fire lit my soul and made me hungry for more. I began soaking up God's Word daily. For the first time in my life, I read the stories of Mary Magdalene, Rahab, Tamar, the woman at the well, and the alabaster jar. I realized that Jesus loved girls like me.

Every Sunday morning, the residents of Victory Outreach Center boarded an old school bus in single-file lines, women first, then the men, and headed into Portland for church. As I listened to the pastor's message one Sunday, I once again felt the deep longing to be free from the bondage of drugs. I rose from my seat and walked down the aisle to the altar, where I knelt and begged God to deliver me.

A soft voice whispered behind me. I recognized Pastor Joe's sister's voice as she began to pray, warring against the stronghold of drugs that was too much to release on my own. My body shook, like the time God had spoken to me about rescuing me from being strangled. I began crying so hard I thought I might throw up. Pastor Joe's sister continued praying until my body quieted and things became still. When I left the altar, I was drenched with sweat through my clothes as if I had just stepped out of the shower. Since that moment, I've never again craved drugs or cigarettes. I was delivered.

As my aunt Loretta and uncle Gerry learned of the miracles I'd experienced, they mailed me books to read. I devoured *The Purpose Driven Life* by Rick Warren, *God's Leading Lady* by T. D. Jakes, *The Power of a Praying Woman* by Stormie Omartian, and other classics about prayer and renewing the mind in truth. I couldn't read fast enough.

After these personal encounters with the creator of the universe, the Bible came alive to me, especially Psalm 40. I'd crawl under my blankets, letting the real-life stories draw me in as I read them by flashlight after lights-out. My aunt and uncle sent me a Bible dictionary, encyclopedia, and concordance. I'd tell the women in the home the stories I was learning and the Greek and Hebrew meanings of certain words and phrases. I read through the Bible three times that year and was allowed to host a weekly Bible study for the residents.

The highlight of my week was leading a *Purpose Driven Life* class for the residents. As I taught, a love for preaching and teaching emerged. It was a gift that burned inside me, yearning to come out, and I felt most alive when I was exercising this passion.

God was doing something in me. I was a new creation. He had restored my shattered heart, and he was renewing my mind, giving me new desires and hope-filled thoughts. I learned about spiritual warfare, generational curses, and my authority in Christ.

On weekends, my mom and stepdad or aunt and uncle would make the five-hour drive to bring Deshae up to visit. They were sharing custody of her during my time in rehab and had put her in the private Christian school where my uncle was a teacher. They would have her during the weekday with my Nannie, and my mom would take her on weekends. She would run through the women's home, and the older women would dote on her. She'd get dressed up and come to church with me. If sister Debbie—Pastor Joe's wife, who had taken my desperate call right before Christmas—was in a good mood, she'd let Deshae sleep in the twin bed in my room with me. Deshae would squeal with excitement when she got to cuddle in Mom's bed. We'd play soccer in the front yard, and I'd swing her around until we both fell to the ground giggling. I missed her so much. Sometimes my family would come with gifts, including good coffee with real creamer—not the powdered kind—and books to keep my mind occupied. We'd all stay in a hotel and eat out. Other family members and friends would occasionally visit, write letters, and send cards with a twenty tucked inside to help me buy shampoo and toiletries. I was grateful for the support they provided. These sweet gestures and visits helped get me through the hard days.

And yet my heart hungered for a healthy family of my own. It was my deepest desire.

One night before bed, I got on my knees and prayed to be married—to have a husband and more kids. I felt as if God had placed that desire in my heart and that it was something he wanted for me too. But instead of waiting on his timing, I had settled for a counterfeit family. I prayed some more and thought about how God wants infinitely more for us than we can imagine, yet we impatiently settle for far less. A song kept playing in my mind as I prayed, one that wasn't my style, but I had heard it often on the radio. It was God's promise to be my hero, to relieve my pain. I loved how God spoke to me, meeting me right where I was, with secular music and words that pierced my heart.

One night, as I spent time with the Lord, my mind drifted to the painful memory of when Bryan had slapped me around, then left me wiping blood from my mouth as I sobbed on the floor. *What more can I do to make you love me? I've done everything for you!* The pain of feeling forsaken . . . not enough . . . unloved . . . came rushing back to me.

The Lord's gentle whisper entered the horrible memory. He spoke to me with firm truth and gentle grace: "That's how I feel about you. What more can I do to make *you* love me? I've been battered and bloody to the point of death *for you*. Why am I not enough?"

His words wrecked me. To think I had left Jesus as heart-broken as Bryan had left me grieved my heart. I sought his forgiveness—I hadn't known I could break the heart of God. Even before the words left my mouth, I felt a supernatural peace. Jesus and his sacrifice were now even more real and alive to me.

I loved being at Victory Outreach. It was tough, but I finally had the structure and boundaries that I'd lacked throughout my life. I loved the daily disciplines of reading God's Word and beginning every morning with an hour of prayer. Our weekly schedule included classes on domestic violence, the twelve steps of breaking addiction, and parenting. But as helpful as these classes were, I remained ignorant about the tangled business of the sex industry that still subtly held me captive.

I'd never even heard of human trafficking. I considered myself to be a prostitute with a boyfriend who beat me. I didn't understand how the complexities of force, fraud, or coercion had played out in my everyday life, and I definitely didn't learn about it from my classes or home directors or pastors. Victory Outreach didn't offer counseling or therapy for trauma. The residents were not given specialized services for trauma bonding, complex, compound trauma, or PTSD. We certainly weren't taught about brainwashing or Stockholm syndrome. I wouldn't learn about these powerful influences for several more years. Victory Outreach was a drug rehab center—and a good one—but this location did not provide the specialized services that victims of exploitation need.

After our morning Bible reading, prayer, and class, we were put on work crews. Several work crews went out every day either to wash cars, clean houses, or do jobs at the center as sister Debbie dictated.

I hated car wash duty, the crew to which I was most often assigned. Every week we'd secure a fast-food location as our host. We'd load up the buckets, hoses, mitts, and signs and head down. We'd rotate each hour from holding signs to washing to rinsing with the hose. Whoever had the hose collected the donation money. We'd wash cars in rain, snow, or unrelenting heat. As I held the signs, I'd sing, pray, and listen to the praise music on the Discman my family had sent me to help pass the time.

These jobs were the way to raise money for the ministry. Some women would get upset and complain that they were using us to make money. Though I disliked washing cars, I didn't mind pulling my own weight. Victory Outreach housed us for free, while most rehabs charged thousands of dollars—money my family didn't have.

I understood the business side of fundraising. It was fun coming in and sitting with Pastor Joe to count the day's money and turn in the receipt for the car wash soap. There were other things I struggled with, such as the five-minute showers and being disciplined for going over—something I became quite familiar with. We'd shave our legs in a bucket in the bathroom to save time in the shower. I often had to wash windows after work crew for being mouthy to the head staff or sarcastic to sister Debbie or too flirty with the men's side. If I didn't perform these after-hours chores, I'd be denied a visit from Deshae. The discipline often triggered the same feelings of being dominated that I had experienced with Bryan.

When I got down and would feel like quitting, Pastor Joe helped me keep perspective. Sister Debbie was less patient with me. I had been studying God's Word so much that it oozed out of me, but as a new Christian, I lacked the maturity to resist turning it against others. I once made the mistake of telling one of the head staff to tame her tongue so she didn't set things on fire (James 3).

Sister Debbie marched into my room and examined the verses I'd taped all over my wall.

"Stop pretending like you know Scripture!" she yelled as she tore the verses off my walls and tossed them on the ground. Her small stature couldn't reach the highest ones, so she climbed onto my bed and ripped them off as I stood there helpless. "If God has a call on your life, He'll tell your leaders first. He is a God of order."

"I'm not sure the word *order* means that kind of order, sister Debbie." I jabbed at her while picking up the papers.

"Oh, you think you're so smart. You're on discipline again!" She stormed out of my room. Anger flooded my heart, and thoughts that mimicked the way I had felt after Bryan went off on me or when I would have to act tough in the streets or in jail whirled through my mind.

These episodes happened frequently in the rehab home. But

it made me hit my knees and draw near to God instead of people. He constantly reminded me that David had become a great king by serving under Saul and learning what not to do.

In late 2003 I was moved into a "transitional phase" and needed to find a real job. I would live at the center but take the public bus to and from my workplace until I had earned enough to afford my own place. Anyone in transitional housing continued to have free rent and food, as well as the support of daily structure, Bible studies, and someone to talk to about the temptation to stop at the bar or smoke on the way home.

Being forced to work next to others on car wash or cleaning crew and reporting to a boss I didn't like proved to be invaluable experiences. It taught me how to hold my tongue and surrender my anger or frustration to God. To be successful, I had to learn how to respond when I bumped up against rules and people I didn't like or unjust situations that triggered me. God was using all things for my good, and I had gained what was most important: my sobriety, my life purpose, and a deep relationship with Christ.

I got a job as a cell phone sales consultant in a shopping mall. I'd ride the bus an hour from Battle Ground, Washington, into Portland, Oregon, transferring several times. I only worked twenty hours a week, but the schedule and distance kept me gone almost all day.

I saved enough to afford a one-bedroom apartment within walking distance of the local church in Northeast Portland and finally got Deshae back. Leaving her was the hardest decision. She was the piece of my life that had been missing for the last year, and now things were looking up. I experienced normal life for the first time since I'd moved to Vegas.

We didn't have a car, so we rode the bus. God provided. To furnish our bare apartment, Aunt Loretta and I found every item on my "wish list" during a weekend yard sale shopping spree. We didn't have a washer and dryer, so Sundays after church we'd pack our clothes in baskets and head to the laundromat. Deshae started daycare and began to read. Life was different—hard but hopeful. I experienced a deep, daily peace that I hadn't felt in a long time.

But eventually I wanted to date again and be a normal twenty-two-year-old girl. I wondered how I could ever get out of poverty. I'd take the bus an hour uptown to get Deshae to pre-school, then another half hour back downtown to the shopping mall to the cell phone store. On my walk into work one afternoon, I passed by a coffee shop. The rich aromas tantalized my senses, triggering a craving for a white chocolate mocha like the ones I drank any time I wanted to in Vegas. A whisper wormed its way into my thoughts.

"Is this how good your God is? You can't even afford a cup of coffee."

A seed of discontent began to take root. I missed money. Even though Bryan controlled all of it, I remembered Vegas as a place where I could buy what I wanted, when I wanted it. I still suffered from PTSD but didn't know it, had experienced major trauma, and was living in poverty with no light at the end of the tunnel. The peace and hope I had experienced stopped being enough.

One day, lonely and broke, I picked up my phone and called Bryan.

He responded warmly. "I wondered when I was gonna hear from you. How are things?"

My stomach fluttered with butterflies. Like Pavlov's dog hearing the bell and salivating, Bryan's voice made me feel something I hadn't felt in a long time.

"I miss you," I told him.

"I miss you too. I want you and the baby to come home. We'll be a family again."

His promise was my kryptonite. No one had explained to me that I was a victim bound to my pimp by a trauma bond that drug rehab hadn't broken. Like cult members or kidnapped victims who've lived with their captor for extended periods, bonds of loyalty form between victims and their abusers. These "trauma bonds" are unhealthy, destructive, and can be extremely difficult to break.

Yes, God had helped me to prune the huge branches of addiction, but the destructive root of trauma was still there. Even the sound of Bryan's voice triggered physical responses in me. Like an adrenaline junkie who'd been invited to jump out of the next plane, I was enticed back to my trafficker and the lifestyle of so-called luxury that he promised me.

We started texting at night. He convinced me to come home, but he laid out clear conditions. He would not pay to move me back again because of how much he lost last time. Strangely, I thought this was fair. If I could get to Vegas, he would take me back. But how? There was no way I was going to be able to save up enough money to buy plane tickets on a twenty-hour-a-week sales job.

The rational side of me hated the idea of being that girl again—the one who answered to someone 24/7. The one who crossed the line every night. The one whose daughter had no idea what her mommy actually did as she slept peacefully in a bed paid for by sale of human flesh. But my days became consumed with a longing to get back to Bryan, to love and be loved.

One day, as I stood at the entrance to the cell phone store, my eye caught a man dressed in clothes that screamed money. He walked through the mall with a lot of swag, apparently alone, and he loitered, stopping to chat with girls. My pulse quickened as he made his way toward my store. I was more than happy to assist "Ricky," the name he gave as I introduced myself and showed him our product line. We discussed pricing, and I recommended one of our most popular phones.

"Great. I'll take it," Ricky said, trying to impress me by counting out cash from his wad of hundreds—a telltale sign that my hunch was correct.

"Great. I'll take a ticket to Vegas." I smiled as I watched him look up from his wallet. I could tell from his inquisitive expression that he wasn't expecting my flippant response.

"What do you know about Vegas?" he asked, cocking his head to the side with a grin.

"I've been in the Game." I flashed him a flirty look and leaned in a little closer.

He scanned me up and down as if he were checking out a new car in some fancy dealership.

After work that day, Ricky drove me home so I could avoid riding the bus. I packed my things and moved in with him. He was my opportunity to get to Vegas and back to Bryan.

At church the next Sunday, one of the Victory Outreach leaders sensed that something was wrong. My usual seat was empty. She immediately came looking for me and was calling frantically.

My phone blew up with messages from my Victory Outreach family. They were worried. As I was reading the messages, sister Monica's named popped up on my phone screen.

"Hello," I answered.

"Beck. What's going on? Where are you?" Concern seeped from her voice as she audibly held back tears.

I was silent, trying to form my words carefully. Before I could give an answer, she blurted, "You're either God's friend or his foe, Beck!" I hung up, scared and painfully aware that I was at a crossroads, but I couldn't do anything but move in the direction I'd been heading.

Aunt Loretta called soon after. "You're making the wrong decision, Becky." Her voice was stern, but I could tell she was crying as she issued her loving warning.

They were right. All of them. I knew I was making the wrong decision, but it was too late. I'd promised Bryan I was coming home, and I'd pulled Deshae out of school. I had already moved my things out. I felt as though I had passed the point of no return. If I returned to my Victory Outreach family now, they'd discipline me and make me start over. I would lose Deshae, my teaching privileges, and all the freedom I'd worked so hard to earn. They'd probably put me back in rehab and I'd lose her again.

What's done is done, I thought. *I've already ruined it. I can't go back now. I'm too far in. I'm going back to the Game.*

CHAPTER 8 choosing up

With persuasive words she led him astray;
she seduced him with her smooth talk.
All at once he followed her
like an ox going to the slaughter,
like a deer stepping into a noose
till an arrow pierces his liver,
like a bird darting into a snare,
little knowing it will cost him his life.

April 2004

From the moment I pulled into Ricky's driveway, I knew I had made the wrong decision, but I was too paralyzed to make a U-turn. *You can do this,* I told myself. *Just push through and get back to Bryan.* I walked to the front door of the run-down rental home. I'm not sure which was worse: the tired, salmon-colored exterior or the filthy interior, complete with dust-caked vinyl miniblinds and a clutter of mismatched Craigslist furniture. This was definitely not what I had imagined when I packed my things.

"Do you have a housekeeper?" I crinkled my nose at the stench of days-old takeout sitting on his kitchen counter.

"You're the housekeeper." He smiled.

What have I done? I just need to get to Vegas.

Ricky put me on the street immediately. As soon as my stilettos hit the track on 82nd Street, the sick-to-my-stomach adrenaline surged through me, coupled with fear. I had never walked the street like this before. Strutting on the Las Vegas Strip in between going in and out of casinos was very different than being on the track. I was petrified. I was used to calling on with services and booking appointments online. This was different. It was frightening. *This is where serial killers find their victims.*

I ventured out into his territory like a junkie who'd returned to the rush of a hit but with more fear than excitement. Money was my drug now, and the need to love and be loved consumed me. My heart was in my stomach over returning to the Game and stooping to this scary street life. It was not what I was used to, but if I proved myself, I'd earn my ticket back to Vegas and back to Bryan.

I hated walking the street, loitering in strip club parking lots and browsing the aisles of porn shops to offer men a visit to their cars. The track was scary. Getting in and out of vehicles without knowing a trick's name—a thin protection most hotel registrations provided—was frightening. I could be held at gunpoint, raped, or murdered at any time. I'd try to get tricks to meet me at a hotel nearby, but more often they'd resort to a thirty-minute rental at a hot tub chain that sat strategically on the track. Shame gut-punched me, and I fell into a deeper rut of depression than I'd ever experienced before.

Denial helped me cope with my situation. I adopted the rules and lingo—*working girl, dates, ads, calls*—to minimize in my own mind the risks I was taking, to make it palatable and normal. I had used these same denial and coping skills when I was using drugs, when I told myself, *I'm not an addict. I can afford my drug of choice.* Back in the day, it wasn't until my dealer was gone and I was out of cocaine that I had stooped to smoking crack to maintain my high. I realized I had hit a low. And here I was again, this time at an all-time low.

Finally, after a month or so, Ricky took me to Vegas.

I couldn't see Bryan fast enough, my trauma bond in full force. Ricky didn't know. I would need to make a move quickly—it was too hard to hide Ricky and Bryan from each other. I wanted to ditch Ricky immediately, but Bryan suddenly wasn't as open to our reconciliation as I had hoped. He met me one night and wouldn't return my affection. I felt heartbroken and betrayed.

"When you start putting money back in my pocket, you can reap the benefits. You know the rules: PIMP stands for Put It in My Pocket. Purse first, a— last, baby." He said it with a smile as if I were astute to these games and rules. It hit me then: I was nothing but a trick to him. The way I felt about buyers was the same way he felt about me. It was all a trick.

"This isn't a game to me, Bryan! This is my life." I tore away from his "loving" grasp and left.

I was heartbroken by Bryan, and my heart hardened again. I couldn't trust anyone. I had to look out for myself and find a way out. I wish leaving Ricky could have been that easy, and maybe it was, but the fear and trauma and shame kept me frozen.

So did the risk. Trying to leave the Game is a little like trying to leave the Mafia or some elite gang. There are great costs to leaving. There are rules. You can't simply say, "Well, thanks for showing me around, but I think I bit off more than I can chew. Time to pack it up. Take care!" You can only run and hope your trafficker doesn't find you, beat you, hurt your family, or kill you. It was different when I left Bryan in 2002. Deshae was safe with my mom, and Bryan had given up on me; he darn near kicked me out for "using up all his money and for fighting with his girls."

I'd figure it out. I just needed time. I didn't even have my own car yet and had been driving Ricky's around. I'd quietly stay with him until I had a plan to get out.

I dialed the 702 number that was ingrained in my memory.

"Hey, Dani. It's Kelby. I'm back." I reenlisted with Girls To You, and just like that I was Kelby again, a familiar persona, like putting on a comfortable shoe. Taylor, Dani, and Maddy were still working the phones. Lenora, the owner, was still calling the shots and trying to get girls to join her stable. They were all happy to see me and gave me calls right away. Within a week or two, they eagerly sent me on a five-girl call to Planet Hollywood.

Three working girls made small talk with me and our buyers in the Planet Hollywood suite living room while waiting for the other girl to show. Once she arrived, we would explain the agency fee and tipping.

I checked my phone. She was almost ten minutes late, and I was getting tired of small talk. Moments later, the suite door flew open, and in walked a stunning blond with shoulder-length curly hair and a dazzling white smile that turned every head. Her tight jeans and short multicolored shirt showed off her flat, tanned stomach, which I assumed was the result of countless hours in the gym.

"Okay, all five of us are here?" the blond said as she strutted in, leading with her chest. "Who's in charge?" She held an orange Louis Vuitton clutch, and her Bluetooth earpiece blinked under her hair.

"We're all in charge," a red-haired man popped off, as if he was not about to be bamboozled.

"No worries, sweetheart." The blond smiled sweetly. "Is each guy paying for himself, or is one guy paying for everything?"

"How does this whole thing work?" he asked. "The lady said $100 per girl."

She gave a slight giggle and tilted her head sideways. "Well, baby," she cooed, her bright blue eyes casting a spell on the man. Her combination of sex appeal and next-door Bambi innocence drew him in like a fly to a July Fourth potluck.

"The hundred is our company's fee. That will get you a strip tease. Your *tip* will determine the amount of entertainment you receive beyond that. The more you pay, the longer we stay, and the more fun we have. Make sense?" She winked and then raised her index finger to shush us as she pushed the blue light blinking in her ear.

"This is Jillian," she answered, turning away from her captive audience. "Yes, we're all here. . . . No, we are not checking in yet. Will call you soon." We had to "check in" with the services to make sure everything was going as planned.

I hoped she wanted to negotiate for all of us together. Surely she could get a higher price than I could. She seemed to have her act together.

"Well, guys," she said turning back around, "my company needs that $500 for all of us to stay, or they'll have to send us on another call. If I get the money, then we can check in and get them off our backs. You can pick your girl and go negotiate your tip privately. How does that sound?" she scanned the men coyly.

The gentleman who seemed apprehensive at first jumped up from his seat. "I'll take you," he said, pointing at Jillian.

She waved at us as he led her into the bedroom. "Check in on your own," she instructed.

I was picked third. *Not bad,* I thought. I hadn't been back in Vegas that long, and my skills were rusty. My primping wasn't at the top of Ricky's priority list. My shoulder-length brown hair hadn't been cut or colored professionally in months. I wore a white capri pantsuit that popped against my olive skin, but my camisole probably concealed my bust a little too much for Vegas standards. I had become used to church attire. My white, strappy Manolo Blahniks that Bryan had bought me so long ago needed cleaning.

That night I sensed I'd met a remarkable woman but had no idea she would forever change the course of my life. I soon came to learn that her real name was Brandi, and we were frequently put together on calls for the service. We even exchanged numbers so we could invite each other along on calls. One night she called me.

"Can you do something for me?" she asked.

"Yeah, what's up?" I offered.

"I'm stealing this call. If the service asks, will you tell them we went on a call together at the Wynn?"

"Sure, no problem."

Many girls would steal a call if the buyer couldn't afford the fee. For example, if he had only $300, and the service fee was $150, that left only $150 for the working girl minus the 20 percent to the phone girl. Many girls would call the service and say another girl had beat them to the buyer (many men shopped around for better rates) or that he hadn't answered the door. When that happened, the service usually required the girl to return to the office within fifteen minutes or face a fine. Stealing a call could get you blacklisted by the service. If the phone girl suspected stealing, she'd do some digging with the buyer or another service to catch the stealer.

I know now that Brandi was testing me. Would I lie for her? Would I cover for her? Could I be trusted? But her offer to include me in the con sparked something deep inside me. I felt flattered and privileged to be asked, as though the cool girl at school had asked me to cover for her skipping class.

I had never stolen a call from a service before. If a man didn't have much money, I'd take the $150 drop, give him a quick strip tease and leave, taking the $150 back to the service. These were considered "base calls," and all the girls, including me, hated them.

Brandi refused to run around on base calls all night making no money, so she'd simply tell the agency the call was a "no-go." Then she would stay and pocket the small amount of money for herself. Brandi also worked the system to her advantage by enlisting with more than one escort service—a foreign concept to me. Bryan had always insisted on one service, telling me to "stay loyal, build relationships there, and sit at home between calls, waiting for your phone to ring."

Brandi would be out from nine o'clock until two o'clock or longer. Between calls from the services, she would "freelance," also a new concept for me, but I enjoyed the additional revenue streams. Freelancing—scouring hotels and casinos looking for a trick—had its advantages: no service involved meant no fees, no tips. Everything a girl earned was hers. But the disadvantages were hefty. There was no protection if a buyer turned aggressive or threatening. As working girls, we could throw this in a man's face if he misbehaved. "My service has your real name, and the hotel has your ID on file." That usually calmed them down.

After I covered for her, Brandi started inviting me out to freelance. We'd meet on the Strip for an early dinner and get to know each other after I had dropped Deshae off at a twenty-four-hour daycare. Brandi had been with her man, Kevin Barker, since she was seventeen, when she was a couch-hopping runaway needing attention. He wooed her with his mansion and fancy car and the promise of turning her into a businesswoman. In the years she'd been with him, Kevin had trained her well, and she believed he was making her better. She'd stopped smoking and was eating right, working out, and taking vitamins.

One evening, while grabbing an early dinner together at the bar of the Four Seasons, I watched Brandi cut her steak into small, delicate pieces. She chewed each one slowly, and between bites she balanced her knife on the edge of the plate and sipped her water silently. She could have held a grapefruit between her shoulder blades, her posture was so good.

I took smaller bites of my hamburger and sat up a little straighter.

She gently touched a series of four purplish-yellow finger prints around my forearm with her French-manicured fingertips.

"Your man treats you like that?" she asked.

I covered the bruise with my hand, looked down at the floor, and silently rehearsed the rules in my head. *Never bad-talk your man with another working girl.* Ricky, like Bryan, would manhandle me when I upset him.

"Does your man have other girls?" I asked.

She nodded. "One of my sisters, our bottom, is retired now and runs one of the family businesses. All of us in the family get out of the Game eventually, with a home and business in our name."

I'd never heard of any wife-in-laws calling each other sisters. I'd never heard of working girls actually getting to live the life their pimps had promised them. I was curious and a little speechless.

"Do *you* have wife-in-laws?" she asked, perhaps in response to my shocked expression.

"Uh . . . I used to," I sputtered. "My current dude had a girl before me, but she hasn't been around lately."

She made eye contact with the bartender and tapped her empty glass to signal that she needed a refill. She looked at me with a closed-mouth smile, making me wonder whether I had said something I shouldn't have.

"I'm surprised you're not bottom," I said. I'd figured she was in charge. I could not imagine another girl being in charge of Brandi.

"No, I'm not. I have two sisters before me. April is bottom and has been here seventeen years. She's retired. The next is Tori. She's been here fifteen and is basically retired, with just a few regulars. I've been here seven."

"*Seventeen years?!*" I nearly choked on my burger. "Fifteen? He hasn't kicked them out?"

"No, sweetie." She giggled. "That's not how our family works," she said as if she were explaining the Girl Scouts' code of honor.

"We even have sister days—go to the spa, hang out by the pool." She daintily dabbed the corners of her mouth with a cloth napkin and placed it neatly back in her lap.

"Sisters? Retired?" I asked. When I worked for Bryan, not only was I not allowed to have friends, but his other girls weren't even allowed to know each other. Over time, of course, we found out, but we'd fight and argue if we ever saw each other in the streets.

"Yes, sisters." Brandi replied. "We're all close. It's more than the game street pimps play to breed competition. We're a family. We have each other's backs, and we stick together for life. April and Tori live in Dallas, and they run our pizza shop. April loves horses and just got a ranch near our home. I have a business we just started here in Vegas."

She looked me squarely in the eyes with a seriousness that struck my soul.

"Kelby, what is your man doing with your money? How are you planning on getting out?"

I had no answer.

In the week that followed, her question haunted me as I worked each night. Every time Ricky took the money I made,

Brandi's question buzzed around my brain. It made my head spin to think of how much money I could have if I'd been working with Brandi and her sisters all along, or on my own. But "renegades" are shunned in Vegas; if you're a girl in the Game with no dude, you're a target for other pimps. Brandi's family was making legitimate investments with their money, and all I had to show for my work was . . . *nothing!*

Soon Brandi invited Deshae and me out to lunch with her. At the time, I thought she was being friendly, but I'd later learn she was recruiting for Kevin and checking whether Deshae was a "good kid" with manners. She did her pimp's footwork to see whether we were even worth his time. Was I a snitch? Was I teachable? This recruiting style is required in most stables, and Kevin was no different.

Days later Brandi arranged for me to meet Kevin after a call. As I walked out of the hotel to the valet, the wind blew my hair back. I was wearing a form-fitting black dress. We approached a truck, and a well-built man in his midforties stepped out of a white Ford F-450 truck. His build made me wonder whether he'd ever played football. He was handsome and mature, not like the guys in their twenties whom I had been dating. He wore a loose gray T-shirt with no logo or brand, and baggy gray sweatpants. Simple, inconspicuous. Already he seemed different from most pimps, who drove flashy cars and SUVs and wore expensive clothes and jewelry.

Maybe he has his act together and has already figured out how to use the Game as a way out, not just wasting money on cars, jewelry, and clothes .

"Dang, Boo!" he said to Brandi. "She's finer than you." I was flattered that my appearance stacked up against Brandi's jaw-dropping good looks. She giggled and opened the door for me. It struck me as bizarre that he openly complimented me in front of her in such a way that put her down. It was even stranger that she seemed thrilled about it. I was fascinated.

We exchanged small talk and hopped into Kevin's truck. On the way to dinner, he pointed at my purse. "I don't want in there"—then he touched my temple and smirked—"I want in here." I thought he just meant getting to know me and not just use me, but I had no clue what was to come.

As Brandi and I grew closer in the weeks that followed and we learned more about each other, I knew I had a decision to make. Kevin wanted me in their family. If I went with them, I knew Ricky would be mad, but life with Brandi's family sounded much better than any life I'd known in the Game up until now. After meeting Kevin, I believed he would be able to protect Deshae and me from retaliation.

One evening I stood in the Rio, watching their nightly masquerade show. The dancers descended from a colorfully-lit mobile showboat that moved across the ceiling as they tossed Mardi Gras beads to the partiers below. The crowd cheered over the loud music, but all I could think about was making my move.

What am I doing? I thought. *I can't stay with Ricky. Bryan doesn't want me. If I go back home, I'll be right back at square one: a poor, single mom. Could Brandi be my way out? Could her family be my ticket to retiring with a business and a home, and Deshae and I not living in poverty? I could work a normal job.*

That day, I "chose up," a subtle, yet impactful phrase created by pimps. It's crazy that it's called *choosing* up; the truth is, I felt trapped. Going with Brandi and Kevin felt like the best of my grim options.

When a working girl chooses up, the transaction gets messy. Sometimes this can mean two traffickers fight over a girl, exchange money for a girl, or simply use threats and intimidation to get what they want. Thankfully, Kevin was intimidating enough for Ricky to resign.

At first they talked on the phone at a distance so I couldn't hear. Before hanging up, Kevin walked over to me and handed me the phone.

"He wants to hear it from your mouth," he commanded.

Ricky left our apartment for a few hours while I packed my stuff. Brandi was not allowed to set foot in another man's home, so she stood outside and ran my boxes down the apartment stairs to Kevin's truck. We were almost back to Kevin's when Ricky got home and called Kevin, complaining that I'd taken items that weren't mine.

Kevin turned the truck around and headed back to the apartment.

"You leave with what you came with," Kevin said to me as if rehearsing some sacred creed. He seemed upset at Ricky for being a punk. But he also told me, "You come with nothing; you leave with nothing. Take off everything, even them crusty drawers you have on."

"But this is *my* watch! My mom gave it to me for my eighteenth birthday," I explained.

"I'll get you new stuff. Just give this fool back everything."

Embarrassed, I undressed in the apartment. I reluctantly unclasped the silver dove necklace that my mom had given me for graduating Victory Outreach and laid it on the white laminate countertop. Taking one last look at these vestiges from my family, I felt as if I was stripping off the last ounce of Rebecca. Covering myself with my hands, I walked back to the truck as fast as I could. With tears in my eyes, I looked around for Brandi, the one person I depended on, but she was long gone. Abandoned and scared, I got in Kevin's truck and dug into the last small bag in the back. Thankfully, I still had jeans and a shirt, which

I slithered into in the front seat. When we arrived at Brandi's townhouse, she acted as though nothing were out of the ordinary and took me to her closet, where I "shopped" for clothes to borrow. Her things were expensive. And she seemed genuinely happy to help me pick out something that complimented my figure and fit my style. The traumatic moments prior were pushed out of my mind to be forgotten. *Keep it movin'.*

"Oh, try this!" She handed me a black Roberto Cavalli dress with a bold floral print. It must have cost her—or him—hundreds. The fabric felt luxurious on my skin. I felt like Cinderella showing off her gown to her Fairy Godmother. Brandi's face lit up.

"Here, use this purse. I don't have the matching shoes— the last girl ran off with them," she said as if it happened every other day.

I smiled back at her. I couldn't have cared less about matching shoes. I would have been happy with a dress off the clearance rack from Target if Brandi had given it to me. I liked her, and I hadn't had a friend in a long time. This kind, intelligent, captivating girl had accepted me into her group. I didn't realize how much I had longed for connection that wasn't sexual or romantic in nature. We formed an immediate bond, and I somehow knew we'd be there for each other through whatever awaited us.

"Doesn't she look great?" Brandi asked Kevin as we came out of the bedroom. He stood up from his chair.

"Wow, you look like a million bucks. Literally," he said with a wink.

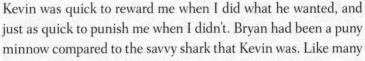

Kevin was quick to reward me when I did what he wanted, and just as quick to punish me when I didn't. Bryan had been a puny minnow compared to the savvy shark that Kevin was. Like many traffickers, he understood how to control my beliefs, my access to information, my thoughts, and my emotions—manipulation tactics that leaders of cults typically use to brainwash their followers. He threatened to give my birthday present—tickets to an R. Kelly concert—to Brandi once because I was "being mouthy." He hung that night over my head as punishment for noncooperation. But I didn't know anything about brainwashing tactics then.

Kevin's authority was absolute. It was the first lesson he taught me. My second day in the townhouse, I bantered back and forth with him and risked making a lighthearted joke. He shot some snarky comment back, and without giving it much thought, I coyly replied, "Whatever!" I thought we were flirting.

Without missing a beat, he snatched me by the throat, pressed me hard against the kitchen wall, and raised me several inches off the ground. His eyes flashed.

"I'm not like those punks you can talk to anyway you want," he growled at me in a low, controlled tone. "You understand me?"

I nodded. As he released his grip, I rubbed my neck.

In the beginning, I was Brandi's student. I rode around in her car, and she taught me that Kevin never wanted to know the details of me going with tricks. He trusted that Brandi would train me exactly how he wanted, by "Kevin's rules":

- Get car keys and pepper spray out before entering the parking garage so you don't get robbed.
- Check condoms for punctures by running them under water prior to use.
- Always keep your hand on the condom so you're sure it does not slip off.
- Never put your clothes on the dirty floor.
- Always lock your money in the glove box.
- Always lock the deadbolt in a hotel room upon entry so no unexpected "friends" of the trick show up.

- Never exchange body fluids, including no kissing or eating off the same fork.
- Never tell a trick any personal information about yourself.
- Always leave flight and hotel information with a sister when going out of town.
- Always try to make the trick fall in love with you.

She went over the ins and outs of doing business their way, including excuses to avoid kissing buyers, what to say to the police if you're arrested, and how to get and keep regulars. "Regulars run you less risk of arrest, and they'll send you money even when they're not in town."

Brandi handled all the money during the training period, and as Kevin instructed, I went with her on every call. I studied the way she walked and how she talked with clients. Compared to her I felt like such a novice, even after a couple of years in the Game, but she was patient and always had my back.

Over time, I'd learn more and more. "Sundown to sunup" was another rule Kevin insisted on. I had to leave the house right after I put Deshae to bed, and I wasn't allowed to come home until the sun came up, regardless of whether it was a slow night or I had hit some really big calls. We were expected to work whether healthy or sick, on Christmas, Thanksgiving, Mother's Day, and yes, even during our monthly cycle.

Kevin once forced me to work while battling the flu. "Swinging hangers," he coldly reminded me when I called home crying that I was throwing up, with a fever and diarrhea. He meant that if I didn't stay out, I'd come home to nothing but hangers swinging in an empty closet, my daughter and him long gone. Sundown to sunup, no excuses and no days off. We weren't allowed to say no. Obey the rules or face the consequences—*swinging hangers*.

My biological family was thrilled when they heard I wasn't getting back together with Bryan but scared that I wanted to stay in Vegas. Kevin directed me on how we were going to "run drag" with my parents. He laid out a specific plan to follow. At first, I was to tell them that Brandi was my new roommate and that I had met her waiting tables—my "new job." After a month, I was to start talking about "the new guy I had met and gone out with." After another month, I'd explain that we were dating each other exclusively. After six months, I'd explain that I was moving in with Kevin. At first he listened in on my family phone conversations to ensure that I followed his orders precisely.

I reasoned that Kevin's intensity was what made him successful. Plus, he seemed to care about me, Deshae, and my family. That summer I'd sent Deshae to spend her break at my parents' home in Oregon. The night before my mom and Ken flew back to bring her home, Kevin gave me the night off so I wouldn't risk being arrested.

They stayed at Circus Circus, and we took Deshae on lots of rides. On their second day, we went to see Siegfried & Roy's Secret Garden and Dolphin Habitat at the Mirage. Deshae was enamored of their stunning collection of tigers and lions. My phone rang as we stood watching the white tigers.

"I need you to come out front right now," Kevin said solemnly.

"I'm with my parents. Is everything okay?" I asked.

"It's important." He hung up.

"Hey, Mom," I said, "Brandi is out front near the valet. She needs my key. We haven't made a copy yet. I'll be right back."

I hurried to the front and scanned the valet parking area. Kevin's muscular build drew my eye to where he was standing, off to the side. His dark eyes connected with mine, and my chest tightened with intrigue. I took a deep breath to suppress the magnetic force compelling me toward him. This relationship was supposed to be all business.

My effort was pointless. I went to him. The fine spray from the misters beneath the hotel awning barely hit our faces before evaporating into the desert summer heat.

"You came." He slid his arm around my waist.

"Of course," I smiled and squeezed his hand. "I'm in this."

"You passed my test." He leaned in and my pulse quickened. "I needed you to show me that you'll choose me over them every time. I'll see you at home," he whispered in my ear. He pulled away, held both my hands, and locked eyes with me. The busyness of the valet's whistles for the next taxi and cars and tourists in and out behind him faded into the background.

In that moment, I believed everything was going to be okay. For the first time since high school, I had a best friend in Brandi and a charismatic man who seemed to have all the right answers, including proof that he helped his girls build a future beyond the Game.

Maybe this was finally my way out.

CHAPTER 9 **wife-in-laws**

But now that you know God—or rather are
known by God—how is it that you are turning
back to those weak and miserable forces? Do you
wish to be enslaved by them all over again?

September 2004

One night, during the first few months, Brandi and I got into her red Mercedes convertible. She dialed the service as she pulled out of the parking lot.

"Hey, Dani, it's Jillian and Kelby. We're both calling on. We're together tonight." She stepped on the gas pedal.

Dani sent Brandi to the Mandalay Bay.

"Did she send me too?" I asked.

"No, but I'm taking you anyway," Brandi replied.

"What do you mean?" I asked. I'd never played the Game this way.

"Watch," she said.

I followed her into the hotel and up to the buyer's room.

"You don't mind if my friend joins us, do you?" Brandi said as she pushed the man to the bed and straddled one knee. "Two for the price of one. I didn't want to leave her sitting out in the car." She grabbed my hand and pulled me to his other knee. She moved my hair off my shoulder and fiddled with my collar, making it appear as if we would put on a two-girl show.

"I only have $500," he said.

"Baby, you don't really think we can do much for that, do you?" Brandi started unbuttoning my shirt.

"Okay, maybe I have $750."

"How about a thousand, sweetie? We take credit cards."

"I can do $900, but seriously that's it," he countered. "I can't have this on my credit card."

"Okay, we'll take $900. But just because we like you." She smiled and extended her open palm.

Brandi showed me the Game through a whole new lens, the lens Kevin required. Emptying our clients' pockets became a sophisticated scheme. Cons were Kevin's specialty, but they were no joke. He was clear: if we didn't carry out his schemes with precision, we'd get in trouble. Though the family's way of playing the Game fascinated me, conviction about their methods was eating me alive. But I shut out the Holy Spirit's voice by telling myself that this was the best way to take care of my daughter. Kevin's grip on my mind strengthened.

"I don't want men to buy you for an hour," Kevin explained. "I want men to fall in love and sign their will over to you. That's the kind of game we play around here."

The money coming in was bigger than I had ever seen.

I quickly earned the right to work on my own. Kevin moved Deshae and me from Brandi's townhome into our own three-bedroom house nearby and hired a nanny. Every night when I came home, I would leave every dollar on the dresser for Kevin. He soon let me keep the "change." If I made $1,860, I'd give him $1,800 and keep $60. If I needed money for anything major—tires, an oil change, groceries—I had to ask. The change was for filling my car with gas and buying a coffee. As with Bryan,

under no circumstance was I to stack money. Girls caught putting money aside were assumed to be saving for their escape.
When one girl I knew was caught stacking, her pimp forced her
into a bathtub, then poured gasoline over her as a form of mental
torture. Even my time at the store or running errands was monitored by being given only an hour. Kevin would call at exactly
forty-five minutes, saying "Where are you?" When I would tell
him I was on my way home, he'd reply, "Honk the horn, turn
on the radio." Once I clicked the alarm on my keychain, trying
to assure him I was getting in the car. "Oh, so you're a liar," he
scolded. I knew I'd be in trouble when I got home.

Shortly after we moved into our new house, our wife-in-laws Tori
and April came for a visit from Dallas. Though I'd been with
Kevin for about six months, I had only chatted on the phone
with them. They seemed excited to meet me, which I thought
was bizarre. I was so used to being pitted against each other for
competition. I was excited to be a part of something, especially
this kind of family dynamic. During their visit they stayed with
Brandi in the townhouse, and one evening they all came to my
home for dinner.

As we shared the meal I'd prepared, Tori looked across the
table at me. "She's beautiful, Pup," she said while glancing from
me to Kevin. My heart swelled with her approval.

"I know, right?" Kevin beamed with pride. "She looks exactly
like Pocahontas. That's it! I'm going to call you Poca."

And just like that, I was in. By assigning me a name of his
choosing, Kevin made me a formal member of their family. Like
a school girl wearing her quarterback boyfriend's varsity jacket,
I wore my new name proudly. Kevin and the girls soon started
calling me Poc.

Receiving compliments from other women in front of the man we'd all fallen for felt uncomfortable at first. I struggled to believe that these people were all enamored with me, happy I was there, excited I was going to be with their man, who moved among our homes at will. Shifting my ideologies to match those more like a polygamous family took intention on Kevin's part.

At the same time, belonging with them filled an emptiness in me. Little by little, I became part of the strange and wonderful family and believed they truly wanted *me*. I was no longer overlooked or unimportant. I was no longer the "new girl," chosen by Bryan but disdained by his other girls. Or the "divorced-family girl," always trying to ignore the whispers and stares of the Sunday school kids. Or the "unwanted girl," tossed back and forth between her emotionally unavailable parents. Or the "brokenhearted girl," nursing her crushed heart after the bad breakup from her high school boyfriend and Deshae's dad.

Would this family be different?

We scraped dinner dishes and loaded the dishwasher together. I stood at the sink with Kevin, and he caressed my hands as I rinsed and loaded. Strangely, the other girls didn't seem to mind. We were a family, one we got to choose; at least, that's what Kevin said. I shot side glances at Brandi, Tori, and April, carefully watching their expressions and body language. More concerned about my new sisters than I was about Kevin, I didn't want to engage him and risk ruining the friendships I'd been longing for.

But his scent, his touch, and his voice formed an alluring melody that charmed me, and I helplessly succumbed to it. He led me away from the kitchen of women as they stowed the leftovers in the fridge. He pulled me up the stairs and into my bedroom, where he closed the door, lowered me onto the bed, and began kissing my neck. I was overcome with a mixture of joy and daring passion. Nervous and uncomfortable yet excited, I returned his impassioned kisses while worrying what the other girls would think. Were they burning with jealousy or laughing as they wiped down the kitchen counters?

"Don't worry about them," Kevin whispered. "What I say goes."

This man can read my mind. He looked so deeply and tenderly into my eyes that it felt as though he saw through to my soul. The man who'd taken ownership over my body was now taking possession of my soul.

Kevin Barker carefully built family loyalty and convinced us sisters that we were being taken care of.

He worked hard to build up our credit scores, focusing on one girl at a time to keep his hands clean.

After Brandi's credit score was high enough, Kevin took us to the Mercedes dealership and selected a car for me. He instructed Brandi to take out a car loan in her name, using fake employment info and matching paperwork. She drove it off the lot, then pulled over, and I got into the Mercedes to drive home. The Range Rover dealership was next. Brandi bought another car in her name for April. Brandi herself was eyeing a prize from Aston Martin. If done on the same day, each loan would take days to show up on Brandi's credit report, allowing one car lot not to know what the other was doing and allowing Kevin to get all his girls in new cars at once.

Per Kevin's direction, Brandi brought doctored pay stubs and bank statements showing that her "business" was highly successful. She listed April as a reference for any loan officers. April knew to answer the phone accordingly. Kevin oversaw every aspect of this with meticulous precision, giving us the exact script with specific wording that we followed in detail. If we didn't follow his dictation to the letter, he'd smack us upside the head. If we used a contraction such as "I'd" instead of "I would" when he directed, that would result in a slap.

Kevin used a variety of marketing methods to advertise his "product." He insisted we follow the "marketing plan," which included freelancing, escort services, and online ads. Like ripe fruit that's polished and positioned in a tantalizing display designed to tickle the taste buds of a Harry & David shopper, we tanned and primped, wore seductive outfits, and struck poses in photographs to draw the highest price from our online buyers.

One afternoon, Brandi and I arrived at the photographer's suite where Kevin had directed us to have our photos taken for some new online ads. When Brandi arrived, she took one look at my spray-tan-gone-bad and erupted into a fit of laughter. I was orange! She quickly pointed out that I looked like one of Willy Wonka's Oompa Loompas. *That's what I get for going to a spray tan machine and not a professional spray tanning artist,* I thought. Brandi continued to snicker as we put on the sexy costumes we'd purchased together.

"You should have seen me in that stupid machine," I giggled back. "I got in with the shower cap on and just stood there. I waited for the little beep but heard nothing. I wondered why it was taking so long and bent down to look for a start button. But before I could find one, the nozzle started spraying me in the face." We couldn't stop laughing.

"I jumped up and rubbed it around my face to make sure it didn't streak, which made things worse. This arm didn't get sprayed as bright at the other," I said, pointing to my right arm. I showed her where the nozzles had left streaks on the back of my calves. The entire thing was a mess.

That's what you get for being cheap. Kevin's voice interrupted my thoughts.

As we finished getting dressed, Brandi stood next to me, giggling under her breath. I glanced in the mirror. There was an uncanny resemblance between the woman in the mirror and an orange zebra. I laughed with her and then thought about working.

"Maybe dudes won't notice?" I asked, looking down at my striped legs.

She busted out laughing even harder.

Laughter and family bonds were forming not only between Brandi and me but for Deshae as well. More than anything, I wanted to give Deshae the family I never had. Deshae was thriving in this home where multiple adult figures showed her affection and care. Kevin charmed his way deeper into my soul by embracing and protecting her as though she belonged to him. He proved true the old proverb, "Who takes a child by the hand takes the mother by the heart."

He treated Deshae as a daughter and took on the role of her protector by making sure no one got ready to go to work in front of her. Most nights I'd leave in sweats, pack a bag, and get dressed in the car. No physical affection between Kevin and the other women was displayed in front of Deshae. He came to my place to tuck her in almost every night, even if he went to Brandi's after Deshae went to sleep. He went to daddy-daughter dances and showed up at her Christmas musical with our "family"—April, Brandi, Little Kev, and me—and presented a lovely bouquet of flowers to her afterward. His overtures were often over the top, like the time he paid Deshae $100 after she did a walking hand-stand across the living room. And birthday parties had to be hosted in the school classroom so no one knew where we lived.

On a slow evening, Maddy sent me to one of the seediest places in town: the Wild West. Nestled between a gas station and the Girls To You office, the Wild West was a mix between a Motel 6 and a Denny's, complete with a craps table. Southwestern-pink rocks and desert shrubs littered its courtyard.

Usually this tacky hotel provided a convenient stop at the end of the night to make change to tip the phone girls. The Cage, where gamblers cashed in or purchased chips, was close to the front door. Also, when security swarmed the Wynn or Bellagio, the Wild West was a quick and easy place to duck into to break a $100 bill. Low-end street pimps hung out all night playing craps, eating breakfast, and often trying to knock other girls. Most pimps stayed near the strip all night so they could meet their girls after each call and take the money—break her of her stack.

Though I wasn't thrilled that Maddy was sending me to the Wild West, I obliged and parked my CLS 500 along the curb roped with white chain link. After climbing the dimly-lit concrete stairs to the second floor, I knocked on the door. The man who opened it seemed fairly normal, not strung out on crack as I'd expected. We sat on the side of the bed, and after a brief negotiation, we agreed on a price. He reached for his wallet under the mattress, a common hiding place for many buyers.

Suddenly, he grabbed the edge of the comforter, threw it over me, and began throwing punches at me like a heavyweight with his punching bag. I screamed as loudly as I could and tried to block the blows, even though I couldn't see where they were coming from. I threw my weight against him and kicked with all my strength until finally he stopped. I stood to my feet as quickly as I could and backed up from the bed toward the bathroom.

"I want my money back!" he yelled, shuffling toward the door to block my exit.

"I don't have your money!"

"The last girl who was here. She stole my wallet," he fumed. His face turned red, and his clenched fists made his veins bulge from his forearms.

"I don't know who was here last." *What was Maddy thinking, sending me to this dump?* "Let me call my company," I huffed, pointing to my purse on the ground.

He nodded.

I pulled my phone out and called in. "Maddy? Who was here last?" I snapped.

"You're the first person I've sent tonight, Kelb. Everything okay?" She sounded concerned.

"No, it's not okay. The last girl stole his wallet, and he's not letting me leave the room until she brings it back."

"I'll call around to other services and ask. Give me a few." She hung up.

I texted Brandi. "Call Wild West 207 Thomas."

"She is calling the other services to find out who it was." I explained. "I'm the first girl *our* company has sent tonight. I can't possibly know every working girl in town."

He sat on the end of the bed making fists. The hotel room phone rang, and he jumped, looking at me. I shrugged my shoulders. "They probably found her," I said, stepping aside.

He walked to the phone and picked it up. "Hello?"

I bolted out of the room and slammed the door behind me. The oldest trick in the working girl's handbook had bought me the head start I needed to get out the door. It takes them a few seconds to realize they're not attached to the phone cord and can set down the headset. I took off my shoes and ran barefoot down the concrete stairs. I saw him emerge from the room, coming after me. He began the chase, yelling for me to stop. Hands shaking, I fished my keys out of my purse. I unlocked the car, jumped in, and locked my doors just as he crashed into my car. I hit the brake and the start button at the same time, and the engine roared.

He slammed into my door and banged on the window so hard I thought the glass would shatter. I shot out of the parking lot. I gripped the steering wheel white-knuckled and took several deep breaths to gather my thoughts.

After a few blocks, I called Brandi.

"Hey," she answered. "You okay?"

"Yeah. Thanks so much. That was scary!"

"I hear ya. Want to meet up?" she asked.

"Yeah, how about the Palms?" I asked.

"Cool. See you in ten."

We sat at the bar and shared a steak dinner, laughing about the night's events and sharing secrets like girlfriends do. Before long, we considered each other best friends. She was the one who made me laugh, made me feel powerful, and served as my greatest teacher and mentor. We'd take Deshae and use a trick's name and room number from the night before to get into hotel pools or spend a day at the spa. If they were mean, we'd charge it to their room. At the same time, she was deeply in love with the same man I was falling for. At least, that's what I thought was happening. It would be years before I learned that I was experiencing trauma bonding and brainwashing.

Long before I joined the family, Brandi had always wanted a family too and had begged Kevin for a baby. When she pushed, he said he didn't want to ruin their relationship with the unknown dynamic of raising a child together. He appeased her with the dangling-carrot promise of having a baby after she retired, which meant making enough money to get the business up and running.

Then he'd lie in bed with me and say having a baby with me would be different, easier, because we already knew what our relationship was like with kids. He already knew how I parented.

"I don't want to have to slap Boo upside the head for driving too fast with my baby in the car. It would just make things messy," he'd say while spooning me. I believed him.

I wondered whether Brandi and I might become forever friends like April and Tori, who'd "grown up" together in the Game since the days they walked the blade together in San Diego.

One night, Kevin, Tori, and April reenacted the "old days." We all giggled as Kevin pantomimed, using a brick-sized 1990s mobile phone attached to a pretend car-battery-sized pack to talk to the girls, like a soldier at war, barking orders to his troop commanders. In those days, the girls would keep a Crown Royal bag full of quarters to check in via payphone between dates. They told Brandi and me their war stories of the tricks who tried to assault them in their vehicles and how Kevin made them wear pantyhose under their clothes with a hole cut out of the crotch. When they were paid, they'd go to the bathroom and put the money in the heel of their pantyhose. If a trick went crazy and stole their purse or clothes, at least they'd have Kevin's money. They'd walk the streets, fighting girls for certain corners, chanting rhymes at each other—the same mantras I was forced to learn and repeat: "Stick, stay, pay. Never go away. Do whatever KB say." We laughed and swapped stories late into the night.

After being approved for a home loan, Brandi got a call one afternoon in the fall of 2005 that she could come choose her lot. We went down to the sales office, studied the different models, walked the available lots, then chose the largest one. A few weeks later, Kevin, Brandi, Deshae, and I returned and walked through the building site. There was no comparison between Ricky's trashy salmon-colored house or Bryan's apartment near the strip or the trailer my mom and I lived in when I was younger and the $600,000 luxury homes nestled into the upscale Aliante neighborhood of North Las Vegas.

As Brandi picked out floors, cabinets, and other finishing touches for what would become the Big House, I witnessed her dreams coming true. I was excited both for Brandi and for the hope it gave me. Kevin would make sure Deshae and I had a good life.

But shadows lurked on the edges of our home. At first, I believed the source of the darkness was anyone's failure to follow Kevin's rules. In addition to his rules for the Game, he also had house rules. T-shirts had to be folded a certain way. Knickknacks had to be arranged just so. The pantry had to look like a grocery store aisle, with food labels facing outward. Our homes had to be constantly photo ready. They were so sterile that a surgeon could have operated on the floor.

April had once been beaten so badly after forgetting to shut the garage door that she thought for sure she had two broken ribs. After beating her, Kevin threw her out onto the freeway, miles from their home, and told her to walk back.

"A police officer saw me and offered to help," she confided in me one night. "I didn't tell him I was in the Game. When he saw I'd been hurt, I made up some story so he wouldn't ask questions." She asked him to drop her off a few blocks away from her house. "I sat on the curb for hours. If I went home too soon, Kevin would know I got a ride and I'd be in more trouble."

April and I never clicked. We were never rude to each other, and we hung out on occasion, but there was something missing between us. I think she was depressed over how her life had turned out. For years she'd been desperate to see Kevin's promises come to pass, and she'd grown more and more detached, watching girl after girl drift in and out of their lives, each one stealing more of his attention. Yes, she was retired from the Game and had a business in her name and some property—a ranch where she had horses. But she didn't have true freedom or Kevin's love. Like some cult member, she'd been brainwashed and worn down day by day until no shred of hope or joy remained.

Tori's optimistic, positive demeanor balanced April's sullen one. Unlike April, Tori easily found good in every situation. Whenever Kevin would hit Brandi or me, Tori was quick to encourage us, saying, "The beatings will stop. He hasn't hit me in years." Her hopeful outlook remained steady despite his endless control tactics, such as the time he threw her out of the house when her insatiable sweet tooth caused her weight to creep over his acceptable 130-pound limit. "You can come back home when you've lost weight," he told her. Or the threats of sending us out to the legal brothels, making social ostracism our punishment for noncompliance.

Tori came from a family of criminals. She and her mom lived with Kevin years ago while her dad served prison time. When the sentence ended, Kevin bought them a home and paid its mortgage monthly. April, an only child, had been adopted. Though I never learned much of her history, it seemed like her family made her choose between them and Kevin.

Kevin was a tenacious entrepreneur who was convinced that his ideas would get everyone out of the Game. Kevin had put April and Tori in charge of a Dallas pizza shop he'd invested in, Grab a Slice. Before the pizza shop, he'd started a T-shirt company, and before that, he had created a device to hold your personal belongings while you work out at the gym.

Shortly after I joined the family, Kevin learned that I could sew. He took me to JOANN's fabric store, where we bought swimsuit Lycra and a sewing machine. He buzzed with excitement and described his latest product idea—decorative, interchangeable motorcycle helmet covers. I sat on the kitchen floor, nipping, tucking, and pinning, and created the exact prototype he'd described. He was ecstatic. I designed a pattern that could easily be duplicated. With that, another new venture was born, one that might be the business I got to walk away with. I enjoyed his cooing over me for the skill my grandma had taught me while making doll clothes each summer. I spent many daytime hours working on "our business" until we eventually moved it to a warehouse and hired one employee under the table to sew with me.

He had me take my prototype to a patent attorney, then he created a website and registered the business in Brandi's name. I oversaw the warehouse, order fulfillment, inventory and shipping, QuickBooks, and got the product into seventeen stores in Las Vegas. He had all the girls deposit money in the business bank account to make it appear more successful than it really was.

Though his creative ideas were endless, he lacked the frugality and focus to make them successful. His marketing strategies and cost projections were unrealistic, and his pride kept him from accepting the very advice that could have helped him turn a profit. Daily he'd flip-flop between praising my business mind and berating me for speaking up, telling me I was stupid and couldn't do anything right or hitting me for not obeying his obsessive-compulsive nature.

He also struggled to accept that none of his cockamamie ideas made the kind of money the Game generated. Trafficking was a business model that suited his narcissistic ego and psychotic need to have ultimate control. The same vulnerabilities that lure girls into exploitation tend to be the same vulnerabilities that lure boys into organized crime, drugs, and gangs. His drive for success, his childhood of poverty with a single mom, his introduction to the Game as a high-school kid, and a series of other vulnerabilities combined to make the perfect cocktail for him to become a pimp, a trafficker.

Kevin grew up fatherless in San Diego but had an aunt who cared for him during the summers. Though she introduced Kevin to Jesus in his childhood, her hyper-religious gestures negatively influenced him, such as when she made him paint her driveway red to symbolize the blood of Jesus. Her strict rules and overzealous behavior turned him away from religion.

Every day after school, for years, he walked by a record shop and went inside. The owner made small talk with Kevin and gave him bubble gum. One day, after his eighteenth birthday, Kevin came home to find the record store owner sitting on his couch. Kevin was shocked and angered to find out that this man was his father, so he veered off into the wrong crowd and got pulled into the Game his senior year in high school. In the same home where his father betrayed him, Kevin beat the first of many women. His mama made him "take it outside" to the front yard. And Mama met each girl in the years that followed, especially when he sent her money each month.

A legitimate future with Kevin was what each of us girls wanted. He made sure we believed in a better future. And perhaps he believed he could make it out someday too.

"I can't wait for the day when you're really mine, Poc," he said one night while we spooned in bed. "I mean really mine." His finger softly drew the letters KB on the back of my neck. "You can get my initials tattooed right here and be one of us."

I wanted all this. It was odd, the way he made me want it. He made me think of this branding as a rite of passage, getting a tattoo, a branding, like all the other girls had on the back of their necks. I didn't think about the beatings or the times I got into trouble. I didn't think about the way he forced me to have sex with him at his whim or follow his rules down to the most ridiculous detail. I didn't think about the dysfunctional "family" my daughter was growing up with or the contribution to the "family pot" of money. I didn't think about all the mantras he forced us to repeat. *A family is only as strong as its weakest link. Loyalty breeds royalty. Snitches get stiches. Stick, stay, pay, never go away, do whatever KB say.*

All I could think about was being one of his women, a part of the cult where "family isn't blood, it's who you choose," as he'd ingrained in us. I knew what it was to be rejected, to be poor, to want to be a part of something bigger and adventurous. I wanted into this club, to be with people who knew me and all I'd been through and loved me just the same. I wanted to make *my man* happy, and I needed him to want me as much as he wanted the ones who had been with him for years.

This is where I belong, where I can be real and honest. I can do this, I thought as he again tenderly traced his initials on the back of my neck.

The nickname, the tattoo, these cult-like rituals did exactly what he wanted them to: replaced my old way of thinking with new beliefs. He made me believe I was part of something powerful enough to save me from living in poverty with nothing. My sisters taught me to dress, walk, talk, and hustle Kevin's way. And these behaviors were reinforced with punishments for noncooperation and rewards for compliance.

Everything in me wanted that tattoo on the back of my neck—and soon enough, I got it. For the first time in a long time, I felt happy. I had everything I thought I always wanted, but only at the cost of my soul.

CHAPTER 10 sundown to sunup

Sin shall no longer be your master, because you are not under the law, but under grace.

February 2006

I awoke in a stupor. The room-darkening shades made it difficult to tell what time it was. I glanced at the clock on my nightstand: 11:06 a.m. I stretched and lay in bed listening to the faint sound of the vacuum cleaner whirring downstairs.

Our nanny, Maria, was at it again. I couldn't imagine what I'd do without her. She took good care of Deshae and made my life as a working mom doable. I checked my text messages to see whether any of the girls had checked in. No new messages. I hadn't heard from Kevin at all.

I hated when Kevin left me in the dark. Jealousy rose up inside me. Was he with Brandi at her townhouse? Had he decided to go to Dallas without telling me? I felt excluded.

I went to the gym, then went to the warehouse, which we had started calling "the shop," where I'd sew and help fill orders. Then I'd run errands, shop for groceries, and pay bills. As I waited in the pick-up line at school, I felt another prick in my conscience. Since I'd left Victory Outreach, a vague, nagging feeling seemed to surface whenever my life slowed down a bit.

Both my addiction to money and the craving to love and be loved kept drawing me back to the fast-paced life of the Game. I had been part of a world—one that normal people knew nothing about—for more than five years. After all this time, working first for Bryan, then Ricky, and now Kevin, going back to being "square" seemed utterly out of reach. Like some Cinderella working girl with her face covered in ashes, I wondered whether returning to a normal life as a beloved wife and mother would take a fairy godmother miracle—someone to transform my Mercedes into a Volvo station wagon and my pimp into a business executive and soccer dad for our 2.5 children. *Like that's ever going to happen,* I thought.

My new family felt a little like the one I always wanted, but at the same time, deep down, I knew something wasn't right. I wrestled over remembering God's promises and making it happen on my own. Would this be a stepping-stone to freedom?

But what if God retracts his plans and purposes for people like me, the ones who get off track? I thought back to my times of teaching at Victory Outreach. Was teaching for me? Or had I gotten it wrong? I loved God's Word, but lately I had grown numb, and Bible verses would rarely pop into my mind.

After I got home with Deshae, I glanced at my dresser, where I'd laid a glossy brochure for an upcoming Christian women's conference to be held at a local church. The speakers smirked at me, as if saying, "You're not like one of us, Rebecca. You think *you* can teach the Bible? Seriously?"

No, God couldn't use me now.

"God's gifts and his call are irrevocable" (Romans 11:29) flashed through my mind.

Not for girls like me. I retorted. *When and how could I ever get back to a place like that? It's too hard. I don't know how—I'm in too deep.*

I took Maria to her sister's for her day off. As I returned

home, I remembered all the days on the public bus with plastic bags of quarters and a laundry basket on my lap. I was grateful to no longer live in poverty.

After giving Deshae her snack and helping her with homework, I cooked dinner, then went to my room to get ready for the night.

I heard the front door open, followed by some footsteps.

"Poc?" Kevin yelled. I could hear him climbing the stairs.

"Hey," I replied from the bathroom. I peeked out and saw that Brandi was with him. *So, he spent the day with her.*

"You heading out soon?" he stated more than questioned. *Clearly not in a great mood. Tread lightly.*

"Yep, probably within ten." I smiled as I brushed on a second coat of ebony mascara.

"You guys have a good day?" I asked. They both smiled and nodded, then he sat down to work on the computer.

I finished my look with a denim bustier and matching denim pants, trying my best to mimic the Guess models I saw in the boutique windows. I teased my hair and slipped on a pair of gray and white snakeskin stilettos. Maybe I looked like I was trying too hard, but this *was* Vegas after all, and it wasn't like I was in a miniskirt and fishnets. Those were reserved for the square girls who'd come to Vegas to get their Halloween kicks: dressing up as Playboy Bunnies or lingeried with feather boas, laughing and flashing their friends. I judged them.

"See, babe," Kevin would always point them out to me, "those girls wish they could be like us. Deep down, they want to be you." He fed us these lines to justify, normalize, and even glamorize our sin. "You're brave and courageous enough to act on those desires. They can only dream and pretend."

With my shoes in my purse, I gave Kevin and Deshae a kiss and left for the night. With only one booking for midnight from the online ad, I was supposed to freelance before and after.

Sundown to sunup, he'd say. That was the rule. I called the escort service as I drove.

"Hey, it's Kelby. I'm calling on."

"Oh, great! Kelby, can you do a bachelor party at ten at the Rio?" Dani asked.

"Yeah, that's fine. Who's going with me?"

"A new girl. She can't go on calls alone yet, so I'm trying to get her acclimated by sending her with some seasoned girls." Dani sounded exacting, as if she'd been given orders.

"Okay. I'll be there," I assured her.

After freelancing for a few hours at the Mandalay Bay, I headed to the Rio. When I reached the room, I could hear the partygoers' loud banter even before the door opened. I walked into two adjoining rooms filled with about fifteen drunk men. I was glad another girl was on her way. If the men's slurred suggestive remarks were any indication of how tonight might go, I'd need the help.

After she arrived, I began negotiating. We took the money, and I checked in while she poured herself a drink and sat down on the couch. She wore tight black jeans and a tank top and looked about nineteen years old. Unfortunately, she wasn't only new to the escort service, as I thought Dani meant; she was new to the Game.

What is she doing? I wondered. We were not there to hang out and party. I began undressing and pulling the bachelor into the middle of the room. I cycled through my standard repertoire of bachelor-party games. She sat watching. I clenched my teeth and my throat tightened.

What the heck? Does she think I'm going to do all the work?

I looked her dead in the eye as the bachelor took a tequila shot out of my belly button. "Get up and get out here, or give me your half." She broke eye contact and looked at her feet. I stood up and flew at her.

"Seriously, if you're just going to sit here and watch me do all the work, then I want your half!"

She got up, walked briskly past me into the adjoining room, and shut the door.

Is she insane? To leave me alone with this many drunk men, their testosterone raging? Does she have no working-girl etiquette?

I bolted to the door and pulled on the knob. *Locked.* No way was she going to try to dart out the other door with half my money. I asked the party host to open the next room through the hallway door. I stood in the hotel hallway, half dressed, with the intoxicated men chanting, "Cat fight, cat fight, cat fight!" I didn't care that I was half naked; I was infuriated.

Mr. Party Host slid the plastic key in the door, and I pushed it open. She sat on the bed, talking on the phone with a panicked look.

"Hang up the phone," I barked.

She put it in her purse.

"If you want to leave, that's fine. But you're not taking half the money for doing nothing. You're making me entertain all fifteen dudes!"

"Fine," she huffed. "I'll come back out, but I can't give you the money."

"Then do the work." I glared.

Back in the other room, she lit a cigarette and settled back on the couch fully clothed.

What is her deal? Is she embarrassed? Does she not know what to do? Will her man give her trouble if she goes back to him with no money after being gone this long?

I grabbed her cigarette with one hand and her arm with the other, trying to get her off the couch. She pulled away like some scared stray crouched in the back corner of a newspaper-lined cage.

"Cat fight, cat fight . . ." the men taunted.

I caught her eye and I saw it: the same fear I felt at age nine as I stood in the Sunday school class, the terror I experienced at eleven listening to my mother's muffled cries as her boyfriend raged, the shameful shroud of dread that covered me the night Bryan made me sign on with the escort service. For a brief moment, compassion tugged at my heart. But then I thought of Kevin and Brandi and what would happen to me if I was out of pocket. It was against his rules to be the only girl in a room with that many men—it was dangerous.

I was incensed by her ignorance about the rules of the Game, and my heart rate shot up. *You just don't do this. It's not what we do.*

I couldn't help myself. I grabbed her by the hair and yanked her off the chair to the floor.

"You're either doing half the work or you're giving my half back!" I stood with my hands on my hips. She got up and started for the door.

"Don't let her leave!" I yelled. "Block the door." A few men eagerly did so as their chants ricocheted off the walls. They'd paid their money and were poised to watch a legitimate cat fight. Refusing to back down, I blasted the horrified girl with a steady stream of threats. Finally, she reached her trembling hand into her purse, took out a wad of cash, and threw it at me.

"Let me out now!" she screamed at the men in front of the door. They laughed and stepped aside. The shaken girl darted out as I picked up the money and redirected the men's attention to me.

Well, at least I have full payment now.

I texted Brandi to see whether she was available and wanted to drop in to freelance the room. But one of her regulars had flown in on his private plane.

I had no choice but to finish the bachelor party solo. Kevin would be beyond pissed if he found out. But I couldn't worry about that now.

When I was done, even though I had an appointment from the online booking a little later at the Palms, I agreed to take one more call for Dani.

"Imperial Palace?" I repeated over the phone while rolling my eyes. Everyone knew Imperial Palace was a crapshoot.

I pulled into the labyrinth of the Imperial Palace hotel and casino. It had taken me months to figure out this place. The parking garage was an entire alley away from the main entrance, which was nowhere near the elevator bank. I carefully stepped out of the parking garage door into the alley, lowering my gaze so the security camera couldn't capture my features. The urine-saturated alley was so shady that I walked briskly to the main building, glancing behind my back to ensure that no one was following me.

The casino smelled like stale smoke and drugstore cologne. The ancient elevators held only a few people at a time and took forever. At the lobby level, I got off and walked around the corner to an escalator that took me to the main bank of hotel elevators. I got in and made my way to the room Dani had given me. I knocked and waited . . . and waited.

After what seemed like forever, the door opened. I looked down to a short, hunched-over man who appeared to be in his late seventies. Movie scenes of old men having heart attacks during sex flashed through my mind. *Can this guy even handle entertainment?*

"So, what kind of entertainment are you looking for, honey?"

"Today would have been my anniversary," he stuttered. His bony hands shook as he took his wallet from the nightstand drawer. I noticed he was still wearing a gold wedding band.

"My wife died last year. All I want to do, sweetheart, is dance." I wanted to cry. How could I do this? How could I take his money for a slow dance? I silently toyed with several explanations I could give Kevin for coming up short. The problem was, I knew excuses of any kind were met with a slap, gut punch, or whack from a yard stick or folding chair—whatever was within Kevin's reach.

A week ago I'd returned home at dawn with what Kevin felt was "short" on my quota for a Friday night.

"Get down and sit like the dog you are," he ordered me through clenched teeth. Kevin never shouted, but when he was angry, his words dripped with threatening disdain. I crouched at the precise spot where his finger pointed.

"Not there." He pointed a few inches away. "There!" I slid over, making sure not to look up.

"So, you like these men, huh?" His voice grew deeper, darker, rattling me to the core. "Do you want to do this forever? You never want to leave this life?"

I shook my head.

"Trick lover." He murmured it under his breath as he walked away.

No matter how sorry I felt for the elderly man, my fear of being hurt, of Deshae being hurt, made me question who was worth it. This man or my daughter?

"How much money do you have, hon?" I asked.

"Two fifty. Will that get me an hour of dancing?"

I smiled and took his money. We danced for a while, about three or four songs. The old man moved me tenderly in time with the music, and we danced slowly. He held my right hand, and he gently laid his other on my waist, treating me like a lady. He seemed to be transported to some distant place as we swayed to the relaxed tempo.

As much as my heart bled for the guy and the pain he was going through, I watched the clock, distracted by the time. For this price, I had to move on.

"All right, honey. Thank you so much," I gave him a quick hug as if I were hugging my own grandparent. "It was my pleasure. I am sorry to hear of your wife, but I bet she adored you." I speed-walked to the door while talking and left, not allowing him to get a word in. I hated this. I pictured him sitting on the end of his bed in tears.

Comfort him, Lord, I silently prayed as I walked to the elevator. I felt terribly guilty.

On my way to the Palms for my online appointment, I collected myself, still thinking about the way the old man adored his wife. *Is it even possible for Kevin and me to get there? Do I even want to get there with him?*

Desires aside, I *needed* us to get there so I could get out of this life. Despite Kevin's abusiveness, there were tender days, the days when I could see a future for us as a happy, married, and in-love couple. He'd hinted at marriage just the other night.

"We can even have a fake wedding." He'd whispered the promise as we lay in bed together. "Your family will think we're legit, and we'll have pictures on the wall for the kids. Then you'll become Mrs. Kevin Barker and change your last name legally, like the other girls have."

I liked the way "Rebecca Barker" rolled off my tongue. Kevin definitely had his moments.

I sighed and glanced at the clock on the dashboard. *I'd better check on my next buyer.* I called the hotel and asked for Doug Smith's room to confirm that he was in fact a registered guest at the hotel.

When I arrived, Doug opened the door with a small, nervous smile. He seemed uncomfortable or maybe disappointed. I couldn't tell which.

"You enjoying Vegas?" I said, hoping to ease his nerves.

He nodded.

This may be harder than I thought. "What do you do?" I asked, trying to fill the tense silence.

"I'm a dentist. I'm in town for a conference," he offered coldly.

I began my negotiation, and we landed on a price. I began to entertain him, but when I thought we were done, he demanded more.

"Uh, no. I think we're done here," I said as I collected my clothes and began dressing.

"Well, *I* think we're not done!" he shouted. "You better give me every dollar back."

The mild-mannered dentist morphed into the Incredible Hulk. He paced around the room, breathing hard. His meek nerves turned into rage. He pushed me back down onto the bed as if to take what he paid for. Panicked, I reached over and fumbled around the nightstand for anything I might use as a weapon. I felt the phone receiver, grabbed it, and with every ounce of my strength, drove it into the side of his head. He fell back stunned long enough for me to slide out from under him and dash for the door. My high heel ripped the back of one of my pant legs as I raced to get them on.

I stood in the elevator, shaken. *My favorite jeans!*

My heart pounded as I raced back to the parking lot while scanning the area for security. That guy reminded me of the type that would find pleasure in murdering girls like me. He exuded a sense of evil. He had a crazy look in his eyes when he grabbed me, as if hurting me excited him. The sight of my car gave me a small bit of relief.

I was still rattled, but my fear turned into a desire for revenge toward the psycho dentist. I opened my phone's internet browser to search the city and state by his area code.

Aha! Colorado Springs.

Next I searched, "Dentist Doug Smith[1] in Colorado Springs."

Bingo! An exact match. He was either too stupid or nervous to come up with a backstory.

I dialed the dentist's office number.

"Hello, my name is Eva. I am a hooker in Vegas, and your boss, Mr. Smith, staying in the Palms Hotel and Casino, room 15210, just got physically aggressive with me when I wouldn't have sex with him multiple times. Just wanted you to know what kind of man you are working for."

I hung up, satisfied. *Two can play your game, Doug Smith.* I laughed out loud as I sat in my car, imagining the look on his office staff's faces when they listened to the messages on Monday morning.

After a couple more no-gos and a couple of base calls that night, the sun was coming up. Yay! I could finally go home.

My thirty-minute drive north always filled me with dread. I never knew what mood Kevin would be in when I returned. Would I face hours of beatings? Would he make me sleep in the closet, or would he want to cuddle in front of a movie? The fear of the unknown never seemed to subside.

When I arrived home, Kevin wasn't there. *Maybe he's been following me again tonight. Will he come home later with the exact details of each call I'd taken? Or is he at Brandi's?*

I didn't want to text her and ask, in case he was with her. That was sure to get me in trouble for "checking on him." My

---

1   Name and location have been changed to protect identity. Any coincidence of a dentist in Colorado Springs named Doug Smith is simply that, a coincidence.

stomach churned as I played out in my head what could happen. I mentally retraced every step of my night, trying to come up with anything I may have done wrong in case he'd been following me.

I sucked in a quick breath as I remembered. *The bachelor party!*

My heart sank. I'd broken one of the rules by being there alone, even though it wasn't by choice. With each silent question, my pulse quickened:

Does that new girl's man know mine?

Did Kevin bug my phone?

Was there a camera in my car when I confessed to Brandi that I had worked the party solo?

As the minutes passed, relief slowly seeped in. The quiet apartment reminded me that he was most likely gone for the night. If he knew about the bachelor party, he'd have been waiting for me.

Even though I still battled a twinge of jealousy, the waves of relief from not being forced to face his questioning—or worse— silenced the other emotions. I yawned, cracked my neck and knuckles, and sat on the end of the bed to count the money.

Crap! I'd almost forgotten to text him that I was home.

I tapped out the words "Home safe. Night. XX."

I paused and stared at the word *safe.*

Safe from what? The police? From being murdered? I was anything but safe. This life was a game . . . a game of Russian roulette. With every hotel room I entered, I took a gamble, not knowing who'd answer the door: a mild-mannered widower or a psycho, sex-addicted dentist.

I stood up, walked around to Kevin's side of the bed, and placed my entire night's wages on the nightstand precisely as I'd been taught: bills in order from highest to lowest, facing up, and all in the same direction. Before closing my window shades, I looked out to see the glow of the sunrise. I laid my head on the pillow and dozed off thinking about the dancing man and longing for the day when someone would miss me that much.

CHAPTER 11 **a home divided**

I waited patiently for the LORD;
    he turned to me and heard my cry.
He lifted me out of the slimy pit,
    out of the mud and mire;
he set my feet on a rock
    and gave me a firm place to stand.

March 2006

G et the kids," Kevin ordered me as I threw back the bedsheets in our dark bedroom. "The feds will come here next." Fear rushed through me.

When federal agents pounded on Brandi's door early that morning with a warrant for her arrest, and the reality of her situation became clear, my mind went to last year's raid on April and Tori in Texas. I hardly understood what was happening. As I quickly dressed, I listened to Kevin give Brandi instructions: *Hide the money. Flush the sim card. Wait for the attorney.*

As he rushed around collecting stashes of hidden money from the curtain hems and beneath the ottoman, I woke up Little Kev and grabbed Deshae. Brandi's hang-up felt like a good-bye, and the thought of authorities taking Deshae down to Child Protective Services while I sat in county jail made me sick.

"Don't come home until someone calls you," Kevin ordered me as I led the kids into our backyard.

Outside, Little Kev locked his fingers and helped me over the six-foot concrete wall. He handed Deshae over to me, then made a running jump over.

This is insane, I thought, wondering whether the neighbors were watching as I crouched in their backyard, trying to compose my next move. I could only hope they were still in bed. But then again, why did I care what the neighbors saw? We had no choice but to follow Kevin's orders. I walked around the neighborhood with the kids for what seemed like forever. Finally, after what felt like an hour, Kevin called and told us to come home.

"Pack up everything," he instructed when I arrived. "Call Maria and give her a month off with pay. And call Bill too," he said, referring to the attorney who handled all our solicitation charges for us. "Poc, this is crazy! I told you, didn't I?" He laughed as he stooped to grab a suitcase from under the bed. "Remember, babe? I told you we're big time now. Feds are only after ya if you're doing big things."

What have we gotten ourselves into? Fear splintered my mind into a hundred different what-ifs, none of them good. *What if I have to go to jail too and sit there for weeks—or months—awaiting bail? What about my baby? What will happen to her?* I tried to calm down by recalling Kevin's frequent promise: "This will all settle down if we can lay low and keep our mouths shut." I'd become much better at that. Kevin had made sure of it.

Once named the best criminal attorney in Nevada, Bill would surely know what to do for Brandi. But it would cost us. Help from the same attorney who represented one of the pimps involved with OJ Simpson's armed robbery conviction wouldn't come cheap.

I phoned the law office at 8:01. The receptionist's voice was annoyingly cheerful. I hardly heard what she said.

"Is Bill available this morning? I am a client of his and . . . I . . . uh, I mean . . ." Kevin glared at me. *Am I telling too much? Not enough?* I stumbled over my words, trying to avoid aggravating him.

"Tell them what's going on, stupid," he grumbled.

I swallowed and cleared my throat. "My sister was just arrested by federal investigators this morning, we—uh, I mean, I need to post bail and figure out what we do from here." I second-guessed every single word. One wrong choice would make things go south fast with Kevin.

"Please hold," she said coldly.

In time a familiar voice announced, "This is Bill."

I reiterated the story.

A few days later, Bill explained one of Brandi's charges. One of her regulars had made monthly deposits into a Texas bank account opened in her fake name—a false ID Kevin had established for her when he recruited her as a minor. Because of the multiple arrests under her alias, which was supposed to protect her real identity, she was considered a flight risk and was denied bail. She'd be extradited to Texas as soon as the state could secure transport, which could take months. Until then, she'd sit at the Clark County Detention Center.

Kevin had April and Tori stay in Texas to handle all the necessary paperwork to defend the family. Bill suggested finding an attorney in the Dallas area.

"Texas is known for its good ol' boys club," he explained. "My representation of you there would do more harm than good; Texans don't take well to outsiders." We took his advice.

Things quieted down a bit. I focused on keeping my head down, working, and not asking too many questions about what was going on. But a couple of weeks later, I was walking down the hallway when I heard Kevin's speaker phone blaring from one of the rooms. I could hear a woman sobbing but couldn't make out her words. Curious, I walked closer to listen.

April?

Between sobs she told Kevin about a CBS News exposé featuring the raid that was hitting all the Dallas news channels.

"The pizza shop's all over the news. They showed up at our home! They're saying it's our front for an organized prostitution ring," she explained.

It was as if April's and Tori's lives had been hidden behind a wall of frosted glass. Though a decade thick, the wall shattered when the media, with one devastating story, took a hammer to it and sent shards flying everywhere. Tori was arrested on charges of conspiracy to commit tax evasion, bank fraud, and money laundering. Kevin sent April scrambling to shut down the pizza shop and pack the Dallas house.

Then he planned to get us out of town until the storm blew over. He instructed me to reserve a two-room suite at a Lake Las Vegas hotel resort where the kids could swim while we laid low. By eight o'clock that night, we were nearly done packing our belongings into the Hummer.

Is this how it ends? I wondered. *Even if a girl makes enough money and invests and buys a home and a legal business, does it all just come crashing down in the end since it's done with illegal gains?*

Kevin knew the feds had enough to charge all of them with tax evasion, but authorities would try to get Tori or Brandi to flip, to give them enough to charge Kevin with far more—racketeering, money laundering, bank fraud, and human trafficking. So far, none of the interrogations had swayed the girls. None of them were talking to the feds or shedding any light on our "crime family." The brainwashed, trauma-induced world they lived in for years had laced their mouths shut. Our new Texas attorney informed us that our family had been under investigation for eighteen months, including a federal agent flashing his badge to the trashman to confiscate the garbage and search for incriminating evidence.

They had turned up some troubling items, such as notes we'd written, saying things like, "Kevin says when you wake up to send Mama $500" and "Kevin wants you to put $300 on a Walmart gift card and mail it to Tori for groceries." Statements like this proved not only that he was the ring leader but that illegally-made money was being transferred across state lines by various means to stay under the radar. Now they would check Western Union for receipts. Unfortunately for the feds, Kevin had already ensured that we made the transfers under fake names. "Mama" was Kevin's mother, who lived in San Diego. We sent her and Tori's family money every month. It's harder for a girl to run when their trafficker is supporting the girl's family, who encourages her to stay.

Despite the ensuing madness of the investigation and missing Brandi like crazy, I persisted in believing Kevin's counterfeit family dream. One Sunday afternoon, Kevin pulled into a luxurious gated community in Lake Las Vegas near the resort where we were staying. We walked through the model homes as we'd done with Brandi's Big House.

"Once all this goes away, let's have a baby, Poc." As we walked through the gorgeous kitchen, he gently took my hand, but it was his whispered promises that took hold of my heart. Once again, he painted a picture of a life I desperately wanted for Deshae and me.

"I only want a son, though, no daughters." Kevin sketched out his perfect family as we walked through the upstairs. "I know too much about what happens out here to girls." He led me into each bedroom, and I pictured one as our nursery. I envisioned holding a baby tightly to my chest and breathing his intoxicating new-baby smell. I craved my own family more than anything.

"You heard of pregender selection?" He stopped and turned to me, studying my face to check my reaction.

I shook my head.

"Doctors can ensure you have a boy or girl these days. Why don't you look around and find a clinic, make an appointment for us to go to an IVF doctor, and find out what that would cost?"

"Are you serious?" I jumped into his arms. "You want to have a baby?" I shrieked.

"I want *you* to my have *my* baby. I love you and Little Mama. I know what we're like as a family . . . and I need you, Poc. I need your business sense. Stay down with me, let this pass over, and we can make it work."

As I climbed back into his Hummer, my emotions soared. I hadn't felt this high in a long time. Never mind a looming prison sentence for possibly all of us, the threat of the feds coming for me next, or my worst nightmare: Deshae in foster care. None of that crossed my mind. I focused on the things that would help get me through. It was easier to live in a fantasy, to live in denial in order to cope. I mean, after all, I had learned to compartmentalize things to get by, and this was no different. As we drove away from the model home, I pictured Kevin's head resting on my pregnant belly and imagined how a baby would transform his heart.

But in the meantime, there were bills to pay. Many, many bills. Though Tori was released on bail, the pizza shop closed after the news hit, and Brandi was still locked up. Our income streams were becoming more of a trickle. The kids swam at our hotel escape, and Kevin lounged in the room while I worked nights. He made sure I stayed busy to save up for the sky-high attorney fees and the future promise of our baby. But as I drove the long stretch between the Strip and the Lake Las Vegas resort each night, the silence forced me to confront feelings that my busyness and the idea of a sweet-smelling baby kept safely tucked away. Deep down, my unsettled conscience formed a pit in my stomach as I thought about having Kevin's baby. Tears welled up, but I quickly flipped on 50 Cent's "P.I.M.P." The bass pulsed, and the raw lyrics helped distract me. They subtly reinforced the Game, with its rules and ideologies that had become my norm.

I sang along with Lyfe Jennings, whose "Must Be Nice" lyrics provided the reminders I needed that no one else but *this* family understood me and my past and accepted me anyway.

I cranked the music even louder and pulled into the resort's gated parking garage. I parked, took a deep breath, and fixed my makeup while swallowing the emotions that tried to climb their way up. I had no choice but to strut past the front lobby in my high heels and tight skirt toward our suite while the night clerk ogled me.

I hate this. I hate this. Act normal.

It was a relief when, in May, Kevin told me the Big House was done and we could move in. The mansion was a pleasant distraction but also a painful reminder that Brandi wasn't there to enjoy it with us. It hit me the moment I first walked barefoot across the beautiful travertine flooring she'd been so excited to select. *I am living in another woman's home.* I felt guilty moving into the house she'd sacrificed so many years to afford.

Kevin had me take the master bedroom upstairs. He put

Little Kev in the downstairs master that would have been my room if Brandi were there. We bought furniture and set up the house while listening to Kevin's favorite mix of old R&B classics by Frankie Beverly and Maze; Norman Connors; Earth, Wind & Fire; and Walter Beasley. Deshae would giggle with delight as her "daddy" spun her around to the old-school music as he used to at the daddy-daughter dance at school. No wonder she loved him. Little Mama never saw the monster behind the mask.

April had moved into Brandi's old Las Vegas townhouse the month prior, and Tori popped back and forth between the Big House, Brandi's old Las Vegas townhouse, and the Dallas house, waiting to settle terms of her plea deal arrangement. We could only hope that Brandi and Tori would continue to keep quiet so authorities would either have nothing or very little on Kevin. Tori tried to take a lie detector in hopes of going to trial, but her results were bad, so her attorney advised against it.

Brandi called weekly from jail while she was in Nevada, then often after she was extradited to the women's prison in Texas. I'd manage to talk to her briefly before Kevin took the phone. I missed her and wanted to go visit her, but Kevin wouldn't allow it. It was too risky to connect our names. Kevin made me drop off money for her at the jail commissary box after hours so I wouldn't be seen. She used the money for personal items and to pay another inmate for braiding her hair in cornrows. I tried to imagine Brandi with bleach-blond hair, one inch of dark brown roots, and braids. She talked in code to Kevin about details, using a secret language I never became quite fluent in. She informed us of the incessant questioning but assured Kevin that she was staying strong. He promised her that we'd get her out soon, that she'd be able to retire, that all she needed to do was "hold it down." Sometimes he'd call me into the room before they finished her brief ten-minute allowance, and we'd get to talk.

"They have a file on you, Poca," she said in code. "A photo of you and Little Mama and everything. They're asking me what your involvement is."

My stomach formed a tight knot as I thought of the implications.

"They want to know how my mortgage is being paid every month," she explained when Kevin came back into the room. After the call, he instructed me to draw up a fake lease agreement and put my name down as her tenant for the year to show that she'd made arrangements to rent out the house after being locked up. I grew increasingly nervous about my name showing up on these legally binding documents, but as usual, I did as I was told.

After the phone call with Brandi, Kevin told me he had an errand for me to run. I jumped in the shower to get ready, and when I came out of the bathroom, there was a ton of cash on our bed. I had seen a lot of money but was shocked at the gravity of hundreds covering the entire bedspread. The attorneys apparently were needing their next big payment. We stood together around the bed and counted out hundred-dollar bills into groups of ten, making one-thousand-dollar bundles. We folded them in half and wrapped the bundles with rubber bands. After we had twenty wads, Kevin had me put on a pair of long tube socks. He sat on the edge of the bed while I stood between his legs, balancing myself by holding on to his broad shoulders. Meticulously, he layered ten thousand dollars on each of my legs and instructed me to go to twenty different Western Unions. I knew from our previous wire transfers to each other that we could send up to $1,000 at a time without showing any identification. I sent all the money to Tori using fake names with no identification, and Tori went and paid the attorneys.

Kevin reassured me they had confirmed that the feds

couldn't touch me. The majority of the tax-evasion charges on the table required purposeful intent to evade for a period of five years or more. Since I'd only been with Kevin's family for nearly three years, the most I could be penalized for was "failure to file," an offense that carries a fine but no jail time. All I had to do was immediately file back taxes, including enough to cover the recent "lease" I just submitted to help Brandi's case.

Kevin and I met with a tax attorney who helped us with this. We met him in the back of an Italian restaurant. He had salt and pepper hair and wore a velour jumpsuit, complete with gold chain. He instructed Kevin on how I should file taxes as a dancer, ensuring that what I reported covered the amount of expenses that had gone out of my bank account. I was thankful for this assurance, but Kevin's daily interrogations made me worry that filing wasn't foolproof. "You're gonna be strong for me, babe, if they come for you too? You're not going to act like some punk, right? They'll threaten to take Deshae."

At home he berated me. "Any call, Poc, *any* call, you hear me, could be a fed." He stood over me, wielding the remote control like a weapon. "If you keep your stupid mouth shut, then they won't have anything, you hear me?" One slight look of trepidation on my face and I knew the beatings would start.

I nodded.

He made me crouch at his feet to drive his point home. "What's your name?"

"Lawyer," I said, staring at the floor.

He hit me in the face with the remote.

"What's your address?"

"Lawyer," I whimpered.

"Where are you from?"

Lawyer.

"Where do you work?"

Lawyer.

Lawyer.

Lawyer.

He hit me again and again. He continued for what felt like hours.

"Please, Pup. Please, can I go to bed? I'm so tired," I begged. He grumbled under his breath and finally let me crawl into bed.

I lay awake while wave after wave of anxiety crashed into my thoughts. *Is he right? If I don't talk will they take Deshae? If I do talk, will Kevin come find us? Oh, God, what if I lose her? Lawyer. Lawyer.*

The weight of carrying the many households' expenses—the rent and mortgages, cars, utilities, groceries, plus our business overhead, the attorney fees, on top of the travel and moving costs—was taking a huge toll on my health. I worked around the clock. Sundown to sunup was no longer enough. Some days Kevin would give me an hour to sleep in the closet where it was dark and quiet. I'd take any call so I could pay his extravagant bills. I had no room to be choosy, and no trick was off limits— from A-list celebrities flying me to the Mondrian on Sunset Boulevard to the businessmen taking me to the Waldorf in New York or the crack heads at the Motel 6, and anyone in between.

I was exhausted and scared. The amount of money I was supposed to bring in was ridiculous. How was I going to do this on my own? I started losing weight, and my hair began falling out in clumps. I'd often drive to the Rio and park my car in the darkest corner to sleep, so if he drove in looking for me, I'd be out of easy sight. I'd blame the low quota on a slow night.

I missed Brandi—my only real friend, my wife-in-law, my sister. Running around the streets by myself with no one to talk to or check in with, no one to eat with—it was lonely. April was nearby, but she got on my nerves. Kevin forced us to be friends, to spend time together, to "work it out" when we argued.

I wasn't sure how much longer I could work all these crazy hours, but how could I ever abandon Brandi and all she'd worked so hard for? Who would pay her attorney fees and her mortgage? What about the business we'd risked our lives to build? I couldn't bear to see her lose what she'd bought with her blood, sweat, and tears. Yes, I was now living in her home, but I had no choice. We didn't dare buy anything new right now. Investigators were watching our every move.

Kevin told me to seek additional legal advice for extra reassurance, so I called an old high-school friend, Anthony, whom I learned was now an attorney in Vegas. April and I went to his home, where he reviewed our paperwork.

"RICO Act," he said matter-of-factly and shut the file.

"What's that mean?" I asked.

"Money laundering, racketeering, bank fraud, tax evasion," he replied. "If no one talks, they'll at least get you guys on tax evasion, the same thing they got Al Capone on." He stood up, signaling that he was done. April handed him a wad of hundreds, but he shook his head and pushed her hand away.

"Good to see you again." He reached out to me for a hug. "Wish it were under different circumstances." He gave a sheepish smile as I hugged him back. April turned to leave first, and as she walked through the door, Anthony grabbed my arm.

"This is serious stuff," he warned. "You need to get out of this." I was a deer in headlights. I nodded my thanks and quickly left to catch up with April before she suspected anything. *Was this what Brandi meant when they were showing her pics of me? Am I next?*

I forced myself to inhale deeply as we pulled into our drive-way. April went back to her townhouse. Deshae greeted me at the door in her usual manner, with kisses, hugs, and excitement.

I walked in, careful not to emote any hint of anxiety, and found Kevin in our bedroom on the computer.

"Hey, Poc," he said in a cheerful tone.

Thank God, I thought.

"Come check this out."

I stood behind him as he showed me the women's federal prisons Tori was considering. Each website offered photos and amenities. *He's picking out prisons for his girls like he's choosing a vacation resort.*

"They get to choose their prison?" I asked, unable to hide my surprise.

"They'll get to request one. The judge will either accept or deny their request. Brandi wants to stay in Texas near her family."

He turned around in his chair and grabbed my hands. "I have something else to tell you. The feds will be filing arrest warrants for April and me soon."

"For what?"

"Tax evasion. We're going to try to cut a deal before that."

What in the world? He's going to cut a deal . . . with April?

He hadn't mentioned anything about this. I felt completely out of the loop. Kevin rarely chose favorites, at least not openly. Brandi made the most money, and he spent the most time with her, so cutting a deal for April and not the other two was shocking, especially since he always complained about her getting on his nerves.

"What kind of deal?" I withdrew my hands from his.

He looked down. "Tori and Brandi are accepting the plea deal—thirteen months. If April and I go to jail, I can't leave my son with no one."

"But I'm here," I said, careful to hide the panic tightening my chest. I wondered whether he was baiting me to test my response.

"I know, but he needs someone who has been with him, and what if they come for you later? We have to have someone who's guaranteed to be out. I'm going to turn myself in if they drop the charges against April."

His loyalty to her took me by surprise. Even though most pimps don't keep girls around who are too old to work, he did. His loyalty had always intrigued me, but never knowing which of us he'd fight for made me question the reality of a future together. *He must actually care about her. I'll never be enough. I can't compete with the history they have together.* With each thought, my hopes spiraled further into a pit of despair.

Kevin knew right away that his decision had wrecked me. I was physically exhausted, and the picture of my perfect family that I'd mentally painted was fading fast. *He's not going to give me a baby. He's not going to give me anything. I'm giving him everything, working myself into a state of complete exhaustion.* So much so that I had collapsed at the Hard Rock one night and was rushed to the emergency room, where I was diagnosed with dehydration and over exhaustion. Kevin showed up smiling to the doctors but pulled me out of bed. I was beginning to fear that my way out was nothing but a mirage.

Later that evening, while getting ready, I sat on my knees on the bathroom floor, hanging my head, barely able to hold myself up. I seriously felt like I might be losing it. A good night of sleep was three to four hours. I was starting to mix up the stories I told my parents. I could tell they were beginning to see through the tangled web of lies I was feeding them. I became paranoid that Kevin was tapping my phone and car, so he could nail me when I got home for saying or doing something out of pocket. I'd check my mirrors and glovebox for microphones or cameras like a paranoid schizophrenic.

"I can't do this anymore," I whispered to no one. The thought of praying didn't even cross my mind. I'd sunk so deep into my pit that I felt I was too far gone for God to hear.

"I can't do this anymore."

I laid my forehead on the cold marble floor. Then I lifted and hit it just so slightly. *I can't do this.* I hit the floor with my head again, a little harder. *I can't do this.* I banged my head against the hard tile of the bathroom floor again. It started hurting but I didn't care. I felt my sanity slipping away like a fleeting thought, a memory of sanity I couldn't hold on to. I raised my head and hit it on the floor again. *I can't do this anymore.*

Tears began to fall as I rehearsed in my mind every pitiful aspect of my dead-end life. It was time to get out.

But how?

CHAPTER 12 **the whale**

How hard it is for the rich to enter the kingdom
of God! Indeed, it is easier for a camel to go
through the eye of a needle than for someone
who is rich to enter the kingdom of God.

May 2006

My phone vibrated across the kitchen counter. I excused myself from the dinner table and walked over to pick up my phone. Joel's name appeared on the caller ID.

"Why, hello there," I answered, using my sexiest voice. Kevin, methodically cutting the fat off his steak, glanced up with a fierce scowl. I pointed toward the hallway, waiting for his nod of approval, which he quickly sent back with a grunt. Some days Kevin hated when I talked to tricks in front of him or the kids, yet he definitely wanted the calls to come in. Other days he wanted to craft my text messages to them.

Because freelancing earned his girls greater profits, he highly encouraged it. Now more than ever, I was happy to get calls from my regulars, especially those with ridiculous amounts of money. Kevin called them "whales."

I'd met Joel Hansen in 2005. His magnetic demeanor and high-end attire caught my eye one night as I was freelancing at the Mandalay Bay. We stood the same height in my tallest heels, meeting eye to eye. He had short, almost completely buzzed light brown hair and a little boy charm and a twinkle in his eye. I crossed paths with him on my way to the casino. In a drunken stupor on his way to his room, he made some sort of catcall toward me. His Salvatore Ferragamo shoes and True Religion jeans were a good sign.

If he spends $150 on jeans and $500 on shoes, surely I can come up with this one.

"Hey, you," I said, moving closer. I could smell the alcohol on his breath as I approached him. "You want some company tonight?"

He quickly agreed and led me toward the elevator. Joel was undeniably attractive, and I was sure he had no problem getting girls. His smiling eyes and dimples were mesmerizing.

In the elevator, I learned that he was participating in an exotic car rally. He was driving from his hometown of Phoenix through Los Angeles and Vegas and then back home. He was proud to tell me about his vehicle, a very expensive Mercedes. He handed me a $5,000 casino chip and invited me to stay until breakfast the next morning.

"Twist my arm," I flirted.

That night, I texted Kevin from the bathroom. *I will be home in the morning.*

I'd finally caught a whale. From that evening on, Joel became my regular. He'd call on me to stay with him every time he was in Vegas, which was often. As our "relationship" grew, he began flying me to other cities he traveled to for work. I would accompany him to dinner, shows, casinos, even business conferences. Sometimes I'd take a commercial flight, but usually he would send his Gulfstream III jet to pick me up from the private Las Vegas airport.

I took Joel's call and darted down the hallway into the bathroom and shut the door behind me. My heart was beating faster at the idea of a night out with charming Joel. He was classy and doted on me, and when I was with him, I felt smart. I felt special and respected by those around us. I welcomed a getaway from the stressed monster who belittled and abused me in my own home and from the exhausting months of picking up as many tricks as I could.

"Hey, can you be at the airport in an hour?" Joel asked.

"Absolutely. Should I pack for the night?" I hoped.

"Yes, I have a meeting in New York. Dress business. There will be other people on the plane, so think of something." He laughed.

"Okay, see you soon!"

Kevin required me to get payment upon arriving to meet Joel. Sometimes he paid in cash. Other times he transferred payment into one of Kevin's business bank accounts, thinking it was mine. Kevin got what we wanted, while Joel wrote it off as an investment. If he knew Kevin would strip search me upon return and take all the money, I'm confident he would have had a very different opinion of the transaction.

Throwing my best "business" clothes into a suitcase, I raced around to get ready while watching the clock. I kissed Kevin and Deshae and gave Maria instructions for while I was away.

This was the type of "work" Brandi had taught me: to get a trick to fall in love with us. But for me, faking a relationship felt deceitful. I struggled with the thought that I was setting a man up for heartbreak.

I pulled my Mercedes into the private airport and parked my car in a handicap space, displaying the fake parking permit on my rearview mirror as usual. I walked into the small lobby where a screen showed the itinerary for the next few flights. I looked at the three on the screen, none of which had G3 listed for Joel's jet. A man in a pinstripe suit with slick black hair sat waiting. He watched me look at the itinerary and pull out my phone to check for any emails about my online ads.

"Waiting for the Gulfstream?" he asked me with a car salesman's smile and a radio host's voice.

"Yes," I replied politely.

"They haven't arrived yet." He stood and extended his hand, "Michael Samson." He acted as if he were applying for a TV anchorman position and looked like one too.

"Rebecca," I said, shaking his hand. I rarely gave out my real name, but because of all the money transfers and hotel room check-ins over the past year, Joel knew my name. Since Michael clearly knew him, I had to keep my stories straight. No one but my real family called me Rebecca, so hearing it somehow made me feel closer to Joel, whom I was growing quite fond of, and yet weird, as though he had access to a person he knew nothing about.

"How do you know Joel?" he asked.

"I work in the Vegas office," I lied, remembering when Joel told me about one of his time-share projects there. "I did some work on the Boca Raton project."

A successful commercial builder, Joel had quickly risen to the height of success. By the age of twenty-nine, he'd purchased a private jet, which he felt caused others to take him more seriously. "Most guys my age are laughed out of the board meetings," he'd told me.

He had married his high school sweetheart at seventeen when he got her pregnant their senior year. They had not expected such a successful business and therefore had never considered a prenuptial agreement. Joel told me they lived in separate homes, but he could never leave her because she would take half of everything. Though he was open with me, I wondered whether he was running drag on me as I'd done with him.

"How do you know Joel?" I asked Michael, quickly changing the subject.

"I'm speaking at the conference," he said.

"Oh, great. I'm looking forward to that."

The jet pulled onto the tarmac, and Joel and his business partner Adam got off. All four of us exchanged greetings and boarded the plane.

"So, Rebecca tells me you guys worked on the Boca Raton project together," Michael shouted above the engine noise while walking toward the jet.

"Yes, Rebecca runs our Vegas office." He looked at me and winked, seeming pleasantly surprised by my ability to think on my toes.

After we settled into the comfortable leather seats, a flight attendant took our dinner orders and poured drinks for everyone. Joel and Michael sat in two captains' chairs facing the cockpit the majority of the flight, while Adam ate his meal and made small talk with me at the table. Adam was aware of our arrangement and had grown to like me.

When Adam got up to use the restroom, Joel moved into the empty seat. Michael leaned his head back and grabbed a quick catnap while Joel rested his hand on my leg under the table, making my pulse race. He seemed genuinely happy to see me.

What are the chances that a guy like this would actually date a girl like me?

Part of me wanted to blurt out everything, including how my daughter and I desperately needed help escaping Kevin's tight grip. But telling him could run the risk of angering Joel, since I'd not been straight up with him about where all his hard-earned money was going.

As the plane descended toward New York City's twinkling lights, I wrestled with the notion of escaping the Game. Why had this guy paid to bring *me* here? Women must fall at his feet.

"I could fall in love with you," he had once said. But Kevin's warning followed close on the heels of Joel's whispers. "Those type of men pay you to leave, not to stay. They have wives and kids at home."

A limo met us at the airport, and we loaded into the back seat, then headed toward the W hotel. The second we hit the W's ultra-modern lobby, I began people-watching while Joel checked everyone in. Businesspeople and travelers sat on low, square couches, some sipping cocktails and talking. Others checked in at the sleek white marble counter. We were mixing with the city's movers and shakers, and Joel seemed perfectly at home in the hip atmosphere.

My handsome date returned with a stack of room keys in cardboard sleeves. "Your room numbers are on the inside," he said, handing one to each of us. "Too bad we're not here longer. Amex comped us a massage."

Even though it would be quick, this luxurious getaway was exactly what I needed, far away from all the stress and drama at the Big House. Thanks to Maria's care, I wasn't worried about Deshae. And Kevin's fierce protective instinct over her caused me never to question his time with the kids.

As we took the elevator to our rooms, Michael exited first, and the three of us breathed a sigh of relief. Joel had obviously requested our rooms on different floors for privacy.

"Boca Raton?" Joel turned to me. "How did you remember that?" he asked with a huge grin.

Our posh, top-story corner room had spectacular views of Times Square. By now I'd been to New York City many times with other buyers, but this visit with Joel was different. I was enjoying and even welcoming his advances. If Kevin found out how this guy made me feel, he'd beat me.

Thank God Kevin can't read my mind.

We awoke early the next morning, and Joel scooted out to connect with Adam for a preconference meeting. Michael planned to meet us at the venue, which left me free. I grabbed a Starbucks and strolled the area until the meeting was over. As I walked near Ground Zero, I peeked through the chain-link fence. It was sobering to be standing in the exact location where terrorists had flown two planes into the World Trade Center buildings, forever changing the meaning of the numbers 9–1–1.

People worked away on an enormous hole, clearing the space and slowly constructing something—I couldn't tell what. The immensity of the hole reduced the workers to the size of ants. They labored away, each one making a miniscule dent in the titanic-sized job.

As I walked back to the limo to meet Joel and Adam, wave after wave of emotions cascaded over me. My heart ached for the victims of 9/11. At the same time, I was grieving too. For some reason, this significant place where thousands of lives were lost was stirring up my own grief.

What am I doing? I've been given the gift of life only to squander it away on material things. Is this what my life has become? A rat race for the finish line? And where exactly is the finish line?

The same magnetic pull that always kept me from leaving, swirled. *I need to get out, but I can't leave Brandi. She'll lose the houses, her car, she'll be forced to get a public defender. What about Little Kev? If I left Kevin high and dry, would he take out all his stress and anger on his son instead of me? How would I live with myself knowing that could happen? Would Deshae and I be safe in my tiny town in Oregon?*

With my head still whirling, I reached the limo just before Joel arrived, flashing his irresistible grin.

My emotions swung in the other direction. *I wish I could be like him, with no worries in the world. And happy, truly happy. Could I ever make that happen?*

When the Gulfstream touched down at the Las Vegas private airport, my heart sank, thinking of what awaited me. As if in direct response to my mental battle with fear, a warm, reassuring hand squeezed mine. I returned Joel's gesture and smiled into his kind eyes.

"You don't belong here, you know." He gazed at me and held my hand tightly. "You're so much more than this, Rebecca."

Those words were what I'd been longing to hear. My heart had ached to hear them from my high school boyfriend, from Bryan, from Kevin. Now I'd found someone who saw me for all that I was. Maybe it was Joel who held my ticket to freedom in his neatly manicured hands.

But beneath the surface lived an ugly secret I was too afraid to let loose. My abusive pimp took every dollar Joel had ever given me. Joel wasn't the type of man you played with. He was serious about life. About business. At best I was sure my secret would make him mad, or embarrassed that I had duped him this whole time into thinking the money he paid was going to me. I couldn't bear the thought that I might drive him away completely by telling him the truth. I rehearsed what he might say out of disgust and disdain.

I smiled, choking back the tears, "I know."

"I can help you . . . get out . . . be normal . . ." He sat straight up to face me, with a seriousness that shot arrows of hope into my heart. Tears became puddles in my eyes that overflowed with every blink.

"I have a daughter," I blurted, looking down. I hated that I'd hidden her from him. I was ashamed of being the type of mother that hides her baby, ashamed of admitting I had kept more than one huge secret from him.

He raised his eyebrows and paused for a moment. "Could you move back to Oregon and be with your family? I mean, would you like living there?"

Anywhere away from Kevin and this crashing investigation.

"As long as we can still take trips like this," I smiled, wiping the tears off my cheeks.

"I was actually looking at some property near the golf course in Bend. I'm sure we could pick you up there." He winked.

Could I actually have a way to escape?

Like a scene in a romantic movie, we embraced at the bottom of the jet's stairs and said our goodbyes. He told me to put some plans together and he'd call soon with details. My mind spun with hope during the entire drive home.

I drove home half elated, on a high from feeling normal with Joel, and yet sick that I still hadn't been completely honest with him. As I got closer to the Big House, panic pushed all that away. My stomach turned upside down as I wondered whether Kevin would be able to tell that I was considering trying to run. *Act normal.*

I went inside and right to the shower, knowing the rules— not to touch anyone, any child, anything while "trick germs" were still on me. I couldn't stop thinking of Joel or his questions. I knew I'd forever be the mistress. He had his Mormon life in Phoenix, his wife, and three kids.

"What's going on, Poc?" Kevin asked suspiciously later that afternoon. He was wiping his finger along the window sill, then examining the miniscule dust bunny with a look of disgust.

"Nothing," I answered quickly, snapping out of my daydreams.

"You're awfully quiet since you been back from that rich trick. Let's go for a walk." He stood up and headed toward the door. "And don't forget to talk to Maria about her cleaning. The windows are dusty again."

You could barely see any hint of dust on the windows, or anywhere in the house, but I knew it was pointless to say anything. I slipped into some shoes and followed him outside into fresh air. Being out of the house was rare for us but good for me, because Kevin never beat me in public.

"I had a dream last night," he began, looking up at the sky with his hands in his pockets. "All those rich NYC tricks were sitting around a conference table laughing at you, making fun of you."

I didn't know what facial expression to make under his microscope. I faked a confused scowl.

"You don't actually think someone like that whale would ever want to be with someone like you, right? To those type of people, you're nothing but a hooker; you'd never be someone they could take home. Remember that." His words pierced my soul and made my stomach turn. I nodded. It was hard not to believe him. I had found photos of Joel's family and blond wife on social media. *Why would he want to be with someone like me?*

"I don't want to be with someone like that anyway," I flipped back. "I want to be here, with our family." We walked in silence the rest of the way, and I was grateful for the sunglasses that hid the tears.

"Going to the gym, Poc," he said as we arrived home. "Be back in a bit." He kissed me, out of obligation perhaps, got into his car, and drove away.

I scooted inside and grabbed my phone. *Is my phone tapped? Is he listening?*

I quickly typed out a text to Joel. *Hello.*

His reply flashed back. *Ready to take me up on my offer?*

Can you talk? I texted while running upstairs to keep an eye out in case anyone came home.

My phone rang minutes later. I jumped.

"Hi, beautiful. How are you?"

"Are you serious? Will you help me get out?"

"Yes, I am very serious." His tone shifted, and I suddenly felt like a banker in the middle of a huge contract negotiation. I paced and tried to sound way more casual than I felt. "I'm going to need plane tickets for me and my daughter, and a car when I get to my mom's. There is no public transportation in that small town. From there, I'll figure out what I want to do, maybe go back to school."

"Okay, how much do you owe on your car now?" he asked.

I had to think of a lie quickly. I couldn't let him pay off Brandi's car. Running off with some clothes would be one thing, but taking a vehicle, that was a death wish!

"Too much." I replied. "Bought it at a bad time. They go now for less than I still owe. My mom can fly into town and help me pack. Then I'll fly home with her. Can you get us a room for a couple days?" I hoped.

"Okay, sounds good. Text me the details, and I'll take care of it." He hung up.

I sat there struck by the thought that I must move quickly. I called my mom, and she picked up immediately.

"Becky!" She sounded surprised to hear from me.

"Hey. I'll explain later, but things aren't working out with me and Kevin. Please don't ask questions right now."

"Okay," my mother started. "Beck, is everything—"

"I'll explain later. I need you to come to Vegas. I'll pay for your plane ticket. But I'll need you to help me with Deshae while I pack my—"

"Yes!" She barely let me get the words out. "I can come right now. Whenever you need me."

We finished talking through the details, and I hung up. When Kevin came home from the gym, I explained that my mom was coming into town for a work trip and she wanted to see Deshae. Kevin knew how my mom and Deshae had bonded during my stay in rehab. It wasn't unusual for my mom and step-dad to visit her. He also knew that too much control from him raised their already heightened suspicions.

"It will only be for a couple days. Can Deshae go stay with her at night? She misses her nana." I held my breath, waiting for him to explode.

"Yeah, sure." Kevin agreed.

"Thank you!" I hugged him. *Whew! So far so good,* I thought.

The easy part was done. My mom flew into town, and Joel put her up in the Four Seasons. Little by little, I transferred a few of my belongings to the hotel without Kevin noticing. One afternoon, while Kevin was at the gym, I asked whether I could spend some time with my mother. He agreed but told me a specific time to be home.

My mom, suspicious of my paranoid behavior—I constantly checked my phone and looked over my shoulder in public—carefully asked me questions, which I knew were out of concern for me and Deshae. But I danced around them. I couldn't risk letting her into my world. I slept a lot while I was with her and even booked a massage at the spa, knowing Joel wouldn't care if I charged it to the room.

It was hard to relax on the massage table, but I did my best to close my eyes and doze off so my mind wouldn't spin like a tornado. The therapist moved her fingers along my back, pressing into the deep tissue of my neck that was holding in layers of stress and anxiety.

I soaked in the Zen-like atmosphere and soothing aromas and began to fall asleep.

Suddenly, someone yanked my hair. I screamed. "What the—" My heart began to race as my worst fear surfaced. *He's found me. I knew this was a bad idea! I knew he'd find out and come get me.* I jumped up, starting to hyperventilate while looking for Kevin in the dark room.

"Oh, sweetie! I'm so sorry. My stool broke, and I grabbed for anything as I fell. I didn't mean to catch your hair!" the apologetic masseuse pleaded.

I snatched my robe and flew out of the room and back into the dressing room. I crouched down in a dressing stall and forced myself to slow my breathing. Eventually, I made my way back to my mom's hotel room and slept there that night. But my sleep was unsettled. Kevin blew up my phone all night long with threatening texts.

I swear to God, Poc. I will find you.

You are a weak hoe.

My mom, Deshae, and I left the next morning.

Thoughts of Kevin's retaliation plagued my mind night and day. On top of being afraid of his vengeance, I forced myself to try to forget what my escape could mean to the best friend I'd ever had. *What kind of friend am I for leaving Brandi high and dry?* When I did think about leaving her, guilt engulfed me.

Deshae and I moved into my aunt Brettani's house, and I spent the first day checking and rechecking my phone. Joel had texted asking whether I wanted to go look at cars. I told him I'd be content with a Camry. I felt it was practical and decent looking, the poor man's Lexus. But he encouraged me to look at a real Lexus. I was testing the waters of his graciousness but didn't want to offend him either. I began looking at Lexuses online and sent him some less expensive options I found locally.

After a few days, he asked about the private airport in Medford and texted me about planning a trip to come get me soon. But no mention of the car. He was silent for the next ten days.

Hey, I finally texted, *just checking in. Are we still on?* I imagined him tied up with work and convinced myself I'd hear from him as soon as things lightened up.

No response. Days turned into weeks and still no answer. Was he ignoring me? Not wanting to impose on my aunt, I'd been buying food for Deshae and myself. But my money was running out. Kevin's money was the one thing I had known better than to take with me. I only left with what I earned the last day I worked.

My concern mounted with each passing day.

I am running out of money, and I have a daughter, I texted. *Don't play games with me. If you don't want to help me, just say so and I'll figure it out.* Our welfare was at stake.

Still no response.

Ironically, the man I dreaded hearing from would not stop reaching out. Kevin's texts and phone calls flooded my phone daily. Desperation and my undiagnosed Stockholm syndrome got the better of me one afternoon, and I answered his call.

"Hey."

"I'm sorry, babe." Kevin said. "I've been stressed with the investigation. You know I want a family, Poc. You are the one for me. What kind of man would I be if I left all these other women who had given years to me? Would you respect me if I did that? Please, Poc, I need you. You're the only one who understands me and my business mind. You're brilliant, and we could do so much together. I want to marry you. Let's have a baby."

"But I don't want you to leave them. I know how much

they've given up for you. That wouldn't be fair to them. I just want a family of my own." I still believed that having a family would fill the gaping hole in my heart. Since money, cars, houses, and adventure hadn't, surely a family would.

His sweet-talking promises ebbed into my heart one after another, wave upon wave, day after day. Like Pharaoh chasing the children of Israel after kicking them out of Egypt, Kevin's ego-driven, emotional chase wouldn't let up.

With twenty dollars left in my pocket and no word from Joel, I was desperate. Kevin called again and reiterated his plans for our life together.

Maybe my leaving shook him enough to realize how important I am. But did it shake him enough to stop the beatings?

My mom bought Deshae and me tickets to a carnival that was in town. Deshae came alive, and as we stepped off the spinning-strawberries ride, she took off running. Smiling at her excitement to rush ahead and find the next ride, I quickly gathered our belongings and turned to run after her. I scanned the crowd for her pink top. Then I froze.

The scene before me played out like a slow-motion movie.

"Daddy!" she yelled, excited.

He's here . . . Oh, God . . . Please don't cause a scene, I thought. *Please don't hurt me; don't hurt my family.*

Kevin locked eyes with me and approached like a hunter stalking its prey.

"How'd you know we were here?" I asked, giving him a kiss in hopes of not upsetting him in public.

"Come on, baby, I know you." He leaned in and breathed heavily in my ear. "I know what time you wake up, what you eat, what you wear. I know you better than you know yourself. I told you from day one, I didn't want in your purse. I want in your mind."

He'd booked a hotel across from the airport. That afternoon,

Deshae and I went and stayed with him. In his own way, Kevin made me feel special again, as if I were the only one, as if our future would be secure if we could only get through the uncertainty of these plea-deal negotiations. The investigation was the reason behind his rage, he explained. Things seemed to be winding down. He told me he'd agreed to twelve months in exchange for April doing probation rather than jail time, but he didn't have a self-surrender date yet.

After Deshae fell asleep on the couch, he sat at the foot of the bed and massaged my feet, something he had never done before. "I've been talking to the others, and they want to move on after prison. They want their own lives," he said as he tenderly rubbed my feet.

I want to move on with my life too, I thought. I was confused and angry about the promises Joel had held out to me. Why would he simply vanish off the face of the earth, especially when he knew I had a child? Sure, maybe he had changed his mind about being with me, but as a father, how could he do that to a child? *My* child?

The next morning, I left with Kevin and went back to our house—well, Brandi's house. My family was concerned, but we told them I knew he was coming, and I covered for him as usual. It was a believable story, but I once again struggled with running drag on the people who loved me most. All along, my family had suspected domestic violence, having seen my bruises on past visits, and they pleaded with me to call if I needed them. I don't know whether Kevin sensed my uneasiness, but soon after we arrived home, he made an announcement.

"Go ahead and make us that appointment at the IVF clinic," he said matter-of-factly.

My heart skipped a beat. "Really?" I tried to hide my surprise. "I'll call the clinic right now," I promised, trying to contain my joy.

He grabbed my hand. "You see, Poc. I'm here for you through

it all. I'm not some whale who drifts in and out of your life whenever he needs a good time. I'm here for good."

I couldn't get to my phone fast enough. I made an appointment for later that week.

The IVF clinic looked like any standard doctor's office, sterile and professional, the waiting room scattered with magazines. After the nurse called our names, we sat across from the doctor, listening to a scientific explanation of pregender determination, allowing us to choose a boy.

"Do you already have a child?" the doctor asked.

"Yes. We have a daughter," Kevin answered.

"Good," he checked off a box on the paperwork.

As the doctor continued, we learned that we would owe about $30,000 by the end of the treatment, and they would gladly take our deposit right away. The first step would be for me to take hormone injections to increase egg production. Then they would harvest my eggs, which would be joined with Kevin's sperm at the IVF lab. They would then test each embryo to determine gender and implant only the male embryos.

"We will implant three to four eggs, and more than likely, two will thrive. This process will greatly increase your chances of having twins," he explained, then waited for our response.

"Wow. Twins?" I said in shock. Suddenly my surprise turned into a whole new vision of my future as a mama. Kevin squeezed my hand and smiled. He paid the $250 consultation fee in cash and, like a perfect gentleman, slid his arm around my waist to guide me out of the office while smiling and greeting others in the waiting room as we left. We walked from the air-conditioned building into the hot desert air and stood together in the parking lot, processing the deluge of information we'd just taken in from the doctor's firehose. *Twins.* I pictured two brown-eyed boys toddling around the Big House's kitchen.

"You ready for twin boys?" Kevin asked as we leaned against the car. "We could make that empty middle room the boys' room. We'll have to give Maria more money. That means you're going to have to work a lot more. Save up the thirty Gs. Save up to take time off. You ready to grind?"

I agreed with an excited, what-the-heck-am-I-doing smile.

"Boss and Champ," he said.

"What?" I stopped rifling through my purse for my sunglasses and looked at him. *He can't be serious.*

"That's what I want to name them, after the twins who play for the NFL. I want to name them Boss and Champ Barker."

From that point on, he referred to our imaginary twins as Boss and Champ. He'd pull strollers and clothes up online at home and show me decorating ideas. I was beginning to believe in a future with Kevin again. He'd serve his time, probably get out in less than a year for good behavior, and we'd get a fresh start with our boys. My excitement grew as I pictured two cribs nestled into the corners of our nursery.

The only problem was the small inner voice that relentlessly nudged my conscience whenever I was still. Part of me wanted to listen to it, but it was far easier to ignore it.

Around this time, Kevin made another big announcement. After eleven months in prison, Brandi was being released! She was denied a request to transfer her parole to Nevada, so she would have stay in Texas. Kevin instructed her to find work there as a dancer and send the money home.

"I'm flying her home," he said one day in early 2007 as winter was coming to an end. He didn't care that leaving Texas broke her parole. "She'll be here next Tuesday."

When Tuesday came, I stood at the Vegas airport, checking my phone and scanning the crowd to catch a glimpse of my sister.

A woman in a baseball cap caught my eye. I couldn't tell whether it was her, but then she looked my way. *Brandi!*

We simultaneously broke into a run and collided into each other, hugging and crying.

"Oh my gosh, Poca! I can't believe it!" She wiped away tears.

"Me too, Boo. You're out!" We stared at each other in disbelief that the moment had finally come. We laughed, cried, and hugged while passersby stared.

Brandi stayed in the Big House with us for a few days, spending much of her time with Kevin

A few weeks after she went home, Kevin sat me down. He looked as though someone had died.

"She needs to hear it from you."

A wave of panic rose up inside me, causing my stomach to flutter. I knew exactly what he was saying but not saying. *He's going to make me tell my best friend about Boss and Champ.* I felt like a giant wrench was gripping my chest, forcing me to concentrate harder so that I could take another breath. I was about to steal her dream of having a baby.

CHAPTER 13 **black and blue**

You are my hiding place;
you will protect me from trouble
and surround me with songs of deliverance.

May 2007

This time when I went to meet Brandi, I dreaded seeing her. She picked me up at the Dallas/Fort Worth airport, and we stopped for pedicures and lunch on our way back to her apartment. I'd never seen Texas before, but being together made me feel back to normal. Yet the truth was breathing down my neck, making it next to impossible to relax and enjoy our time together.

When we got to her tiny apartment, I sat down on the bed.

"So, do you know why Pup sent me out here?" I asked, grateful for the trash can next to her bed. I felt sick to my stomach and figured it might come in handy.

"Yeah," she said, sitting down next to me. "It's okay, Poca. You've held it down for me, and you want a family too." Her voice was tender and quiet. Her kind eyes reminded me why I loved her so much. She was always selfless. *Was this* part of her true character or something Kevin had brainwashed into her?

"You deserve a family too!" I said through tears. She started crying.

"I'll have one, just not now."

We laughed and cried and lay in bed like schoolgirls sharing secrets. We were both craving the same thing. Deep within us, our Creator had placed a desire to be loved, to be part of a family. But the enemy of our souls had twisted that desire into a contorted idea of "family," tempting us away from God's path again and again. He'd swapped out God's destiny and replaced it with a fake version. And yet somehow, despite that, we'd formed a deep bond that helped me survive this messy, crazy Game.

Despite Brandi's understanding and support, I knew I was taking something from her that she deserved more than I did. We tried to go back to normal after I came home, but the geographical distance between us only highlighted my sense of loss. We never again mentioned having babies, either out of respect for privacy or because it was too tender of a topic. And Mother's Day was right around the corner. For Christmas and Thanksgiving and all the other holidays, we were together as a family, all the "aunties" and the kids. Kevin even celebrated each woman's anniversary with the rest of us, like a polygamist. But because of Deshae, Mother's Day was my special day.

When it finally arrived that year, Kevin woke me up with a warm smile and an affectionate touch. I rolled over, thinking of all the ways we'd celebrate. I'd been looking forward to this for weeks.

I ran errands as usual, went to the gym, and checked on orders at the shop. I came home to a bouquet of red roses and white lilies from Kevin. I was excited to have to work for only a few hours before getting to come home and take the rest of the night off. We planned to go to a movie.

The escort service sent me to the Bellagio first, which turned out to be a bust. While leaving the Bellagio, Maddy called. I was relieved; Kevin wouldn't be happy if I came home with nothing. The last thing I wanted to do was ruin my chances of celebrating.

"Hey, Mad. What's up?" I answered.

"Oh, good! You answered. Are you close to the Mandalay Bay by chance?"

"Yes, actually. I'm just leaving the Bellagio. I can be right there."

"Okay, great! Thanks, Kelb!" she chirped.

I arrived at the Mandalay still slightly annoyed by the first trick who'd wasted my time. If this was another no-go and I went home with nothing, Kevin would wonder why I was gone for so long. I grabbed my back phone out of the center console.

He answered, "Hey, what's up?"

"My call was a no-go, but Maddy got me another. I'll be back shortly." I was glad I remembered to call him.

"Good job, Poc. Text me," he replied.

I walked into the Mandalay Bay. As I neared the hotel entrance, a group of undercover cops walked toward me. *Uh-oh.* EMTs rushed by with a stretcher. I recognized one of the vice cops from a previous arrest. We locked eyes. He grabbed me by the arm, turned me around, and walked me out. I winced from his tight grip.

"I'm leaving!" I pulled away defiantly.

"I've got a girl upstairs—strangled to death. She was just thrown out into the hallway naked. No ID on her—we don't even know who she is. Is this how you want to end up?" I shook my head. "We won't even be able to tell her family." He had tears in his eyes. "Seriously, get out of here."

I stood, shocked.

"I'm not talking about this hotel. Get out of this city, out of this life." And with that, he released my arm and walked away, shaking his head.

I couldn't get to the car fast enough. I pulled out my phone from the glove box and, with shaking hands, texted Kevin. "Coming home."

This wasn't the first time I'd been made aware of crimes against working girls. Other women had been murdered in the same halls where I worked. Maddy had sent a brunette to a local who killed her and kept her body in the closet. I was on that night. It could have been me. Another girl, whom I'd worked with a ton, didn't die but was raped and tied to a bed, left naked in the sleazy motel. The trick left with her car and house keys.

As these scenarios looped through my mind, a verse from Isaiah popped in too: "I will give Seba and Ethiopia in exchange for your life. Others died that you might live" (Isaiah 43:4 NLT 2000).

I drove home crying as the presence of the Holy Spirit filled my car. "I don't want to be here, Lord," I prayed. "Please provide a way out."

I arrived home and inhaled the fragrant aroma of Kevin's bouquet. Now more than ever, I had to believe that an end to this crazy life was in sight: our new chapter with our twins and a growing business. I had gotten our product into many stores across the city and was overseeing production with April daily.

Since it was Maria's night off, we thanked Little Kev for watching his sister and kissed Deshae good night. Kevin asked me to drive, and we headed toward the late-night theater on the Strip. We talked and laughed all the way about the boys and the business. We joked about Boss and Champ being in their car seats in the back. We imagined them crawling through the house and decided where we'd need safety gates. Our dual staircase would need one on each side.

Kevin always complained about my driving, to the point where I wondered whether he asked me to drive as a way to pick a fight. But tonight was different. Even though I was driving, he was in a good mood. We needed this time away to distract us from the prison time that loomed for him and Tori.

"Where are you going?" Kevin asked when I stopped at a red light.

"To the theater. Isn't that where we're going?" I asked with a pleasant voice.

"You need to turn left here." He pointed.

I put my left blinker on and tilted my steering wheel toward the turn lane, where a long line had formed.

"What are you doing?" he asked again, increasingly annoyed.

"I'm hoping someone will let me in."

Without warning, his fist flew at my face. My mind went blank. I was caught completely off guard. Another blow, then another, and another . . .

The pain came in waves but was masked by the utter terror. I held my quivering hands up over my face in a pathetic attempt to block the blows. He threw the truck in park and jumped out.

I heard him mumbling, "Oh, you think I'm stupid? I'm stupid, right? I'll show you stupid."

I looked up and noticed blood spattered across the driver's side window, my shirt, and seat belt. I sat frozen in shock. Circling around to my side of the car, he opened the door, pulled me out by the hair, and heaved me down to the asphalt. People drove by. No one noticed; no one stopped. Surely *someone* was as shocked by his behavior as I was?

He climbed into the driver's seat. I thought he was going to leave me standing there on the side of the road with no purse, no phone, and no money. But we were too far from home to walk, so I frantically ran around to the passenger side and jumped in. Kevin turned the truck around and headed home. *What will happen once we get there?* I began to have second thoughts about my choice to get back into the car. Maybe it would have been better to be left on the side of the road. But there was Deshae to think about. Everything in me wished I could rewind to laughing together on our way to the movie.

I sat quietly. I knew better than to talk unless spoken to. *Why did I say anything? What did I even do wrong? What happened?*

After thirty minutes of silence, we pulled into our driveway. "Get out," Kevin commanded. "Go inside."

I obeyed. He walked behind me, pushing me into the downstairs guest bathroom.

The sight of my face in the mirror made me gasp. I was unprepared to meet the disfigured woman staring back at me. Though Kevin beat me almost daily, most of those occasions left me with a black eye or a few bruises. But tonight, I was unrecognizable. My face was mangled. I didn't even know beatings like that happened in real life; it was worse than I had ever seen in the movies.

"Look at what you made me do," he snarled as he grabbed the back of my hair, forcing me to stare closer. Salty tears streamed down my cut face. It hurt to cry. It hurt to move.

"Clean yourself up," he demanded as he walked out.

I ran the water until it was warm and soaked a washcloth to gently wipe the blood from my swollen face. But it made little difference. Even cleaned up, I looked like I had just stepped out of the ring with Mike Tyson.

His face appeared behind me in the mirror. I jumped.

"Pack an overnight bag, and get in the car. Oh, and change your shirt."

My hands shook as I obediently crammed some sweatpants and a few necessities into an overnight bag. Fighting brain fog, I struggled to figure out what I might need. I rushed to the car and got in. Deshae was sleeping in the back seat.

What was happening? What was he doing with us?

Please, I begged God, *please keep her safe.*

Was he throwing us out? Where was he taking us? I wanted to curl up in a ball and cry and beg him not to hurt us. The mama bear in me felt like jumping in the back to grab my baby and run, but I knew he might do more damage if I reacted. He was so strong that there was no physical way to get away. I forced myself to breathe and sat quietly while my brain rehearsed all the horrifying things that might happen.

We drove toward April's, and a bit of relief surfaced. Kevin called and told her to come outside. When we pulled up, he picked up Deshae, still asleep, and handed her to April, who did what she was told. In the side mirror, I saw her looking at me with a perplexed expression. She was as equally confused as me.

As the Hummer sped back down the road, I sat frozen in the passenger seat, my heart beating as if I'd had three Red Bulls. The air conditioning blew a stray hair into my right eye, but I didn't dare risk brushing it away. Any tiny thing might upset him.

This man is going to kill me. He's going to take me out to the desert and kill me.

We pulled up to a Courtyard Marriot, and I knew my face was bad when he went inside. I had never seen Kevin rent a hotel in his own name—*ever*. He came back to the car and told me what room number to go to. Was he coming with me? Was he leaving me? Would he keep Deshae or leave her too?

I took a few seconds of quiet to shoot up an arrow prayer. *Please, God. Please, I need you now.*

He grabbed the bags and emotionlessly ordered, "Get out." He walked with me toward the hotel, looking over his shoulder. Was he going to berate me all night? Keep me up with no sleep again? I didn't know whether I could handle another night of this. My mind was growing foggier by the minute, and I struggled to focus on taking one step, then another. I was no stranger to sleep deprivation. Like a drill sergeant trying to break down his soldier, Kevin had nearly driven me to the edge of a breakdown many times.

In the room, he began his typical routine. He lined up everything symmetrically on the nightstand, his clothes folded in perfect squares, his shoes aligned along the closet floor. Next came the wet wipes to disinfect the remote control, door knobs, and light fixtures. I followed his lead.

"Go get us some ice," he said without looking up, almost in a whisper. He seemed distant, full of thought. Maybe even remorseful? I retrieved the ice and set it on the wood-veneer desk.

"Put it on your face and lie down," he directed. "I'll be back."

I jumped as the hotel door shut. I pulled on my sweats and climbed into bed while icing my face. After a while, curiosity got the best of me. I tiptoed to the bathroom and peeked at the damage in the mirror. The redness had gone down, and I could see the damage a bit more clearly now. Two severe black eyes, bruises all over, a swollen nose, and a jet-black top lip that stuck out like a duck bill. I didn't even know lips could turn that color. I tried a sip of water, but it wasn't worth the pain.

I climbed back into bed and tried to quiet my mind. I couldn't stop the tears. *This is crazy,* I thought. *I can't live like this.* I felt paralyzed with fear and confusion. People ask why you don't run—they expect you to grab a grenade, bomb the hotel, jump out the window, and run for freedom like the hero in the movies. When you live in a tornado of trauma, it's like you just need a moment to take a breath and gather your thoughts, but it never comes. I believed I was a victim of domestic violence and the Game was just my man's hustle. I couldn't see the truth.

About an hour later, Kevin returned. I stiffened as he sat on the bed next to me. I held my breath, bracing myself for what might be coming.

He gently moved my hair out of my eyes.

"Oh, babe . . . Poc," he whispered. "I'm sorry, baby. I'm so sorry."

The words I wanted to say got stuck behind the lump in my throat, and the tears returned. He gently brushed them away, careful not to hurt my swollen face. "I want you to listen to something. Will you come get in the car with me? We can go get some food."

My shattered heart didn't know what to say. He asked, "Will you?" as if I had a choice. I didn't get to choose anything with him. Not what I wore, not what to cook for dinner. I hadn't chosen anything that mattered in a very, very long time. And I was tired. I was very, very tired.

We got in the car and started driving. He put on Mariah Carey's "Fly Like a Bird." After a few minutes, I realized we were driving in circles. I was drawn in by the haunting spirituality of this song about the reality of the world's pain, along with the hopeful prayer to a God who could lift us out of the muck and help us fly above it. The lyrics seemed to speak directly to us.

A tear fell down his cheek. Something deep inside me softened. I wondered whether he felt bad, bad enough to stop. Did he realize that his anger had been taking over for quite some time?

"Forgive me," he said. But he didn't look at me. He just stared ahead at the road.

"I forgive you." I said the words but felt numb. I didn't want him to kill me or drive us both off a cliff.

We drove to my favorite Chinese food place in the Venetian, and I called in the order. I waited in the bottom level of the parking garage while he went in. I knew if the Hummer could have cleared the low ceilings on the upper levels, Kevin would have parked there, far away from passersby. As people streamed by the truck, I did my best to stay still, not allowing them to see my face.

The elevator doors opened, and he emerged in his baggy gray sweat pants and plain oversized gray T-shirt, with one hand in his pocket and one holding the to-go bag. He walked toward the car, looking left and right as if tonight were any other night. He was the king of calm, just as he had been at the IVF clinic, smiling and working the waiting room. Just as he was with the other parents at Deshae's school, who never noticed our odd family sitting beside them while we too took Christmas recital photos. These people he smiled at while he nodded his friendly hello as he crossed the parking garage, they had no clue about the women working for him around the clock. Why *would* they suspect anything? Nobody would. He was that good.

We ate dinner back at the hotel. He told me we would stay there for a couple of days and April would keep Deshae.

When we returned home, we told Maria and the kids that I had been in a car accident.

The days marched on, and before I knew it, it was October. In our home, that meant football season, because Little Kev was on the high school team.

"Hey, Dad." Little Kev was getting ready for football practice. "Can I borrow the Caliber to drive to practice?" We'd bought a Dodge Caliber for the business. April often drove it after returning her Jaguar because there was no more money to pay for expensive cars.

Even though the fields were only five blocks away, I was surprised when Kevin agreed to let his fifteen-year-old son drive there without a license. Kevin clearly didn't care about the law, but why would he jeopardize his own son's ability to get his license?

"To and from practice only," Kevin instructed. "You hear me, Dada? None of them little friends in your car either."

"Yes, Dad! Thank you, Dad. Bye, Poc." Little Kev bounced

out carrying his cleats. What he didn't know was that Kevin purposely had cleaned all the handles on the car so he could check them later for fingerprints.

That night Kevin sent me to rent a few movies from Blockbuster. He let me have the night off as he tried to maintain the facade of being a changed man. Sitting at a stoplight, I looked over at the car beside me.

Oh no.

Little Kev was driving our car, but he wasn't alone. Several of his football buddies were with him. He turned and saw me. Like a quarterback after throwing a game-losing interception, he threw his head back against the headrest in defeat. A few seconds after the light turned green and I pulled away, my ring tone jingled in my purse. I dug out my phone and answered it.

"Yes?"

"Please don't tell my dad," Little Kev begged. "Please don't tell him!"

"I have to, Dada." I replied sadly. "If he finds out that I knew and didn't tell him, I'll be in trouble."

"But Poca, he'll beat me!"

"No, he won't!" I was convinced that Kevin had his temper in check now. Not only had I never seen him lay a hand on Little Kev, he was always hyperprotective of the kids. "But you'll probably lose your car privileges until you're sixteen."

Back at home, I told Kevin, and he was rightfully upset. His fifteen-year-old son had not only driven in areas where he could've been pulled over but had put other kids in danger too. He could barely drive alone, let alone with a car full of kids! Kevin called him and told him to get home right away. He hung up the phone and paced by the front door. I nervously huddled by the kitchen, pretending to get items ready for movie night. The front door opened, and I heard Little Kev start to explain.

Kevin immediately grabbed his son by the scruff of his neck and began heaving punches at him. Little Kev fell to the ground, screaming. Kevin kept going. I watched, aghast, as he continued to beat his own son as if he were a grown man. From the corner of my eye, I turned to see Deshae standing frozen at the top of the stairs. Fear was etched across her face. I flew to her.

"Baby, it'll be okay. You stay in here," I said, walking her to her bedroom. "Do not come out until I come back to get you." I shut the door.

When I went down, Kevin was dragging the young boy kicking and screaming to his room, leaving a trail of blood. Kevin kicked the door shut behind him. I stopped, straining to hear their voices. The sounds of struggle and pleas continued.

I stood paralyzed, trying to decide how best to protect the children. *This is my fault. I have to do something. I should have never told on him! Should I jump in?* A few minutes later Kevin emerged from the bedroom, seething.

"Clean up this blood before it stains my carpet!" He stomped up the stairs to our bedroom and slammed the door.

I did as I was told, then went into Deshae's room and cuddled her in her bed while she watched cartoons, petting her hair and telling her how special she was to me. I told her I'd be back, and I got up and went into the kitchen to ensure that I had cleaned up after myself.

Little Kev came in. The left side of his face looked like a meat cleaver had been taken to it. He could see the shock on my face.

"It's my fault. I shouldn't have driven with my friends." He stared at the kitchen floor, avoiding eye contact.

"Dada, don't ever!" I couldn't hold back my tears. I put my hands on his shoulders. He looked up. Tears pooled in his big brown eyes. "Don't ever blame yourself for this. Your dad has issues," I whispered, afraid he'd overhear us. "What are you going to tell the school?"

"Football practice," he said, not skipping a beat. I wondered whether he'd had to use this lie before.

I was sick with guilt. Little Kev grabbed some food and went back to his room. I went upstairs to check in with Kevin. He sat motionless on the floor, facing the wall, leaning up against the bed, tears streaming down his face.

"What is wrong with me, Poc? I have anger issues," he bowed his head low and laced his bloody fingers behind his neck.

I sat down next to him. My heart hurt for Little Kev, but for some crazy reason, for the first time, I felt bad for Kevin too. I had never seen him bothered like this over his anger, nor had he ever admitted to how badly the spirit of rage consumed him. He rested his head on my shoulder, and we cried together.

"I need anger management classes or something," he sobbed.

"I can find one in our area," I offered.

"Don't leave me, Poc. I need you."

"I'm not leaving," I promised.

His head on my shoulder got heavier as he pushed me to the floor. He climbed on top of me and told me he was going to have sex with me. I dared not say a word. Just like that, any hope that he'd never again harm those he loved evaporated.

The next day, while Kevin was at the gym, I tucked myself into a corner of my walk-in closet and called my aunt Brettani, whom I'd stayed with the last time I tried to leave Kevin. She worked as a children's advocate at a domestic violence shelter in Oregon.

In a hushed voice, I told Aunt Brettani everything about Dada and the fight. The scene haunted me; I was unable to contain it or forget it. Armed with professional expertise, she took off her auntie hat and put on her advocate hat, urging me to think through an exit plan and to create a code word with her for safety.

As we finished our conversation, she said, "You know he's going to hurt Deshae, right?"

My mind began spinning. "He would never. He loves her." I spoke the words to convince myself as much as to persuade my aunt.

"Until she's fifteen and talks back for the first time." Like a sharp knife, her words cut through my denial. She was right. For now Deshae was young and moldable. What would happen when she hit her teen years?

As I hung up the phone, my mind became a thick fog of thoughts. I didn't know what I thought about my situation, other than I finally knew I had to get out as soon as I had an opportunity.

Kevin gave me Christmas night off. We sat down with the kids for dinner.

"I need to fly home and tell Mama," he said between bites, not looking up.

"What are you going to tell her?" I said under my breath as the kids got up from the table to go play with their new toys.

"That I'm going to prison for tax evasion. That's the truth! I *am* going to prison for tax evasion." He looked up at me, annoyed disgust across his face.

I nodded, feigning a meek smile.

Kevin had hidden the situation with the feds from his mama, who seemed to know everything else. When she visited, she never seemed shocked that we all lived together. Apparently, having multiple women come and go from her son's life didn't bother her in the least. After all, we kept sending her money each month.

"I'm gonna leave Sunday, spend New Year's with her. You'll be busy working." He finished his plate, and I stood to clear the table, my mind spinning. This was it—my opportunity. Would I muster enough courage to run? To run once and for all? I chewed on how to make an escape. I had less than a week. Day and night, it was all I could think about. I started wiring my mom $50 daily, small enough not to make Kevin suspicious. And I burned the receipts immediately, while still at the counter. I couldn't risk being caught.

Kevin called me that Sunday afternoon from the airport to tell me he'd see me in a couple of days. I listened intently for the background noise to confirm his story. When I heard gate announcements, my heart began to race. It was all I could do to exchange pleasantries before hanging up. I paced back and forth for an hour, waiting fifteen minutes past his departure time. I hit his name in my recent calls list, and the phone went straight to voicemail. *Go time!*

"Deshae!" I called. She came running in with a questioning look on her face.

"I want you to pick five favorite toys," I said, frantically grabbing clothes from my closet. "We're going to go see Nana!"

I pulled out two suitcases, one for each of us. This was all I could take, all I could carry on the plane. After packing all our important paperwork and toiletries and a few outfits, I stood in my closet, scanning the shelves.

Thousands of dollars' worth of purses and shoes were lined up in neat rows. *They're just purses. Just things. They are replaceable,* I preached to myself. Frustrated that I was caught up in something trivial when my daughter's life was at stake, I cried and talked to God. I spoke to him as if he were standing in the closet with me, urging me to leave the purses.

"But you don't know what I had to do for these, Lord!" I cried out loud. As if I needed to remind God of what he did and didn't know. "These are more than just material possessions. My blood, sweat, and tears went into these. If I don't leave this house with something to show for what I gave, this will all have been for nothing!" I cried as I put the purses in a big cardboard box and decided to mail them home. I finally understood how Brandi had felt, having to leave behind so much that she had worked for.

That night, I walked in to freelance at the Wynn Hotel, wondering whether it would be my last night in the Game. Whatever money I made would have to be enough for us to live on until God worked something else out.

At the roulette table, an attractive, fortyish man wearing a well-made suit stood laughing with two friends. His short fade was combed stylishly into a fauxhawk, and his tall muscular build oozed more than confidence, bordering arrogance. He glanced over, and I teased him by playfully sticking out my tongue as Brandi had taught me. He checked behind him for the person I was flirting with.

"You," I mouthed, and smiled my sexiest smile.

We made small talk after I approached him. "I like your accent," I said. "You from the UK?"

"No way!" he scoffed. "You've just insulted my Irish bloodline. How dare you? I do live in London, but I'm a Paddy through and through." He smiled, and I laughed along, enjoying the banter.

Conall captivated me. Paying for a companion was new to him—but the chemistry between us was there, much as it had been with me and Joel. And since Kevin was out of the picture, I didn't have to go home in the morning with a certain amount. Still, I went and got my back phone out of the car in case he called. I wouldn't answer but would call him back later from the bathroom and tell him it was a slow night.

I gave Conall a ride from the Wynn to the Four Seasons, where he was staying. Allowing a trick in my car was completely forbidden by Kevin, and I panicked the entire ride. I was breaking nearly all Kevin's rules. Would he know? Would he catch me? Would I actually be able to run tomorrow?

He didn't call. Conall and I spent the entire night together.

The next day, I stopped by a mailbox store and shipped some boxes. It was time to call home.

"I need you to do something, Mom," I said.

"What's up, Becky?"

"I need you to charge two plane tickets on your credit card for tonight. I promise I will pay you back." Once again, Mom jumped at the opportunity to get me out of my "domestic violence."

Later that day, Conall and I spent a few hours enjoying Vegas together, sight-seeing. He was enamored, and my mind raced the whole time. As we ate lunch together, I shared my big news with him.

"I'm leaving Vegas. I'm done with this life," I confided.

"So, what's your plan?" he asked.

"I don't really have one yet," I said.

"I can help," he offered.

Yeah, sure. You'll turn out exactly like Joel. I politely declined his money.

When I got home, I knocked on Maria's door. I'd been dreading this conversation, but knew I had to tell her. Before I began to mutilate her native tongue with my choppy Spanish, I started crying.

I took a deep breath and explained as best I could that I had to leave Kevin. Her brown eyes telegraphed sympathy. I could tell she knew much more than she'd let on. I felt guilty. She depended on us, and here I was leaving her high and dry. Many people had been depending on me, and I was going to let everyone down. I handed her an outstanding letter of recommendation and pulled out the wad of cash I'd made over the last day and a half from Conall. I gave her $800 of the $1,800 from the Irishman. Only a thousand dollars to live on until I found something else.

I called April and asked her to take me to the airport. I

knew if I took the car and left it there, I'd be in big trouble. She was confused and angry at me. I had written up a list of all the things I did at the shop so she could keep the business running. I knew she'd tell Kevin immediately, but I'd be gone before he returned. He needed to turn himself in soon to meet the conditions of his plea deal, which meant he'd be less likely to come after me this time.

"What are you going to do?" she asked.

"Why do you care, April? You're good. Kevin took a plea deal for you. Boo is out and back to making money. Tori will be out in a few months. You all can go back to how your life was before I came around."

She sat quietly, looking straight ahead.

"Maybe I'll write a book," I stated plainly.

April's neck snapped around, and she stared at me wide-eyed. "About what?"

"I don't know yet. I've overcome a lot—drug addiction, losing Deshae. I keep feeling like God has something more for me."

I sat in the Las Vegas airport with Deshae, laying her head on my lap. Aunt Brettani was going to pick me up in Oregon, take me with her to a family and friend's New Year's Eve party, then let me stay with her for a bit because my parents were living in an area too rural for me to find work. My phone vibrated with a text message. I glanced down, afraid to see Kevin's name on the screen.

Conall's name appeared next to his text message. "Happy New Year. When are you going to meet me in London?"

I smiled and looked up at the TV in the airport just in time to see the brightly lit New Year's ball dropping in Times Square.

This is it, Jesus. A new year. I need a new life, for real this time. Please, help me.

CHAPTER 14 **prodigal daughter**

He got up and went to his father. But while he was
still a long way off, his father saw him and was
filled with compassion for him; he ran to his son,
threw his arms around him and kissed him.

2008

I sat on the end of the twin bed that was squeezed into a small half-bedroom, half-closet space. In the beginning I'd had grand ideas of how I was going to make a living, but day by day, the reality of being poor began to sink in. Money was the one addiction I couldn't shake.

I was grateful my aunt and uncle had allowed me to use this space as a temporary home. My uncle worked nights, and he'd often use the tight space to catch up on rest during the day, so it was a sacrifice for them to squeeze us into their home. Deshae shared a room with her cousin, more like the sister she never had. The girls were close in age and got along great. On Sundays we rode with the family to church, and I spent my time in worship in a puddle of tears. I had missed being in the presence of God so much. While this church in Oregon was not the lively purpose-driven church I was saved in, their heart of worship allowed me to bask at God's feet without feeling a need to be involved in multiple ministry groups.

But the reality of daily struggles sank in fast. How in the world was I going to support my daughter? I had no money, no car, no clue where to begin or even how to navigate this small town. Kevin was calling; the IRS wanted payment. I was a mess.

Conall and I had continued chatting, though his location in London made connecting difficult because of the time zone difference. He was a widower with two kids, one off at college and the other in high school, or secondary as they call it.

"Why don't you and Deshae come here for a while? It'll be a good rest and getaway," he persuaded. In March we visited during Deshae's spring break, but I was broke and had no purpose. As our trip ended, Conall suggested we live with him. I wondered whether London might offer the fresh start we needed, far away from Kevin, with a man who wasn't in the Game and could look out for us.

The only problem was, I had started to hear God's voice again—at least I thought it was him. "This is not the plan I have for you," the Holy Spirit whispered. But the chance to live in London was too great a temptation to resist.

"God," I prayed, "If I don't go to London, I'll wonder *what if* for the rest of my life."

I took Conall up on his offer, packed our things, and moved Deshae and myself to London that summer. Deshae wasn't as excited as I was and cried the entire six-hour drive to the San Francisco airport. She begged to stay with the family she loved: her aunts, cousins, grandparents, and nana. How could I blame her? I'd ripped her away from them for years, given her the hope of reunion, then switched plans on her again. The guilt I carried for dragging her through such tumultuous upheaval weighed on me. *This will be it, though,* I silently vowed. In London we wouldn't be poor. I wouldn't have to work. Kevin was still finalizing his plea deal—by the time that was done and had served his sentence, we'd be long gone and hard to find. This was our perfect opportunity to prevent him from finding me and to reduce my stress about money.

Conall greeted us with a warm embrace as we exited customs. Even though he was middle-aged, he took care of himself by working out daily. His perfectly tailored sports coat and fitted black T-shirt showed off his muscular build. His Gaelic-themed tattoos peeked out from his sleeves when he removed his jacket, and his green eyes danced as he smiled. As we walked to his Range Rover, he made small talk with Deshae about the in-flight movies she'd watched .

Because he was an adventurous man, Conall's idea of settling in together that summer meant frequent jaunts to Cyprus, Ireland, and all over the UK. I was living the *Pretty Woman* dream, attending fancy horse races nearly every weekend. I even went to Ladies Day at Royal Ascot in a fancy hat. *Maybe the tables have finally turned for us,* I thought, as we spent our summer exploring Europe.

I liked London. Conall's house in North Barnet was a slender row house that was a good size by British standards. It also had a big back yard and was within walking distance of Deshae's primary school. Conall bought me the same Mercedes CLS 500 I'd owned in Vegas, and I soon got used to driving on the left side of the narrow roads. I went to the gym and the market while our Slovakian au pair, Zofie, cleaned the house. I began the necessary paperwork for Deshae to start Year Five, the UK equivalent of fourth grade. Conall's Irish accent began to rub off on us. Deshae and I began to speak with a hint of his brogue, which made us feel cultured. We lived a high-class lifestyle, just as in Vegas, but without any abuse or forced prostitution.

For the first time in a long time, I could breathe. I didn't look over my shoulder and wasn't tormented with triggers and fear. I slept. I ate. I worked out. I started reading my Bible and praying daily as I'd been taught to do at Victory Outreach. God welcomed me back as if I were the prodigal son of Luke 15. It didn't matter that I'd only been saved a certain amount of time. I learned that God wasn't checking to see whether I'd clocked a certain number of hours in prayer. I could hear the voice of the Lord again immediately, as if my loving heavenly Father ran to meet me right where I was. I didn't have to work my way up a spiritual ladder to prove I was good enough for him. This Jesus was the One who'd delivered me of my drug addiction. He was the Jesus I remembered and embraced. I loved being with him.

I cried out to him as I began to face my past. "Why was I so foolish? Why did I fall for so many lies, God?" In prayer, I came face-to-face with God, creator of the universe, who began healing my heart in ways I couldn't have imagined.

After one of my morning quiet times, I heard the mail drop through the slot in the door. I skimmed the local newsletter for some kid-friendly outings around town, but a postcard caught my eye—*How Many Brothels Are in Your Borough?* It was an awareness piece on human trafficking and forced prostitution. I sat down on our comfy couch and slowed my reading, shocked by this "Big Brothel" report.

Something deep inside stirred as I pored over the exposé. The Eaves organization had begun something called the Poppy Project. It was designed to provide support, advocacy, and even places of refuge for trafficked women. I immediately fired off an email to the contact in the article. To my surprise, they responded right away by asking me to come in and share more of my story. I jumped at the chance to learn more about how I could help. I paid a visit to the Poppy Project the next day.

The tube ride into Camden from North London took a while. I found the building and wound through the maze of doors and stairwells until I saw an intercom. After I announced myself, they buzzed me through.

A dark-haired, petite hipster, maybe only a year or two older than me, met me.

"Hey! Rebecca?" She smiled, pushed her glasses up, and swept her long, dark bangs out of her smiling eyes. "I'm Abby. Thanks for coming in," she said. Her pronounced British accent made her seem even more hip.

I extended my hand. "Nice to meet you."

She guided me through the corridors. "Eaves is a center with lots of different programs to help end violence against women," she explained. "I think you're familiar with the Poppy Project?"

I nodded. We climbed a set of stairs, then passed through another secured door. Finally we arrived at a large, open office space. A honeycomb of cubicles buzzed with workers typing at computer keyboards and chatting on phones. Several private offices lined the perimeter. Abby led me inside a corner office, where a robust woman with short, wavy black hair sat typing at her keyboard, her back to us. I glanced at the business card in the brass holder on her desk. "Denise Marshall, Executive Director, Eaves."

Abby left, and I waited a moment or two while the woman finished typing. My stomach fluttered, but before I could change my mind about talking with her, she swiveled around.

"I'm Denise," she said, extending her hand. Her kind eyes smiled behind her dark-rimmed glasses.

"Hello. I'm Rebecca."

She gestured to the chair beside her desk. I sat. She scooted her large leather chair out from behind her massive oak desk and leaned in, giving me her undivided attention. My heart skipped at the realization of what this powerful woman might ask me.

"Rebecca, I'm so glad you reached out to us. Thank you for coming in." Her Irish accent, soft smile, and gentle eyes eased my nerves. Her perfume—a comforting blend of cloves, cinnamon, and jasmine—transported me back to my grandma's porch swing, where we had often sat eating warm apple pie.

As my story tumbled out, I felt exposed. But strangely, the more my words flowed, the more my confidence grew. Denise introduced me to some new vocabulary. I understood that I had felt tricked and forced into prostitution, sure. I recognized the injustice in my past. But when she suggested that I'd been trafficked, I felt that was a reach. Trafficked girls were shipped from other countries or kidnapped and locked in rooms. She used words like *coercion* and *fraud*. I kept nodding as if I had a clue what they meant. The conversation left me slightly confused, overwhelmed, and yet oddly empowered.

Thirty minutes into our chat, I balanced a cup of tea with milk on my right knee and checked my watch. I hoped Conall would be cool with my coming here. After all, Denise was a fellow Irishwoman. She offered me a tour and introduced me to a flurry of staff members as we walked the building. When we returned to her office, she told me about an upcoming event in a few weeks. We agreed that it could be an opportunity to share my story. I thanked her and headed back to the tube. The whole ride home, my head whirled with all I'd experienced. I had no idea there were organizations, such as Eaves, whose sole purpose was to help marginalized and exploited women. When I was in Victory Outreach teaching *Purpose Driven Life*, I had a strong feeling I wanted to help women. Was this my purpose, to help by sharing my testimony? What *was* my testimony anyway? That I had made a series of terrible choices?

I began preparing the best way I knew how. I opened my Bible and pored over the pages. I missed my days of preaching at the women's home and grew excited about the potential of sharing more of my story publicly. I drank in God's words and prayed them back to him. I read, prayed, and searched my soul. I didn't simply want to share a sad story. I desperately wanted to bring a word of hope that would shift people's perspectives the same way my pastor's words had shifted mine. Even though I wouldn't be speaking at a faith-based event, I recognized God's providence. I was desperate for him to use my words to open the hearts and minds of those who would listen.

As I drew nearer to the Lord, I grew uneasy with how our North London lifestyle failed to meet my daughter's needs. Deshae had started school and was making friends fine, but I could tell she missed home like crazy. I would flit about to the horse races or the spa or shopping or working out while she stayed with Zofie.

Living here had its charm, and Deshae experienced new cultures, especially when we traveled. Watching her swim in the Mediterranean filled my heart with hope that she too could finally have a normal life. But we both lacked the peace and normalcy of true family life. The occasional visit from my mom gave us a fleeting dose, but as soon as she left, reality would hit. I knew in my heart that God had something else in store for the rest of my life. But what? I needed to find out exactly what that something else was, so I prayed and waited. I had a feeling it meant leaving the UK. But until I could figure out how to make it on my own, I was stuck.

I was stuck not only financially but in a dead-end relationship. Conall provided for us and often talked of marrying me, but he had expectations. His sexual appetite demanded more and more from me. He began to manipulate me by getting upset if we didn't have nightly sex. He controlled the money. He wasn't just arrogant; he was mean. He'd honk at elderly women crossing the street to hurry them up. My suspicion of illegal business crept in as men with duffle bags of cash would come by frequently and heightened when we attended a funeral in Ireland for a member of the Irish Republic Army. Shame and self-hatred came knocking on the door of my heart again. I had traded the violence for sexual and financial abuse and exchanged one crime family for possibly another. *This isn't what I signed up for.*

As I daily pressed into the Lord, the mud-caked lenses through which I viewed my life began to clear. While in prayer one afternoon, I brought my situation before God. I wanted a family more than anything. Why was that desire so strong? I craved the rewards of being a wife and mother—the normal life many other women possessed. But why did that life seem impossibly out of reach *for me?* "Why not, God? Why can't I be like every other girl I see around me? I just want to be normal!" I prayed.

A Scripture popped into my head: 1 Samuel 8. This was not familiar, so I opened my Bible. I read how the children of Israel were crying out for a king, saying, essentially, "We want to be like the other nations around us." Conviction gripped my heart. I continued reading how God told Samuel that he would give the Israelites what they wanted because he loved them. But the prophet warned: *it will not be like you expect.* I tossed the words around and let God's warning sink in. Marrying Conall would not be anything like what I was hoping.

Weeks flew by, and the yearning to pursue my calling to speak out and to seek God more weighed heavily on my heart and mind. But Conall grew more and more concerned about me speaking out about my past, not wanting people to know "what kind of girl you used to be." Afraid he'd freak out, I sneaked away to Oxford University for my first speaking gig with Eaves. I arrived and was informed that I'd be publicly debating a dominatrix. I was never more grateful that I'd chosen to take debate in high school.

That evening, I came home unable to hide my excitement about the event. Conall was furious. He just glared at me and shook his head. When I refused to give in to his sexual demands that night, he lost it.

"I should just leave ya both the way I found ya!" Conall shouted in his thick Irish accent as he grabbed a blanket and headed to the couch. I took a deep breath. All night I tossed and turned, worrying and wondering about our next steps.

The next morning, I stared at my mascara-stained reflection in the mirror, realizing this was not the life I wanted either. *That's it.* I washed my face and talked to God. I heard the Lord clearly. "Time to go home." I knew *home* meant the small town where I'd grown up in Oregon.

"I'm scared, Lord," I replied instantly. "Where will I work?"

Both of my parents had just been laid off due to the 2009 recession. Jobs were few and far between. I had a criminal record of prostitution-related charges and a huge gap in my job history. As a twenty-eight-year-old single mother, I could forget about dating. Whom would I ever date in that small town anyway? Did any guys my age live there? Where would I live? How many times would I have to reach out to Aunt Brettani? How would I get around? There's no tube or subway in Grants Pass, Oregon. What about my calling to help trafficked women? I doubted any existed in the area!

Going back home made absolutely no sense. None.

I shuffled downstairs, silently whining about the thought of relocating again. But I couldn't shake the notion that Oregon was exactly where God was sending me. I needed stability for Deshae.

I was learning more about how God loves to work in seemingly dead-end situations, like when Pharaoh's vicious army closed in on Moses and the Israelites. Completely blocked by the Red Sea, God's people could see no feasible way of escape.

I knew we needed to leave Conall, but I still felt trapped by the Red Sea that stood between us and Oregon.

Had God allowed me to wander into these desperate places? Maybe so I would learn to lean hard on him instead of relying on men and worldly possessions?

Anxiety gripped my stomach as I imagined myself working three jobs and sleeping on someone's couch. Helpless and afraid, I grabbed my Bible, knelt down, and begged God to show me how he expected me to pull this off. The words *Psalm 34* ran through my mind. This was again a passage I was unfamiliar with. I looked it up in my Bible. Clearer than day, the Scripture beckoned:

> The young lions lack and suffer hunger;
> But those who seek the LORD shall not lack any good *thing*.
>
> Come, you children, listen to me;
> I will teach you the fear of the LORD.
> Who is the man *who* desires life,
> And loves *many* days, that he may see good?
> Keep your tongue from evil,
> And your lips from speaking deceit.
> Depart from evil and do good;
> Seek peace and pursue it.
>
> PSALM 34:10–14 NKJV

At that moment, the last streak of mud dripped off my spiritual lenses, and my next move became crystal clear. In my innermost being, I knew I needed to leave London and go to Grants Pass. I needed to pursue a godly life like never before. The words took root in my heart as I read them. I believed with all my heart that God would provide for us, that we would lack no good thing.

"You'll be married by September." The thought flashed through my mind, taking me completely by surprise. Surely that wasn't the Lord but rather my own wishful thinking forming another bubble that life would surely burst.

It wasn't long before my confidence wavered. Images of being on welfare plagued my mind. I begged God for confirmation that I had heard him right. It was a big decision, and I didn't want to be the old impulsive me. That Sunday I set out for church. But not just any church—Victory Outreach London. I figured if I came this far without visiting VO London, I'd greatly regret it. I identified with this Spirit-filled denomination. With Deshae in tow, I put the address into my navigation app and set out on the hour-and-a-half drive, determined to hear a word of direction or confirmation from the Lord for my next steps.

The minute I entered the church, I felt as if I were back in Portland, Oregon. The music was the same, and the spirit was the same. Men's and women's home residents sat along each side of the congregation, just like old times. I felt at home.

The preaching began, and I found out that Pastor Mitchell was an American. He talked about his time coming to London. He had been there seventeen years. His friends were there, his family— London was his home. He spoke of God's call on his life and the sacrifice of doing things you don't want to do in order to fulfill his purpose. He delivered his words with deep conviction. I could tell he had been mulling over this message for quite some time.

The minutes flew by. When it seemed like he was nearing the homestretch of his message, he looked down and paused.

"I'm going back to America to follow the call of God on my life. I've been offered a position at Victory Outreach headquarters in California. This has not been an easy decision. I love it here. I love all of you, all my friends, my family. But I have to pursue the call of God above all else."

A hush fell over the church. It was Pastor Mitchell's voice I heard, but it was as if God were speaking directly to me. His words collided with the whisper I'd been hearing within my soul: "Time to go back to America to follow the call of God on my life."

I looked around. *Could it be?* The timing was too perfect. The one time I go to VO London desperately seeking a word from God was the one time their pastor preached a sermon on going back to America. This had God's fingerprints all over it. Driving home that day, I made up my mind.

"I'm going to trust you, Father," I prayed. "No matter how hard it gets, no matter how humbling it will be. Every ounce of fight in me wants to run the other way, but Lord, in the deepest part of my heart, I know you're asking me to surrender, and my answer is yes. I will answer your call on my life."

Conall and I both knew what we had wasn't working. Saying bittersweet airport goodbyes and starting fresh elsewhere was the best we could hope for. In February 2009 he drove us to Heathrow Airport and gave me some cash to help us get settled. Within six hours, we had an ocean between us. My London chapter was over, but my new chapter to pursue Jesus and lean on Him as I never had before was about to begin.

CHAPTER 15 **we shall overcome**

*Ask and it will be given to you; seek and you will
find; knock and the door will be opened to you. For
everyone who asks receives; the one who seeks finds;
and to the one who knocks, the door will be opened.*

2009–2012

Deshae and I arrived back in the US on February 23. I'd lined
up a job interview before touching American soil. A mom-
and-pop manufacturing company I'd found online was willing
to delay my interview process until I returned. That same small
closet space of my aunt's home became my new bedroom, and
my daughter bunked again with her cousin. Excited to begin
our new life with a new job, I didn't balk at our cramped living
quarters.

This time around I trusted God's plan and was grateful for
my family's enduring willingness to help me start over. Their
gracious hospitality and ability to step in and help at any time
was a gift. My stepdad came over and hung shelving to better
accommodate my things. Aunt Loretta and Nannie helped watch
Deshae when needed.

But after my excitement waned, I once again faced the reality of poverty. I had a sense that choosing to be poor, choosing

homelessness without a fork or pillow to my name, could prove to be one of the hardest decisions of my life. But I had no idea how it would stretch my faith. The unshakable truth of Psalm 34:10 became my daily manna: "The lions may grow weak and hungry, but those who seek the Lord lack no good thing." When I stood in the food-stamp line, I'd remind the Lord that he promised me I'd lack no good thing.

I landed the customer service job and started working right away. But my first paycheck, a measly $250 for an entire week's work of dealing with disgruntled customers and rough coworkers, spiraled me into despair.

"How can I live on this?" I cried out to God. "How does anyone live off this?"

His familiar voice came as a thought: "Millions of people do it every day without selling themselves. You can too. Figure it out." My woe-is-me paradigm began to shift. God was right. If millions across America can do it, I could too. This was my first step in breaking my addiction to money. I looked into budgeting classes at the local community college and decided to take an occasional night class when I qualified for financial aid.

In a few months, thanks to my experience from running Kevin's manufacturing shop and my God-given ambition, I was promoted from customer service rep to general manager. I thought things were looking up until I learned another lesson of poverty—my $50 per month raise decreased my food stamps by $150 per month.

But through hard work and careful budgeting, I managed to scrounge enough to rent a tiny, dingy, government-subsidized apartment. It wasn't beautiful, but it was ours—and quite the contrast to my former living space in Vegas or London. Gone were the days of travertine and jaunts to the Waldorf or Ladies' Day at the races. The cockroaches that resided in the apartment when we moved in would scamper as we turned on the lights. The constant yelling next door could be heard through the thin walls. My yard sale and thrift store finds worked, but there was only so much I could do with beans and rice.

Poverty drives people to seek comfort in drugs or alcohol, and I fell prey to this temptation. My occasional girls' nights out with old high school friends included too much wine, something Kevin had never let me indulge in. Part of me longed for the more typical twenty-something years that had been stolen from me. I began to drink more, and more frequently. Then I began to drink alone.

Aunt Brettani, my pillar during my escape and recovery, stepped in again. "I'm concerned about your drinking." Her intervention hit hard. She'd loved me, invested in my life, and earned the relational capital required to call out my personal habits.

I stopped buying alcohol. I had a call on my life, and I had slipped. I traded in my nights of sipping wine for journaling and praying. I cried out to God, begging him to change the life habits the Game had created. I asked him to take a flashlight to my heart and remove all that had consumed me.

"God, is this all you have for me?" I'd lament. "Is this what you saved me for?" Yes, I hated the Game, but this alternative wasn't much better. I was living in extreme poverty, with no end in sight, no dreams to allow hope to carry me through, no place to use the gifts that I wondered if I still even possessed. Yes, I was physically free, but I was still hopeless and depressed. I had slipped and resorted to drinking as a comfort instead of relying on God. My mind still battled the brainwashed lie that possessions made life worth living.

And then God whispered something that would change everything.

"If you give me the same amount of time you gave the enemy, I will never be outdone," God challenged me. He was right.

Immediately, I pictured a giant mess of papers scattered all over the floor and Jesus picking them up. I realized that it had taken years for my present habits to form. I couldn't possibly expect Jesus to clean up in a few months what had taken the enemy six years to create. He needed time to work out the mess I had created with my life.

"All right, Jesus, you've got six years," I joked back, while reminding God again of his promise to return to us one hundred-fold everything we give up for His name's sake (Matthew 19:29).

I began learning to shut out the enemy's voice. Every time I heard the accuser say, "Is this how good your God is?" I'd reply, "Get behind me, Satan! These cockroaches are temporary, but my God's promises are eternal" (2 Corinthians 4:18). I was learning to fight the battle in my mind and had the scars to prove it.

I wasn't proud of my yard sale couch or thrift-store pots and pans, but with every humbling, honest step I took toward independence, a deeper determination stirred. I used half of the $3,000 Conall gave me to purchase an old beater, which got me to work and Deshae to school. The fan belt was going out and screeched when I started the engine. Deshae would duck down and hide in the front seat as we pulled up to her school, and we'd laugh and make fun of our "little red banshee."

We attended church weekly. One Sunday afternoon, as we were making our way out of the sanctuary, I took note of a nicely-built man who had an Adam Levine vibe. We had exchanged greetings prior to my move to London, but I told him I wasn't staying. He sat behind the sound board and looked about my age. *Surely, he can't still be single,* I thought. Before I knew it, he'd approached me, flashed a brilliant smile, and introduced himself.

Matt's blue eyes were gentle and kind. After some get-to-know-you talk, he asked, "Would you ladies like to grab some lunch sometime?"

My heart leaped, and the smile on Deshae's face spoke volumes. She'd taken an instant liking to this handsome man. We exchanged numbers and later set a date. Deshae had plans that Saturday morning, so he asked whether I would mind riding on his motorcycle, his only mode of transportation. I was thrilled!

When Saturday came, I awoke to gray skies and the threat of rain. Matt called.

"Not the best day to take you for a ride, I'm afraid. So I'm borrowing a friend's car. I'll pick you up at one. Sound okay to you?" he asked.

"Of course!" I lied. I was bummed. The thought of zooming down the curvy back roads on a motorcycle excited me. I still struggled with how boring being a "square" was, and I yearned for excitement and adventure.

I let out a heavy sigh, set aside the helmet I'd borrowed, and closed my eyes. "Lord, I want you to show me a sign like you gave Abraham's servant when he searched for a wife for Isaac (Genesis 24:14). I'm tired of dating. I'm done with men who coast in and out of Deshae's life. I want a family, and I'm sure that's your desire for me too. I've fallen for the fake, microwave version too many times. Please, God, if Matt is someone I should take a chance on, if he's someone who will be part of our future, let him show up on his motorcycle today and not in a car."

It was a bold prayer. But then I've never been feeble about asking God to show up. Especially not since Deshae and I had moved back to the States and I'd watched him provide for our needs without fail. At one o'clock the loud rumble of a motorcycle engine made my adrenaline surge. I ran to the front door and peeked out into the small parking lot. As I opened the front door, a shaft of sunlight moved out from behind the gray clouds, and I spotted a muscular young man parking his bike.

Once again, God had answered.

We grabbed a to-go lunch at a small market and rode until we came to a scenic overlook. We climbed over the wall and marveled at the majestic Rogue River. As we picnicked, we shared the God-sized dreams for our futures.

"I believe the Lord has told me, pretty clearly, to share my story with anyone who will listen. My past isn't pretty, but I know I went through it all for a reason." I detailed a bit more and held my breath, remembering how Conall had reacted to my calling.

Matt looked intently at me with his kind blue eyes and listened to every word. When I finished, he turned and looked out over the river. The longer he took to speak, the more I feared his rejection. After a long pause, he turned back to me and said, "If God is telling you to speak, who am I to tell you no?"

Soon Matt became part of my daily rhythm. He adored Deshae, and our relationship as a couple quickly deepened. "You're beautiful," he'd say, to which I'd roll my eyes. "Can't you think of anything other than that?" I'd complain. I had become jaded to what seemed like shallow compliments that would demand something of me in return. "I'm going to redeem that word," he said as he pulled me in for a kiss.

One rainy April afternoon, we snuggled up on the couch to watch TV. Matt very matter-of-factly said, "We should get married."

No candles. No roses. No carriage ride through Central Park. This wasn't the proposal I had dreamed of, but the thought of a new life with a man I'd grown to love thrilled me more than any romantic proposal could. He was patient and up for a challenge, but more importantly, he loved Jesus, and I wanted someone who relied on the Holy Spirit to be his guide.

A few weeks later, we sealed the engagement with a ring. A diamond was far too expensive, so we opted for a gem that signified beauty wrought from hardship—a gorgeous pearl. One evening after we'd agreed to pray about our wedding date, I heard a knock at my door. I opened it, and Matt stepped inside wearing a huge grin, "Does August mean anything to you?" His eyes danced with joy like he had a gift he couldn't wait for me to unwrap.

Immediately, the promise God had whispered in London came rushing back. *You'll be married by September.*

My eyes filled. "Yes . . . yes it does!" I grabbed him and hugged him so hard we nearly toppled over. We set our date for August 29, 2009, two days shy of September.

As the weather heated up, my feet grew cold, and the prewedding jitters hit hard. I lay prostrate on my living room floor with Misty Edwards's worship music blaring. I told God I wasn't getting up until I had direction. Matt and I were so different. He was quiet, and I was loud. He was patient and I was impulsive. I had big dreams and he was okay with being mediocre.

"God, you haven't failed me yet," I prayed. "You continue to lead me through these difficult places. You've never led me anywhere that wasn't for my good. But I'm feeling lost right now. You know I struggle with being single, but I'm willing to wait, Lord. I need you to speak clearly."

Two hours later, as I cried before the Lord, weeping and begging for guidance, a thought pierced my silent, face-down worship time like a shaft of light cutting through fog. "The most effective boats have both a motor and an anchor." In my mind's eye, I saw a boat with two motors, going in opposite directions, fighting for control. Next I saw another boat with two anchors, sitting stagnant in a molding green pond. God's wisdom became crystal clear. Quiet, reserved Matt anchored my high-energy demeanor. He buoyed us and would keep our family steady when my impulsivity threatened to carry us away to choppy or dangerous waters. And I challenged him to venture into uncharted places where he wouldn't normally dare to go.

Our wedding day came, and we exchanged our vows surrounded by the overflowing love of family and friends. Matt wrote out vows to Deshae too and gave her a necklace with a pearl pendant that matched my ring. Our new life was starting, and I couldn't have been happier. I was finally experiencing the pure and radiant gift of marriage that God had planned since the beginning of time. This was the love I had wanted my whole life.

We wasted no time trying to start a family, but when I didn't get pregnant immediately, I feared I was being punished for my past. But after a few months, we found out we were expecting, with a June due date. I looked up the baby's birthstone: a pearl! Another providential God-wink at the plans for our life together.

Married life and parenting were not as easy as I had hoped. I had issues. As our toddler grew, Matt would discipline her, and I'd trigger. And I felt the need to put on a performance in the bedroom, which often made me push him away. His patient, prayerful response was humbling. He knew he couldn't change me but that God could. The Lord prompted me to drive around, saying out loud, "My husband loves me, and he's on my team." This countered the brainwash and negativity that plagued me with fears of mistrust.

Little by little, my triggers slowly diminished. With the help of a facilitator, I went through several intensive, guided inner-healing prayer sessions called Sozo to show me where Jesus was during the hardest moments of my life. Seeing his presence in those times reassured me that he was always with me. Jesus showed me where he was the day Kevin beat me horrifically. He showed me that I had turned my high school boyfriend into an idol that I worshiped instead of the true God and that I had partnered with rage as my protector through my entire journey.

These inner healing sessions revealed deeply embedded lies and allowed me to rebuke and bind them and speak truth and life over those areas. This process turned my bitter "why me?" or "where were you?" cries into a thankful heart for God's steadfast protection over me and Deshae.

The challenges of parenting and marriage were tools in God's hand. Through daily trials, he patiently smoothed my rough edges. Before long, my thoughts took on a new clarity, and I slowly took on a new likeness. The closer I grew to Jesus, the more I began to see his life taking shape in me and through me. At first, I was hard on myself for being loud and impulsive. Certainly, I must offend the meek and humble Jesus I read about in the Bible. One day as I was in prayer, God put my shame to rest with his gentle whisper that I had come to know. Jesus had turned over tables because of his righteous indignation (Matthew 21:12), rebuked his disciples for not praying (Matthew 26:40–41), and was accused of disrupting the religious routine in his day (Mark 7:5).

"You're not as far off from me as you think." I beamed at the thought that I reflected this unique aspect of God and embraced exactly who he created me to be.

One afternoon in fall 2010, my phone rang while I was folding laundry. I glanced at the caller ID. Unknown. *That's strange,* I thought. Debating whether to pick up and risk the telemarketing tango, I felt the nudge to answer.

"Hello?" I said with some hesitation.

"Poca?" the soft voice asked.

I recognized the voice immediately. "Boo?!" A flood of joy and relief brought tears to my eyes. "Boo?! Is that you?!" I laughed. "How'd you find me?"

"I hired an investigator." She giggled.

It was almost too good to be true. I shook my head in wonder. Her infectious laughter . . . her bubbly voice . . . I had lain awake many nights questioning whether I'd ever hear them again. She was moving on with her life in a positive way too. She wasn't totally free of the Game, but she was working on it.

I told her about Deshae, Matt, and the new baby. We planned a date for her to come to Oregon and talked daily to make up for the years we'd lost. I had my best friend back, someone who knew me, all of me, and understood my struggles and my inner thoughts as no one else could. Matt was concerned it was a set up.

When Brandi arrived in my small town in Kevin's bright-blue Hummer, I feared Matt may have been right. But I pushed through the fear, reminding myself of all we had been through. I trusted her.

I was already pregnant again and invited her to my ultrasound appointment. The next day, we waited together in the darkened exam room, the glow of the ultrasound machine bouncing off my gel-covered belly. The technician rolled the instrument until we heard the familiar echoing beat of the baby's heart. Brandi's laughter turned to tears, and she reached over and grabbed my hand with a warm squeeze. Our eyes locked in a knowing glance that spoke volumes.

"You know Kevin wanted you pregnant to keep you from running," she told me later.

"How can you be sure?" I asked.

"He took me out to dinner while there on parole. He convinced me that it had to be this way so you wouldn't run off. He promised me I could have a baby after you—I just wouldn't be first."

Kevin's manipulation knew no end.

We were in awe of how our lives had turned out. We stayed

up night after night, reminiscing about the good, the bad, and the ugly. Years of enduring life in the Game cemented the fierce bond between us. We curled up in blankets on the couch and shared stories into the wee hours of the night. "Boo," I said after we'd fallen silent for a while.

"Yeah?" She was looking up at the ceiling.

"I think we were trafficked."

"You're out in left field." She rolled her eyes and laughed. "We were just prostitutes."

"But what would have happened if we said no?" I asked.

She shrugged her shoulders and laughed again, this time a little nervously. "Yeah, right."

"I'm serious, Brandi." I sat up and faced her. "If I didn't want to go to work tomorrow because I was sick, Matt wouldn't beat me. He wouldn't strip search me and take every last dollar while leaving me to throw up on the side of the road. I think trafficking looks very different based on the community and culture and what part of the world you live in." I told her about the documentary *Nefarious*, which shows what trafficking looks like in various countries. It had opened my eyes. "Just because we were in Las Vegas and not a third world country doesn't make the force, fraud, or coercion any less real."

She sat contemplating but not replying.

Around the same time, Kevin completed his jail time and went back to business as usual with Tori, who was also released, and April. I had no doubt he was still trafficking girls. My survivor's guilt was relentless, but it compelled me to use for good what the enemy had intended to steal, kill, and destroy (Genesis 50:20; John 10:10).

I researched the statute of limitations for human trafficking victims and was told that it was too late for Brandi and me to go to the police. Instead, we both lived with the consequences of our experiences while our trafficker got off with none. Not quite the justice we would have chosen. To pacify the fake lease we had created, Kevin made me file taxes showing I made enough income to cover the mortgage on Brandi's house while she was in prison. Consequently, I carried a forty-thousand-dollar tax debt, which incurred taxes and penalties for each month it went unpaid. And though she was free from Kevin, Brandi would always have a felony on her record, plus a quarter of a million dollars in tax penalties. To make matters worse, when I ran for good, unbeknownst to me, Kevin switched the house utilities into my name and refused to pay. This stacked up even more debt, ruined my credit, and prevented me from being able to set up utilities in my name, which meant I had to rely on Matt.

By the summer of 2012, Brandi had left the Game for good and finally got her dream of becoming a mother too. A week or two after her son was born, she called me.

"Hey, Poca." She sounded shaken.

"Hey. You okay?" I held my breath and hoped for the best.

"It's April," she said. "Kevin slapped her across the face when she came back from McDonald's with pickles on his burger. He sent her back to get it remade, but the idea of going back was too much for her, so she took off. She's here. She doesn't have anything—just the clothes on her back and her phone."

"Oh, thank God!"

"She's here, Poca. She made it out too."

I decided to cash in some airline miles to visit Brandi and April. Days later I deplaned with my infant nestled in tight against me and hustled to baggage claim. Brandi stood by the carousel clutching her newborn.

Careful not to crush either child with our overzealous embrace, we rejoiced enthusiastically. I stood back and took in the miracle of these four lives—two brand-new and two *renewed*.

We chatted nonstop the entire ride to Brandi's parents' house. When we pulled in the driveway, a tall, slender, middle-aged brunette came out to greet us. April's face was gaunt, and the dark circles beneath her eyes spoke of the horror she'd been through.

Still, our tearful reunion was bittersweet. Upon seeing our sisters, none of us could stop crying. April's frail state—clumps of her hair missing from stress, jumping at every loud noise— reminded me of how far I'd come and how much healing was still ahead for her.

Her brainwashed vocabulary and addiction to money were also painfully familiar. She uttered phrases that sent shivers down my spine and filled my mind with images of Kevin. She labeled her experience as domestic violence. For April, true freedom was far from reach. Watching her painful struggle deepened my drive to share what so many women like April need to hear. I found out that Kevin had secretly married April before serving his sentence. By marrying her before he went in, he ensured he could legally continue to live with her after he got out, since felons are generally not allowed to interact with one another while on parole unless married. I also learned that he'd been sentenced to twenty-four months, not twelve, to get her a deal for felony probation only, no prison time. I wondered what other lies I had believed.

April's behavior reminded me so much of Kevin that it was hard to be around her. I kept hearing Kevin's command in my head: "No drama, Poc. You two work that crap out." I struggled but was determined that we would celebrate her freedom. The history we had in common gave us a strangely sweet sisterhood.

But not everyone in the Game sees their experience the same way. April still believes she was in domestic violence and just happened to have three wife-in-laws. She wants nothing to do with the anti-trafficking movement.

Tori is still with Kevin, being trafficked.

Life in Grants Pass was good. Matt and I had a circle of friends who were also raising kids and juggling jobs and family responsibilities. We shared our lives and our struggles and helped each other navigate the daily trials. I was surprised and delighted to discover that I was just like these "normal" women, with similar fears and longings.

I quit my job as GM at the local manufacturing company to start my own business—an elective 3D ultrasound center. Matt and I took out a small personal loan, and I rented a building that my family and friends helped paint and decorate. I leased an ultrasound machine and learned how to get great pictures and determine gender. The company was soon paying for itself with a small profit. But we pinched pennies and trusted that God would allow me to have flexible hours with our growing family. It was healing to discover that I could run a business and that I wasn't stupid, as Kevin had tried to make me believe.

One morning I grabbed a cup of coffee, put on worship music, and got into my devotional before the craziness of the day began. This regular time spent with Jesus was even more dear to me now that I had two littles pitter-pattering around the house and Deshae in middle school.

As I sat there reading, the sun came up. For many, a sunrise is one of the most beautiful displays of creation. Some wake up early and run or hike great distances to see this majestic array of colors and light. But that morning, as the light peeked through my living room curtains, my stomach churned in a queasy mix-ture of tension and anxiety. I heard Kevin's rule in my head. *Sun up. Time to go home.*

Tears welled up, and I swallowed nausea back down into my churning stomach. A familiar wave of dread swept over me. Would I ever forget what it was like to be more afraid of going *home* than getting in a car with a stranger? Would I ever not recall what it was like to tiptoe into the house after a long night of dealing with unpredictable tricks or wondering whether I'd be beaten in my own home?

The next thought arrived in a familiar whisper. "How can you sit here and do nothing? How can you sit in your nice, comfy surroundings, drinking your warm cup of coffee when you know what it's like?" The Holy Spirit ushered in His words with author-ity, love, and weighty conviction. He wanted better for me and for those who routinely woke up to dread. My anxiety left, and my pulse quickened with fierce determination and hope.

You're right. How can I? I did know the fear that crippled a working girl's heart, mind, and feet. I knew the ins and the outs of trafficking, the ups and the downs, the red flags, the warning signs and yet, here I sat—doing nothing. I thought of the true meaning of home, the place that is supposed to be one of refuge and safety.

A Bible verse came to mind: "They triumphed over him by the blood of the Lamb and by the word of their testimony." The truth of Revelation 12:11 echoed in my heart like the roar of a mighty lion staring down the enemy of my soul. I bowed my heart in surrender. I knew immediately what I had to do.

I paced the living room floor, waiting for my husband to wake up.

"I think I'm supposed to sell the business," I told Matt the moment he emerged from the bedroom.

"Oh yeah?" He smiled and pulled me in for a morning hug. "I love your creativity." He laughed and walked over to pour his coffee.

"No, I'm serious. I think I'm supposed to write a book and start sharing my testimony. I want to put the business up for sale." I was excited to show him the business plan I'd drafted while he slept.

"Oh, you're serious?" He sipped his coffee and his grin faded. He knew I meant business.

That day, we marched into battle for the lives of trafficked women. We prayed and sought direction. Within thirty days, and after a couple of false alarms, our company sold for the exact amount we owed on it. I began sharing my testimony anywhere and to anyone who would listen: at the local Mothers of Preschoolers (MOPS) group, local youth groups, and high schools.

Habakkuk 2:2 played constantly in my mind. "Write down the revelation and make it plain on tablets so that a herald may run with it." I grabbed some paper and began writing out the steps I'd taken toward freedom. There were ten. The guide became *Roadmap to Redemption*, a faith-based workbook for survivors. I was able to point women and groups to the book so they could give it to survivors who wanted to move toward freedom and healing. I'd written the first rough draft of my first book!

But I soon learned that surviving a fire doesn't make you an arson expert. I'd escaped the nightmare of human trafficking, but that fact alone didn't qualify me to empower others in professional arenas I knew nothing about, at least not with widespread impact. My training had only just begun.

The desire to share my story in a way that freed others burned inside me. I was so passionate about this calling that even the occasional random lady in the grocery store wasn't off limits.

One day I was surprised to get a call from former congresswoman Linda Smith, founder of one of the largest anti-trafficking organizations in the world, Shared Hope International. She wanted to meet me—this "local survivor" she had heard about—and invited me to have coffee with her.

Eager for this once-in-a-lifetime opportunity, I rose before dawn to make the near five-hour drive. I sensed that this cup of coffee might have the potential to change my life course. We lingered at the café for what felt like hours, and I was enamored with her professionalism and desire to help women like me.

During our conversation, she asked how long I had lived in the area. I told her that I actually lived nearly five hours to the south.

"You drove five hours for coffee?"

"Yes, ma'am, I did." Right away she recognized my drive and determination.

A few months later, Linda Smith's office invited me to speak and present the awards at the first annual Shared Hope anti-trafficking conference in Washington, DC. I was thrilled and slightly terrified.

Upon arriving at the Shared Hope conference in November 2012, I was quickly swept up by the energy and passion of advocates, allies, politicians, and trafficking survivors. This was my initiation into the domestic movement to eradicate modern-day slavery. The decadent reception hall teemed with policy makers and legislative heavy hitters who rubbed elbows with world-class abolitionists as they sipped their morning coffee. As things kicked off, state-by-state trafficking report cards were issued by press release, a kind of state of the union for the spellbound attendees.

To my delight, a fellow survivor stepped to the podium to deliver the keynote message. Shamere McKenzie spoke with elegance and grace. The audience was visibly moved and emboldened by her words. She partnered calls to action with her personal story.

Dozens of workshops in my conference packet piqued my interest, but I attended those with the greatest potential to equip me for my new calling. A colloquium on Capitol Hill brought me up to speed on current trafficking issues. I was drinking from an educational fire hose, but I tried to swallow every ounce.

At Linda Smith's invitation, on our last day in DC, I was blessed to join a tour of the congressional floor and Capitol Building. The last room on the tour was huge—the Statue of Liberty could have fit inside. The walls of the room were lined with murals painted by Italian masters. Each painting captured a moment in American history. It started with Christopher Columbus landing in America and ended with the Wright brothers and the advent of aviation. The tour guide explained each one, then directed our attention to a painting that rested in an easel, not on the wall like the rest: Pocahontas.

In the painting, she wore a glistening white dress that cascaded down the altar steps of a church. At the top of the stairs, she knelt in front of a priest, his hand dipped into a baptismal font, preparing to sprinkle holy water over her. We listened to the tour guide tell the story of the Native American woman who had captivated the English and helped to bridge the gap between them. The guide's lecture reverberated off the walls. "Then Pocahontas was baptized and given the Christian name Rebecca."

At the precise moment he spoke my name, the Spirit of God came on me with such force that I could barely stand. I was undone. Tears came, hot and heavy. I was fully exposed in the midst of baseball-capped tourists taking selfies and senior citizens in I Heart DC T-shirts. Dozens of eyes stared at me. They stared because they didn't know.

They didn't know my old name was Poca.

They didn't know that for years I'd been beaten by my trafficker.

They didn't know how he'd renamed me, stripping me of all my identity—how he'd owned me.

I wept in wonder and thanks. I wept at how the mighty hand of God had never let me go. My God, who through it all, knew I would be given back the name *he'd* chosen for me, the name and identity that he had intended. He knew I would emerge triumphant. It all came together in the end—the old and the new. The transformation for Pocahontas and now for me: Rebecca.

CHAPTER 16 learning curve

You intended to harm me, but God intended
it for good to accomplish what is now
being done, the saving of many lives.

2012–2013

My transformation didn't happen overnight. It required making daily choices toward God, his Word, and his truth. It was hard and scary, and it went against what my earthly, fleshly self constantly craved. Choosing life, and life more abundantly, required dying to self, and that took far longer than the counterfeit version of life the old me kept falling for.

Early in my healing journey, I opened my eyes one night to the darkness of our bedroom and gasped to catch my breath. The sheets were twisted around my legs, and I fought to uncover myself. My nightmare resurfaced. Still breathing hard, I sprang free of the covers and rose from our bed and headed to the bathroom.

Standing at the sink, I inhaled and exhaled deeply. I stared at my reflection in the mirror, cupped my hands under the cool water, bent down, and splashed my face with water. I felt a hand on the curve of my back, and I flinched, spritzing my T-shirt and sweats with water.

"Babe, it's me. You okay?" Still groggy, Matt squinted at my startled reflection. His eyes were soft with concern.

"No. I'm not okay."

"Did you have another one?"

I nodded.

"Do you want to tell me?"

I shook my head. I didn't want to relive these recurring nightmares, and somehow speaking about them made it worse. A war raged within me: do I push the dreams away or admit that my trafficker still owned a part of me? He stalked my nights, hellbent on coming after everything I held dear.

Matt kissed me on the shoulder. I turned around and hugged him before he walked me back to bed. As we climbed back into bed, he took my hand. "Father, I pray for my wife, whom you love. Give her peace, Father. Take away these night terrors that plague her, and give her the rest she needs so badly."

Sleeping was hard. Being a wife was hard. Being a new mom was hard. It was *all* hard.

If the towels weren't stacked neatly, I got mad. If my dinner didn't turn out how I had pictured it, I freaked out. I was constantly irritated and frustrated at the smallest things. I battled thoughts of rage toward others. Ephesians 6:12 told me I wasn't battling against myself, my family, or even my trafficker, but "against the rulers, against the authorities, against the powers of this dark world and against the spiritual forces of evil in the heavenly realms." I became increasingly aware that God was for me, urging me to stand firm. But the enemy was relentless in his attempts to keep me from my calling.

Eventually I sought prayer, first from some women at my church and then from my pastor. I knew there were things, maybe demonic spirits, bad habits, and thought patterns that felt foreign to me, but somehow, they held power over me. We prayed, and they anointed me with oil, and God's powerful Holy Spirit filled every space in my heart.

But that was only the beginning of my healing.

Every time I'd speak at a conference, I'd stay for the duration, taking advantage of the workshops that helped better equip me to fight human trafficking. I learned the legal definition of *sex trafficking*, or modern-day slavery, defined as "the recruitment, harboring, transportation, provision, obtaining, patronizing, or soliciting of a person for the purposes of a commercial sex act, in which the commercial sex act is induced by force, fraud, or coercion, or in which the person induced to perform such an act has not attained 18 years of age" (*22 USC § 7102*).

This caused me to reflect on the distinctions between force, fraud, and coercion *in my own life*. Did Bryan use fraud to get me to Vegas, pretending to be a music producer and luring me away from my family and friends with pressure to "dance" while promising me it wouldn't be prostitution? Yes. Did Kevin use force if I wanted a night off, was sick, didn't obey his rules, or bring in enough money? Yes. Did all of them physically use force in some capacity? Yes. Was coercion—the threat of harm—behind Kevin's numerous "swinging hangers" remarks? Yes.

In my hotel rooms, I would journal and pray about how my traffickers had employed fraud to cut off my support systems, used force to keep me from running, and applied coercion at every nightly destination—not just once when I arrived to the new city but every single time.

Learning how trauma affects the brain fascinated and horrified me. I wept at the feet of Jesus when I realized how deep the roots of my mental trauma were. Tears of gratitude flowed to God; he alone had protected me from killing myself. He'd also protected Deshae and even saw fit to give me a sound mind despite all the pain I'd endured and caused others.

I learned about brainwashing and how pimps, like cult leaders, use rewards for cooperation and punishments for non-cooperation, not only with physical abuse but also with sleep deprivation, social ostracism, and repeated mantras. I thought of Tori being sent away for gaining a few pounds and how Kevin once threatened to give my birthday present to Brandi if I didn't obey his rules and how sleep deprivation had caused me to pass out and wind up in the emergency room.

I studied Hitler's propaganda tactics, which slowly indoctrinated the culture of the time, and began to recognize our own cultural indoctrination in the United States. I took a hard look at our hypersexual culture and the way society makes light of pimps and pimpin'. The music I grew up with—Reba McEntire's *Fancy*, R. Kelly, Snoop, Eazy E.—helped shape my perception of the objectification of women and normalization of commercial sex. Kevin also used it to glamorize and normalize trafficking. I recognized the power that music, videos, and movies had on my young, impressionable mind. With easy access to pornography on the rise, I questioned how far sex-for-sale had come and where it was headed. I wondered about the damaging ripple effects of billboards and marketing campaigns—what used to be called "soft-core porn"—on the four-, five-, and six-year-olds who were exposed to these images plastered on television commercials and mall window dressings.

Continued healing came as I researched the Adverse Childhood Experiences study (ACEs) and examined my own childhood. This led me to pray over lies that had taken root in my heart as a child: the abuse I witnessed, the alcoholism, the divorce, the poverty, the heartbreak, and the secrets I kept for my parents during their own troubled lives, which taught me that we kept secrets in our home when we knew others wouldn't approve. The lack of boundaries and party girl mentality I embraced for the adventure and attention that I craved. Though my parents both eventually found their own strength and healing, that didn't negate the effect these experiences had on me. These deep roots shaped the way I thought and responded to a myriad of issues throughout my exploitation. Naming those inaccurate perceptions allowed me to take control over my own thought life and identify where maybe I learned wrong.

On my knees, I would picture nine-year-old me walking to the pay phone while my dad was in the bar. The adult me would cry out, "I bind the enemy in the name of Jesus from my heart. I come against the lie that I am not worthy, that I am not wanted, that I am unimportant. I bind that lie in the name of Jesus, and I ask you, Holy Spirit, to fill that void in my heart with your love and acceptance. Show me how you have desired me, how I am worthy simply because I am yours. Thank You, Jesus, for coming into my life and healing my heart. Thank you for steadying me as I walk along."

I eventually went to a therapist who specializes in trauma and who recommended Eye Movement Desensitization and Reprocessing (EMDR) to unlock memories that had been stuck in my brain. God used many gifted people and ministries to walk me through every aspect of my healing. Though it was far from easy, I was grateful for the new freedom I began to embrace. My personal healing became an even greater necessity as I identified faulty thinking and systems in our culture. I was determined to offer my story in a way that would make a difference.

The crime of prostitution is an industry, and where there is an opportunity to make money, the spirit of corruption will follow. Force, fraud, and coercion have many faces. Many American women involved in prostitution are likely being trafficked but slapped with cuffs and called criminals while their brainwashed minds (and our prejudiced minds) protect their captors. There are terms for this brand of brainwashing: *Stockholm syndrome, capture bonding, trauma bonding,* and *complex, compound trauma.*

Healing and freedom from my past gradually came as I put into words all I had been through. What the enemy used to harm me, God began using to free me and countless others. Over time, I began receiving the occasional phone call and email from groups who had heard me speak and asked me to mentor women in their community who had also escaped trafficking. But I couldn't live on the road and also be the wife and mom God called me to be. Even so, the desire to work, to fulfill the passions he had placed in my heart, burned inside me. It was a pull, but I trusted that where he guides, he provides.

I researched and talked with some people I met at conferences and decided to start a nonprofit. I wanted to equip communities to identify domestic trafficking, and I wanted to empower women to live fully restored lives.

In the beginning I didn't know exactly where my "lane" would be. I began exploring many different avenues to share my experiences. I shared my testimony in my community and lived off donations, since we didn't have enough to pay me a wage yet. I was overjoyed that people wanted to hear how to combat exploitation in their communities. Was God calling me to speak to students and colleges? I wondered whether policy reform was for me when I was invited to speak at my state's legislative hearing to help pass Senate Bill 673, a law that would increase penalties for buying children for sex and prohibit the arrest of a child for prostitution, because children can't consent. I trained my local child welfare office, while wondering whether I was called to assist in foster-care reform. With no idea where to start, I tried anything and everything that came my way. My husband was tremendously supportive through it, and we pinched pennies and accepted help from family while we went after the call of God.

Not long after I'd begun speaking locally, I received a call from an employee at the local department of family services where I had trained before.

"We have a client named Allie, up in Portland," he explained. "She's a fourteen-year-old who's coming home here soon, and I was hoping maybe I could connect you so she has someone when she returns."

"Of course," I agreed. "Anything I can do to help."

I learned that while attending a party between her eighth- and ninth-grade years, Allie met a twenty-something boy who showed interest in her and told her she was pretty. She had already determined that she was going to run away that weekend to escape arguments with her mother, a common coping mechanism Allie had become accustomed to. That night, Allie went home with the older boy, who'd previously turned the bedroom and bathroom doorknobs backward to lock people in. Three weeks later local police found her locked in the bathroom, shot up on meth, being sold online by the hour.

Now she was being held in a secure Portland facility that could assist her physical and mental needs better than anywhere else in Southern Oregon. The state needed her testimony against the trafficker at a grand jury hearing. Because of her history as a chronic runaway, a locked facility was the best option, apparently.

I made arrangements to visit her. On the drive there, I flipped through the radio stations as my signal went in and out. I found a station and an old-school gospel song came on the radio.

"Oh, this is my jam!" I said while turning up the volume.

Where do I know this song from? I praised the Lord, excited to hear an old favorite. Then I suddenly realized why this song was familiar. An eerie feeling set in.

Kevin used to play this in our home.

"No!" I said out loud. I did not want to revisit the feelings this music was stirring up.

Immediately, a warm presence washed over me. I sensed God's familiar voice saying, "He is my son and I love him. I am not happy with his choices, but he is my son and I love him. I died for him."

I began to pray. "Lord, I forgive him for the hurt . . . so much hurt. I don't know much about his childhood trauma or how the culture indoctrinated him. I do know that we don't fight against flesh but against principalities and the rulers of darkness. I come against a spirit of corruption over men, in the name of Jesus. I come against the spirit of violence toward women and the sexual immorality that has deceived and taken captive the hearts and minds of our next generation.

"Lord, I pray for the young men who are being lured into the Pimp Game, into gangs, into selling drugs. I pray for the men who believe buying sex is our American cultural norm. Father, I ask that the Christians around them would be faithful and that you'd raise up a generation of defenders and protectors who would mentor our young men and women and become the role models they need to go after their rightful place. In Jesus's name. Amen."

As I spoke the amen, I realized I'd been shaking the entire time. My fingers were gripping the steering wheel so tightly that my palms were sweaty. I wiped my brow with my forearm and reached over to my glovebox for a napkin. I dabbed under my eyes, trying not to ruin my makeup. The radio station was no longer audible but had disintegrated into a steady static. I turned off the static and pulled into the parking lot feeling a thousand pounds lighter. As I parked my car, I became nervous. I had never worked with teenage girls before.

Inside, the front-desk clerk greeted me. I introduced myself and asked for Allie. An attendant buzzed a door, then led me through to a visiting room with a conference table and a few chairs with worn, maroon upholstered seats scattered about the room. I sat there staring at the blank walls until a petite, attractive brunette sauntered in and slumped into one of the chairs near me. She stared at her feet and messed with the hem of her shirt.

"Hi, I'm Rebecca." I smiled and stretched out my hand. She barely grasped mine, feigning a handshake with her finger tips.

"Hi, I'm Allie." She glanced up just briefly enough for me to smile back. Though her brilliant blue eyes and long eyelashes were stunning, I recognized in them a familiar world of pain and nervousness.

This may be harder than I thought. I took off my blazer. She looked up and stared at my right arm.

"Cool tattoo."

Good. It's working. I began to describe the meaning behind the half-sleeve tattoo I got to celebrate my ten-years-clean-from-drugs anniversary. I pointed to each piece.

"The earth signifies my love of travel"—I pointed to each symbol as I described its significance—"and the hummingbird is a sign of prosperity and unique design by the Creator." The classic 1930s beauty with Native American war paint and traditional geisha flowers in her hair represented the past, present, and future for me. It was a portrait, which I'd seen in an art store, of a girl called Fearless. But I changed the flowers in her hair to match my daughters' birth months in the traditional geisha calendar known as Kanzashi. Past, geisha. Present, warrior. Future, beauty.

I pointed to the next inked image on my upper arm. "A

chandelier can triple its light by reflecting it." Allie was paying attention, her blue eyes bouncing between my arm and my gaze. "This script is from the line in the song 'Alabaster Box' by Cece Winans."

I told her the story of the prostitute in the Bible who rubbed a very expensive oil from her alabaster box all over Jesus's feet. She washed his feet with her tears and dried them with her hair (Luke 7:36–50).

"Allie." I leaned closer to her and looked intently into her sapphire eyes. "In the days when Jesus lived, that jar of oil was valued at an entire year of a man's wages—it was expensive. Maybe something only a prostituted person or wealthy person could afford. The day I ran from my trafficker, I couldn't leave my purses or my shoes behind," I continued. Allie was mesmerized. I knew she was taking in my words, forming an unspoken connection between us.

"It wasn't because of their value; it was because I knew the blood, sweat, and tears . . . I knew the cost. When Mary poured the oil out for Jesus, she was letting it all go—all that she had done for it, she let it all go for him."

She opened up a little before we hugged each other goodbye. I promised to write, and I did. On the weekends, we spent time getting to know each other and growing closer through phone conversations.

Allie was to be released after her fifteenth birthday. As the date approached, Allie's mom and I were concerned that her return to a strained relationship at home combined with small-town bullies and gossip was a recipe for disaster. Our fears proved correct. Her mother soon asked the social worker whether Matt and I could take her in, allowing a new school zone and different family dynamics with someone who was supposed to understand a bit more.

Becoming foster parents wasn't exactly on our master plan, but we agreed that the Lord would lead and direct us as we stepped out. We became emergency certified and fingerprinted. The $300 I'd spent upon my return from London to have a lawyer expunge my record was a blessing. God knew what was coming, and thankfully, in Nevada, you need only to be crime-free for three years to qualify for your misdemeanors to be sealed.

Matt set up bunkbeds for Deshae and Allie, and she settled in. We began a structured routine, including attending school and doing chores. To counteract the negative voices in her head, we read a Proverb a day and made a dream board to sketch out her future plans. But night terrors plagued her.

Life with Allie was rougher than I expected. Having a "new girl" in our home triggered old behaviors, and my thoughts regressed to when Brandi taught me our house rules. Allie also struggled with dissociative identity disorder. "Candy" wanted to "make Daddy happy" by running away from our home and going missing for the weekend. Other times, she'd climb onto my lap like a little girl, stroke my hair, and call me Mommy. We weren't equipped for the long-term mental health care Allie needed. Her mental health issues were present long before her exploitation, but were only compounded by it.

"Some Christian you are!" she screamed at me one day during a heated argument.

I restrained my fleshly impulses, but I later confessed to Matt, "I want to fight her. I almost told Jesus to hold my coat while I showed that little girl . . ." Matt laughed at me. "I'm serious, babe. I legit want to fight a child. What is wrong with me?" I folded myself into my husband's arms and cried. This was harder than I'd ever imagined.

Nearly every weekend, Allie would run away and I'd go searching for her. One night, I found her at a local drug house.

Another time, she ran from Deshae while they were building a snowman. She called me another time from a local motel at 2:00 a.m., sobbing, "I need you to take me to the hospital." I did, and they quickly diagnosed her as pregnant and having an STD.

"I'm fifteen!" she screamed at the doctor, tears streaming down her face. I sat in the hospital and held her while she cried.

When Allie's sixteenth birthday came, we celebrated with a party, her favorite cake, and a trip to the spa. She had never experienced anything like that and was thrilled. It felt amazing to see her light up as we celebrated and pampered her.

Slowly, she began showing signs of healing. One January evening, she emerged from the bedroom in pajamas. She handed me a stick of eyeliner. I saw dozens of rows of self-harming cut marks peeking out from her shorts hem. Though shocked, I forced a calm face. I had no idea that she had struggled with cutting too.

"What's this?" I asked, holding out the eyeliner.

"I feel like running, so I'm setting up a roadblock for myself." She smiled. "I put on my pajamas because I won't run in pajamas, and I always take my eyeliner when I go."

Tears welled up in my eyes. "It's healthy to recognize unhealth," I said as I got up and gave her a hug. "I'm proud of you. A few months ago, you wouldn't have even recognized that feeling, let alone done something to stop yourself!"

She beamed with pride and hugged me back.

Allie's relationship with her mom improved as Allie sought therapy and found healing. Eventually, they were ready to try again—and just in the nick of time. After her last pregnancy ended in a miscarriage, Allie found out she was pregnant again by a boy over eighteen. We could no longer knowingly let her date the guy we now knew was over age. She screamed and spit in my face in front of my kids, grabbed my phone, and ran. I grabbed her and took my phone back. The time had come for her to go home. I wasn't ready for this. Our family needed a return to peace, and I knew it was time to ask God for my next step.

Walking alongside young women who long to be loved requires a calling. It isn't about rushing in with guns drawn on the bad guys to "rescue the voiceless." For me, this calling is about being a cheerleader and an advocate. It's a call to help victims navigate an unknown world while providing support, guidance, and opportunities to overcome the many hurdles of an abused past, through patience and grace.

Today, Allie is engaged and has three beautiful children.

Soon after Allie returned to her mom in 2013, Matt and I found out we were pregnant again. Another girl! Three baby girls within four years made four daughters total!

I cried in the car on my way home from the ultrasound.

"God, I'm scared of having daughters. What if my girls turn out like me?" I pictured old me and Allie and the hardship that came with the sin and abuse and generational ties in our spiritual bloodline.

"I like the woman you've become," God reminded me. "If they turn out like you, it'll be okay." My Father, who sees "the end from the beginning" (Isaiah 46:10) saw the new me, not the old me. With every gentle encouragement, God's truth empowered me to be a new creation determined to raise daughters with a fearless passion and drive to go after all that God has for them.

I wondered how God would continue to make a path to preach and share my testimony and travel with multiple children, but I knew he always makes a way where there is no way (Isaiah 43:16–19). I had grown closer to God than I thought possible and heard his voice more clearly than ever.

Morning devotions were great, but I had a craving to study the Bible in more depth, so I looked into attending seminary. I discovered Bethel Seminary's online accelerated master's program. I didn't meet all their requirements, but I applied anyway, believing if God wanted me in, he would open the door. I eagerly awaited the response, constantly refreshing my email inbox after the submission deadline. Nothing came, and eventually I let it go. One day I was picking up toys scattered about the living room when my phone rang. I didn't recognize the number but answered in case it was law enforcement or a training opportunity for my newfound nonprofit.

"This is Rebecca."

"Hi, Rebecca, this is Scott, academic advisor from Bethel Seminary. I'm calling to congratulate you on your acceptance into the school!" His smile was audible.

"Seriously?" I cried. "I got in?"

"Yes, the board met, and although you don't meet all the criteria, we felt strongly that your voice would be a great addition to our program."

That day, I enrolled to obtain a master's degree in Christian Thought. I couldn't believe I had become a seminary student! My heart leaped. I ran to my Bible and opened to a highlighted, handwritten note with "1–27–03" scribbled in the margin. Ten years later, Jeremiah 31:33 was coming to pass: "I will put my law in their minds and write it on their hearts. I will be their God, and they will be my people."

I believed with all my heart that God could be trusted. Bad habits were hard to break, but God showed me that he would bless my faithfulness by stepping out and being faithful in small things. He would bless me even if I wasn't hearing him correctly, because he sees my heart. He is a good Father who never punishes his children for trying their best.

"What if I'm wrong, Lord, and I hear you wrong?" I asked him. "What if I make a mistake?"

"Do you think I won't bless you for trying to follow my voice?" he responded. When I would beat myself up for being that rude, hardened, impatient girl, he'd remind me that he knows better than I do how my brain works. He knows how and why my childhood and exploitation has led my brain to think the way it does. He wasn't mad; he wanted to help renew my mind and rewire my neural pathways.

I sat looking at my toddlers. God reminded me of how he delights in my progress. "When your youngest tries to walk and instead stumbles and falls, do you get mad at her? Or do you clap and cheer and get out your camera to capture the moment of progress? That's how I feel about you, even when you mess up. I celebrate your progress."

I saw this principle at work in my life. What you practice gets stronger, whether that be running, exercising, shooting a basketball, or painting. Or in my case, hearing the voice of God and being obedient so that the Lord can finally trust *me*. If he said wait, I could wait. If he said don't go, I wouldn't go. The more I talked and listened to God in prayer and in his Word, the more familiar I became with his voice. He could speak from anywhere and I'd know it was him. He had become my friend.

CHAPTER 17 **the expert**

They triumphed over him
  by the blood of the Lamb
  and by the word of their testimony.

2014–2015

As training requests continued to come in, my belly continued to grow. It became clear that while stories of overcoming are powerful, I wanted to do more than inspire people. I wanted my narrative to include a call to action that would actually change lives, state procedures, and our culture as a whole. I wanted professionals to walk away with tools to identify and respond to suspected exploitation victims. Three training programs were created out of this desire: one for law enforcement, another for medical professionals, and a third for community service providers.

With that, the Rebecca Bender Initiative was born in January 2014, one week after the birth of my fourth daughter.

The requests to mentor other women in groups or churches also kept coming. People were looking for more than my self-published guide. One afternoon while taking an online course for my masters, I sensed the Holy Spirit's voice. "If you can get a master's online, you can mentor online. And you can't possibly be the only survivor who lives in a community where services don't exist."

That's it, I thought. An online school for survivors would enable me to mentor women regardless of their location. I used my existing ten-step guide, *Roadmap to Redemption*, and added six more lessons on professional development areas that I had gleaned from my work in the anti-trafficking field. That made sixteen classes in total, offering registrants one full semester of deeper healing, professional development, and career exploration. I looked into the same technology that my seminary was using and started advertising at conferences and on social media. My first group of seven women logged in from all over the country, and I was thrilled to train them from my tiny town.

My trainings for community professionals also increased. I found my work rewarding and was humbled to be equipping law enforcement and medical professionals with information that would save lives. My life had come full circle, and fruit was pouring forth as a result of my being obedient to God's voice. I was in awe.

Around this time, I attended a Christian writers and speakers conference for women. The music was powerful, and I worshiped God, praising him for his faithfulness. The music swelled as the majestic presence of the Lord moved over me. I fell to my knees, yielding to his Spirit.

"I want you to take the year off from speaking," he whispered.

"But, Lord!" I cried. "My speaking career is picking up. Besides, I already have four events booked, and they've been promoting them."

"Do what you have, but take no more. If your hands are too busy, you will not be able to take hold of what I have coming."

I cannot begin to adequately describe the battle of the will I faced in saying no to opportunities that my heart had longed for. The Game was hard, healing was hard, but this was a whole different kind of hard. This was sacrifice and dying to what my flesh wanted. But this time, I was sacrificing "good things." These were things I was sure would bless others. And yet God had said, "Take no more."

As speaking and training requests continued to pour in—engagements I had prayed for and waited to receive—I kept returning to the same truth: *blessing comes from obedience.* Then I would say the hard no, sometimes hesitantly.

Following a suggestion from Lysa TerKeurst, president of Proverbs 31 Ministries, I channeled my energy into creating a speaker's team and sent out others to teach. I stayed behind to build the infrastructure needed to sustain my growing nonprofit ministry. I was blessed to have the time to build our foundation and resumed community training after the year was over.

Obeying God isn't always easy. There are no shortcuts to learning that obedience and sacrifice go hand in hand, and I was being trained in both. I needed boundaries from a loving Father whom I trusted to teach me a healthy fear of the Lord. It took me time to understand that Jesus wasn't some angry police officer or abuser holding a punishment over me. "When I was a child, I talked like a child, I thought like a child, I reasoned like a child. When I became a man, I put the ways of childhood behind me" (1 Corinthians 13:11). To partner with God on the call of my life, I would need to completely rely on his guidance.

I invited Brandi to train with me at the Dallas Conference on Crimes Against Women, where I had been invited to give perspectives about the inner workings of a trafficker's organized crime. We invited both the federal agent who had arrested her, Mark Parsons, and the US attorney who had prosecuted the case, Andrew Stover, to attend the training, and they both accepted.

Agent Parsons attended with his wife and son. With tears in their eyes, they sat and listened. It was clear they'd been affected by what we both shared. Afterward, we all went to lunch together. They were shocked to hear our stories but inspired to see where we were today and how far we had come.

Mark's wife looked at us across the lunch table. "Hearing y'all's story was powerful," she said with a soft but powerful voice. "I remember my husband bringing this case home. To think you came from a home just like ours. This really can happen to anyone." I could tell she was fighting back tears.

Their son, who was in his early twenties, jumped in. "Yeah, when Dad would bring your trash home from the investigation, my sister and I would sit around and put the torn-up pieces of notebook paper together like a jigsaw puzzle, and my mama would pray over you."

My heart was deeply moved by this Jesus-loving family from Texas who, throughout the entire investigation, prayed for us. Tears welled up as I recalled something Aunt Loretta had told me: "I always prayed for the Christians around you to be faithful." God not only heard Aunt Loretta but graced us with the chance to meet the living answer to her prayers.

Relationships grew organically. The FBI, Homeland Security, vice schools, and law enforcement detectives started calling to pick my brain on cases or hire me to interview trafficking victims. In time, I was sworn in on the stand as an expert in court cases. I began flying around the country as a human trafficking expert. I was truly humbled to receive multiple awards from various social justice groups and was honored by the FBI and then again by Congress.

But I wasn't the only one. There were other survivor leaders who paved the way before me. Seeing hundreds of advocates and allies and leaders fighting long before I was trafficked, was moving.

In fall 2016 I took a call from a local detective, Jim Williams, who wanted to bring me on as a trafficking expert for a case involving a twenty-two-year-old female victim. The next day, we met at the district attorney's office to learn more about the case and my role. Jim needed me to serve as a subject matter expert for the prosecution. I gathered a wealth of specifics on the victim, Felicity*, and met with her the following day.

She wore a light brown wig and a long shirt with leggings and flats. We swapped stories, and mine seemed to open the door for her to give me details that would be helpful in her defense. The district attorney's victim advocate, Peggy, sat in too and explained the trial procedures.

Prior to the trial, I learned that Virgil Rucker, a forty-three-year-old pimp, had driven Felicity and her two children, ages four and six, from Stockton, California, to Medford, Oregon. Out of the local Motel 6, Virgil began selling her online by the hour.

At midnight, while smoking a cigarette from his hotel room's balcony, Virgil heard a commotion coming from a nearby room. Two teenage girls were tangled up in a fight on the balcony, and he quickly assisted in breaking it up. The fifteen-year-old intoxicated female stood thankful but scared, blood running down her face, while the other girl went back into the hotel room and shut the door. He invited her to come in and clean up. Unsure, she looked inside the open door to his hotel room and saw Felicity and her two children.

*Victim's name is an alias to protect her identity.

"I figured, how bad could it be if a family is there?" she testified.

The young girl cleaned up with Felicity's help and admitted she was scared to go home and wake up her mom with this drama. Virgil offered to let her sleep there for the night. A couple of hours later, she awoke to him raping her. She made eye contact with Felicity, who was also awake and looked just as scared. Crying, Felicity turned away. The next morning, Virgil drove the fifteen-year-old victim home to find out where she lived. During the trial, the DA made sure the jury knew that perpetrators often use this tactic to threaten their victims.

On the drive home, the victim told Felicity's children about her puppy and asked whether they would wait outside her house to see the puppy while she went inside. Virgil drove away while she went inside and called 911.

Because rape committed against children under the age of sixteen carries a much harsher sentence, the defense claimed, "See, she wanted it. They liked each other. If anything, this is statutory rape, but not rape of a fifteen-year-old." During cross-examination, the defense attorney questioned the young woman about the puppy conversation. "If you didn't like him, why would you want them to stay around and see your puppy?"

"I didn't have a puppy," she testified. "I was lying to Virgil to keep them in the driveway while I called the police, but he didn't fall for it."

The teen continued her testimony, telling how she went to the hospital, where doctors confirmed that she was indeed raped. They collected semen for law enforcement. Police investigated the name on the Motel 6 room and began looking for not only the rapist but the woman with the two children who may have witnessed the crime.

When the detective found Felicity, she asked him, "Why

haven't you been looking for *me*?" She explained that she'd been trafficked by this man since she was sixteen years old.

When she took the stand, she began responding to the DA's questions, and her trauma was apparent. All eyes were riveted on her.

"Virgil shaved off my hair in the middle of the night as my punishment. That's why I wear this wig. He made me get his name tattooed across my chest." She pulled her shirt away from her neck to reveal the branding. "He wrote out a recruiting letter and made me send it from my Facebook Messenger to other girls."

After a very long and grueling day, Felicity and I were both spent and ravenous. I offered to take her out for Mexican food, and we hung out, joked together, and blew off some of the day's stress while eating tacos and sipping pineapple soda. We made a Walmart run to pick up some essentials for her, then I dropped her off at the hotel.

"You get some rest, because tomorrow's going to be another big day. Good night."

She shut the car door, and I made sure she safely entered the lobby before I drove away.

On my way back, I couldn't shake her hollow look as she'd said good night. We were both silently dreading listening to her trafficker's testimony the next day. But things were off to a good start, and I had enough hope for both of us.

The next morning, I phoned Felicity to give her a heads up that I was on my way. No answer. I texted. No answer. *Crap . . . I should have prepared her more for trial. Poor girl. She's probably freaking out this morning.* But even I hadn't known what to expect since this was my first trial too.

Nervous, I drove over to her hotel, calling the detective to get her room number. After zipping into a parking place, I flew out of the car to the room and knocked a few times. Countless scary scenarios of why she wasn't answering raced through my mind. After no answer via phone either, I waited and knocked again. Still no answer. My adrenaline threatened to steal my peace, so I called the detective again. Before I could finish explaining the situation, he said, "I'm on my way."

He arrived and showed his badge to the front desk clerk, who forfeited the room key. At Felicity's room he knocked loudly. Nothing. As he inserted the key, the door suddenly opened, and a face appeared.

With short hair sticking out in a hundred directions, Felicity stood there completely naked, looking as if her winter hibernation had been interrupted.

"I'll let you handle it from here," the detective said. He handed me the room key and walked away.

"Come on, girl," I said, rushing into the room, "We have to go! You're going to miss his testimony." The contents of her purse were strewn across the bed she hadn't slept in. I scooped them up. Chocolate cake was all over her sheets.

She yawned and stretched her arms over her head with a laugh. "I crashed hard last night! I hadn't eaten or slept in days, so after that chocolate cake, I was out!"

We raced around the hotel room. Felicity threw on a dress and her wig and brushed her teeth while I repacked her purse. "Throw your makeup in a bag, and put it on in the car," I directed.

We scooted out the door and stopped by a donut shop that was on the way to the courthouse. I knew it would be a long day, so I grabbed a couple of donuts, a small coffee, a carton of milk, and jumped back in the car.

"Here, eat this." I handed her the bag, and we sped off. When we got out of the car and rushed toward the courthouse, I realized that her teeny tiny tank-top dress was a little too tiny.

"Here," I said, handing her my jacket. After she put it on, I scanned her from head to toe. Not exactly the professional image we were hoping for, but at least it would tone down the street look attached to so many stereotypes. For the same reason, I opened the back of my minivan and dug through my Goodwill donation bag, searching for something to cover my tattooed arms. "Put on these leggings too." I threw some to her. We stood in the parking lot, me rushing her while she put the leggings on and swapped her hoop earrings out for my pearls.

Virgil took the stand, testifying about his service as a church youth leader and his passion for mentoring kids in music. He supposedly knew nothing about his own email. He blamed Felicity for all the recruiting evidence law enforcement had uncovered in his inbox. The district attorney asked him about his six-month sentence in a California prison for beating Felicity's children. He denied ever being imprisoned.

"Are you stating, Mr. Rucker, that the California state prison records are inaccurate?" the DA asked with more than a hint of sarcasm in her voice.

"It didn't happen in my heart," Virgil replied.

I watched the jury roll their eyes. *This should be an easy win*, I thought.

Even though things were looking good for Felicity, this was the DA's first trafficking case. She repeatedly used words like *date* and *escort* to describe calls during which Felicity was forced to engage in sexual acts or face Virgil's strict punishment of her or her children. I took notes throughout the trial and subtly slipped them to the DA during a break.

"You have to stop sugar-coating this to the jury. 'Dates'? This isn't coffee and a movie. She is being sold for sex acts. 'Escort'? This puts an inaccurate picture in the jury's mind. She is a trafficking victim."

When the court reconvened, the DA began her opening

statement by turning to the jury, "I need to apologize." She held my note in her hand. "I've been using the wrong words. These aren't dates that Felicity is going on. This isn't coffee and a movie. She is being sold for sex. She is also not an escort; she is a trafficking victim."

Tears welled up in my eyes. Our work was making a difference to the legal system, to the community members who made up the jury, and to Felicity and her children. From that point on, the DA began referring to the online ads that were used as evidence of prostitution as "Virgil's ads." She referred to them this way so frequently that even Virgil's attorney began referring to them as "Virgil's ads."

When the testimonies ended, the only thing left to do was wait. After five grueling hours of waiting in the victim advocacy room, eating fast food and watching bad TV, we got the call. The jury didn't want to wait through the weekend. They'd have a decision by the end of the night. We spent two more hours waiting. Finally, at 7:00 p.m., the bailiff announced that the jury had reached a verdict.

We filed into the courtroom and sat. Felicity took my hand. Her knee was bouncing. I sat in such a way as to block her view of her trafficker. The judge asked each juror, one by one, "Members of the jury, how do you find count 11379 on rape in the first degree?"

"We find him guilty," the foreman responded.

"How do you find count 11380 on involuntary servitude?"

"We find him guilty."

One by one, all thirteen counts were read. By the seventh count, Felicity and I looked at each other, our faces wet with tears. "We're gonna win this!" I whispered with a smile.

Thirteen guilty convictions and a thirty-one-year sentence later, it was finished.

We practically skipped out of the courtroom. Detective Jim, who was also crying, leaned in and hugged me.

I looked at him steadily to make sure he wouldn't miss a word of what I wanted to tell him. "You know, you didn't only help bring justice to Felicity. You changed the course of life for her kids. Virgil will no longer be able to harm any future victims," I said, wiping my tears. "You've set a legal standard in our county that countless prosecutors can refer to for generations to come. You did that!"

"No," he replied, pulling me in for another hug. "We did that."

Felicity and I headed to the hotel to grab her things, then I took her to the airport so she could get home to her kids and family.

"Where are you living?" I asked. "With your mom?"

"No. I'm in the Travelodge," she said nonchalantly.

"Where are your kids going to go to school?" I asked, confused how she had enrolled them with no address.

"We'll use my mom's address to register them, but I can't stay with her. She's the one who introduced me to Virgil when I was sixteen."

"How are you paying for the Travelodge?" I asked.

She flashed me a sideways look, and I knew.

"I'm gonna call you TT. Tricks at the Travelodge." I smiled, trying to show her that I understood. Of all people, who was I to judge? I would not encourage her decision, but neither would I sit in judgment of her.

"Yeah, TT girl." She laughed. A look of disappointment flashed across her face.

I pulled up to the airport departures curb. Felicity got out of my car and reached into the back to get her bag.

"You know we have help for you if you want it," I said. "I can get you and your kids into a shelter temporarily." I put the car in park and turned to the open side door, hoping she'd consider my offer.

"Rebecca . . . I've never known any other way." She leaned through the passenger door and hugged my neck.

"All right, TT. Well, you call me when you're ready, okay?"

She nodded, swung the bag over her shoulder, and walked away.

I watched Felicity walk into the airport and sat frozen for some time, letting the reality of her next steps quietly burst my bubble from the trial victory.

As I drove away, I thought about the weight of everything survivors must overcome and all the hurdles to reentry. I was dumbstruck with gratitude for God's astonishing grace. It was much to take in, especially given Felicity's return to the only life she'd known.

I understood. Navigating a world you know nothing about, taking risks on homelessness and hunger with children hanging in the balance—choosing the unknown is impossible when you can return to the quick fix.

My new life is full. I help young women and communities identify trafficking in their neighborhoods. I help law enforcement officials, the FBI, and district attorneys prosecute traffickers by taking the stand and working with victims to prep for trial. I help other girls like me find their "Now what?" through my online academy. But the greatest reward of this new life is that I have surrendered all I had to the King of Kings, who has restored my life, called me out of my darkness, and circumcised areas of my heart that were not of God.

Working as an anti-trafficking professional gives me purpose, but it is also actually the very thing that saved me, the very thing that taught me to look deeper into my own trauma and seek healing for the complexities of my experience. I got involved to help others in the movement, but the movement ended up helping me. The young girl who years ago would pursue anything for love is now a woman who has been completely redeemed by His pursuit. I have experienced God's love through my faith, my husband, my kids, my friends, my calling, and even in my learning how to love myself. God used all that to show me what true love looks like, but I had to turn away from it all to truly pursue him. This has always been his original intention not just for me but for each and every one of us—to throw all caution to the wind and run after him.

HUMAN TRAFFICKING LINGO

304: Looks like "hoe" upside down on a calculator, often used in ads or texting.

b--ch: A term used endearingly toward one another to refer to a "working girl."

blade/track: The area in which a girl walks to try to catch a "date," usually a street or street corner.

bottom/bottom b--ch: The girl there the longest, the bottom of the totem pole that all others are built upon. They are required by the pimp/trafficker to recruit potential victims, report violation of rules, and may be forced to help punish.

branded: A tattoo on a victim that indicates ownership and indoctrination into the family. A rite of passage.

caught a case: Went to jail for prostitution.

choosing fee: A fee charged to enter the stable. Many traffickers relate it to a "signing bonus."

chose up: The act of joining a trafficker's stable or changing traffickers/stables.

daddy: A term a male trafficker/pimp might require his victims to call him.

date: The appointment set up to exchange sex for money.

family/folks: A group of victims under the control of a trafficker/pimp. The term is an attempt to suggest a family environment.

the Game/the Life: The lifestyle and industry of human trafficking.

gorilla (sometimes guerrilla) pimp: A violent trafficker/pimp.

grooming: When a trafficker is dating a girl to win her trust and gradually expands her boundaries before turning her out.

hoe: Derogatory term traffickers use regularly with their victims. Refers to a person in prostitution.

in pocket/out of pocket: Abiding by (in) or breaking (out) the rules that the trafficker has set.

john/trick: A man purchasing sex from a prostituted woman or child.

kiddie track/runaway track: The place where minors or homeless youth are identified and/or sold.

knock: To traffic, convincing a girl to get involved in the Game and go home with a trafficker.

lot lizard: Derogatory term for a prostituted woman or child at truck stops.

PI: A pimp.

quota: The amount of money a victim must give to their trafficker/pimp each night.

reckless eyeballing: Looking at other pimps, which is considered out of pocket.

Romeo/finesse pimp: A trafficker who uses fraud and deception to lure his victims in by pretending to be their boyfriend.

seasoning: The process of breaking a victim's spirit and gaining control over him or her via rapes, beatings, manipulation, and intimidation. Alternate meaning: experienced.

sister: Anther female in a pimp's stable.

square: A person living a "normal" lifestyle.

stable: A group of victims under the control of a pimp.

stack: To put money aside in order to make a move.

trade up/trade down: The act of buying or selling a person for a pimp's stable.

turn out: To be forced into prostitution; also, a person newly involved.

wife-in-law or wifey: A term prostituted women are required to call the other females in the stable.

working: Performing sexual acts for money.

ACKNOWLEDGMENTS

I could not have done this without an incredible team who believes in this project, believes in the transforming power of Christ, and wants to be a part of bringing his message to the masses. Maresa DePuy is a phenomenal writing collaborator and a true gift from God. Thank you, Maresa, for taking my heaping piles of messy memories and bringing order to it box by box, unpacking and organizing my story. You pulled out things I forgot were there and dusted them off and found a place for them. You waded through the memories that may be too graphic to share and risked your own inability to unread them. Truly remarkable. Thank you.

Thank you to my agent, Blythe Daniel from the Blythe Daniel Agency, for taking a chance on me! You saw the long-term vision and stuck with me while we let God find the perfect place for it in his timing.

Thank you to my editor, Carolyn McCready, for noticing a girl from your neck of the woods and trusting that God wanted to do something great with his story of redemption. I'm grateful for your kindness and encouragement while I tossed and turned over titles and direction for the story and for your patience with this new author. Thank you to everyone in the Zondervan family— Kim, Denise, Robin, Bridgette, Andrea, Caleb—for all your hard work on this project! It would not have been the same without your wisdom, discernment, and patience.

Thank you, Erin Healy, for your beautiful gift of breathing life into the order of events I would lay out matter-of-factly. You helped find my voice and ensure it was clear, painting a beautiful journey for readers to grasp the truth of coercion and trafficking in America.

Thank you to Johanna Wilson from Bethel Redding for the incredible help putting together the Self-Reflection Questions. I am honored to have met you and developed the friendship we have. Love you, girl.

I also want to acknowledge my family. I continue to have the most supportive relatives! Thank you for taking my daughter and raising her for a year while I went into a women's shelter, for babysitting while I pursued the call of God, for paying tuition for seminary some semesters and giving me Bible dictionaries and concordances before the internet was a thing, for letting me sleep in your homes for months and buying me groceries when I couldn't yet pay for my own. Thank you above all for all the prayers and encouragement and support. I could not have done it without you. I know that not every person escaping her trafficker has the same good fortune, and I don't take you for granted. I'm so grateful to God for you. Love you, Phyllis and Wayne Saffer, David Saffer, Joyce and Kim Alexander, Gerry and Loretta Bjornstad, Cedar and Brettani Shannon, Grandma Glenda, and Dave and Dorine.

Thank you to retired Federal Agent Mark Parsons for giving me reminders and clarity on his part of the investigation. But also, thank you to the Parsons family for continuing to pray for us, for girls like us, and for being such a great support system after we were able to escape. Thank you to US Attorney Andrew Stover for using our case to help prepare others on how to identify sex trafficking in their communities. Thank you both for the use of your real names and your willingness to train alongside us and take interviews and calls relentlessly to get this message out!

I also want to thank our team at RBI (Rebecca Bender

Initiative): Kathy Bryan, Melanie Huggard, Deni Anderson, Chelan Russ, Lauren Hall, Jessa Dillow Crisp, Angie Conn, Laura Harville, Christa McCormick, and our entire RBI Board of Directors: Nick Lembo, Trina White, Angie Lott, Scott Peterson, Al Winn, Will Hart, Ashlee Kleinert, and Elizabeth Phillips. Your support, help, input, and patience while I equip communities through this project are beyond words. The constant wordsmithing and dry-erase boards have helped get readers into my shoes. I love you guys and am honored to partner with you in the good fight.

And to my friends, my tribe, thank you for your encouragement, support, read-throughs, and prayers. Thanks for believing in me and being there while I tried to find my new normal! Tracey Moss, Chris Musillo, Jill Moschella, and April Thomas, you were my first group of friends (and still are) who loved me while I worked through my mess. Thank you.

Thank you to Bekah Charleston. When people say "ride or die," that's you. I love you with all my heart. God knew what he was doing when I met you fifteen years ago and how it would all turn out in the end. I am so proud of the woman you have become and am excited to cheer you on along the journey toward the call and purpose you feel in your heart. Love you, sis.

Lastly, I want to thank my husband, Matt, for believing in me and in my testimony and for always holding on and supporting me in the many adventures God brings our way. From our first date, you supported me, saying, "If God is telling you to speak out, who am I to tell you no?" When you find a man like that, ladies, put a ring on it.

And to Deshae—you have come alongside me through it all. From my telling my story to you, to our community, and to the world, you have been open to hearing my heart through it all. You are brave and strong to look deeper than my "excuses" and see the psychology of trauma and culture and childhood experiences. You're wise beyond your years, and I'm so thankful God made you just the way you are.

APPENDIX 1

Are You or Is Someone You Know Dating a Trafficker?

Circle all the characteristics that apply to your situation. One item on its own does not indicate trafficking, but three or more may be cause for you to look deeper into who you are dating.

- He has a fancy car, clothes, or jewelry.
- He frequently spends nights away or out of town.
- He portrays the negative aspects of rap culture.
- He claims to have a job, but not in a place one can visit (e.g., he says he owns a record label, magazine company, billboards, restaurants, sometimes in other cities).
- He has dreams of making it big and being successful. He will encourage you to become part of *his* dreams.
- Your dreams and goals for life will be put on hold for his.
- Sometimes he promises to make *your* dreams come true (e.g., finishing school, modeling, marriage and family).
- He pulls you into his life: everything becomes "we" in your conversation. (When a person internalizes a dream, she will work harder to achieve it.)
- He isolates you from family and friends by moving away.
- He tries to fast-track the relationship. (Moving and

talking of marriage within a short time frame should be a cause for concern.)
- He limits your access to relationships. (Healthy partnerships expand your circle of friends.)
- He carries multiple cell phones.

Maybe a woman you care about is in a relationship that has you worried. Could she be at risk of being trafficked? Look for these warning signs:

- She's tired during the day from working at night.
- She suddenly has expensive things: Gucci purse, diamond bracelet, name-brand clothes, or nails and hair done on a regular basis.
- She's increasingly interested in or talks a lot about his dream. "We're going to . . ."
- She has an older boyfriend, usually one not in school.
- Her morals and values have slowly declined.
- She sports a new tattoo or "brand" of initials, his name or a saying, especially about money or "the Life"/"the Game."
- She keeps her eyes down while in public.
- She starts to become secluded. You see her less and less.
- She seems to have plausible reasons for always canceling appointments.

If you believe someone you know is being groomed or is in danger, please call the National Human Trafficking Hotline to find a local detective and advocate in your community.

1-888-373-7888

APPENDIX 2

THE POWER OF COERCION

Are you or someone you know experiencing abuse? Circle how many you can identify with to see if coercive tactics are being used in your relationship.

These statements were taken during a survey asking men who had been convicted of domestic violence to share how they would use gaslighting, force, fraud, or coercion to control their victims. These are the top forty unanimous answers out of hundreds of questions asked and created by the Jackson County Domestic Violence shelter. Rebecca Bender has adapted them to fit human trafficking.

I would isolate her, breaking her ties with any support she had:

- I convinced her family and friends that I was the good one.

  (Survivor: "He met my parents, and they liked him." "He helped my family during hard times.")

- I took all the money so that she depended on me for everything.

  (Survivor: "At first, I felt I was a contributor to the home, but then I questioned why he had to control *everything*. He insisted that he take me to the grocery store. He paid the power bills; he mocked me if I didn't eat what he ate.")

- I would start a fight before she visited with friends and family so that eventually, she simply stopped visiting.

  (Survivor: "I felt too guilty about leaving after an argument. I was also too embarrassed for my family to see my bruises.")

- I moved her way out in the country or to another city. When I left, I took her car battery with me.

  (Survivor: "At first, I felt excited to be on a new adventure, a new town. After a while, I felt I had no one to turn to—nowhere to go.")

- I convinced the people around her that she was crazy, imagined things, and needed counseling. I could prove it by pointing out her erratic behavior. That way, she had nowhere to go if she tried to leave.

  (Survivor: "I remember thinking, Am I crazy? I couldn't follow the conversation because he kept talking in circles.")

- I convinced everyone around her that she was incapable of caring for the children because of her stupidity, mental illness, and laziness.

  (Survivor: "He convinced me that I would lose my child if anyone knew what was going on in our house.")

- I ripped the phone cord out of the wall during a fight when she tried to call for help or broke her cell phone.

  (Survivor: "He even controlled whom I called on my cell. I felt sick to my stomach as he read my text messages, wondering whether the smallest thing would set him off.")

- I had her back me up on illegal things so that I could hold it over her head if she tried to leave.

(Survivor: "He would tell me that he'd turn me in if I tried to leave.")

I'd make her doubt her sanity and capabilities:

- I'd convince her that she was crazy by playing mind games with her. I'd hide her things and tell her how incompetent she was so that she'd believe me when I told her that she needed me. (This is known as "gaslighting.")

  (Survivor: "I felt that something was *wrong* with me. I questioned my sanity.")

- I kept her up all night so she was easier to control the next day.

  (Survivor: "I remember feeling crazy. He'd fight with me when I returned from work. I kept wanting to just go to sleep.")

- I turned the kids against her by making her the bad parent and tricking the children. I would make her discipline the children by threatening to hit them harder, then I'd threaten to report child abuse if she left me.

  (Survivor: "I thought, if I hit them, it'll hurt less; if I let him do it, it will hurt more." "I feared the day when my little one got old enough to talk back to him.")

- I made her feel guilty about wanting to break up our family, that she was a bad mother and wife if she wanted to leave every time things got difficult.

  (Survivor: "He'd say people who love each other stick it out through rough times—that we could get through this, and I'd think, He'll change.")

- I told her how fat and ugly she was all the time, and how

badly she did things around the house. I told her how embarrassed I was of her.

(Survivor: "I wanted him to adore me, so I tried hard to do things to get his approval." "He didn't let me come home until I lost weight.")

- I told her that no one else would want my sloppy seconds, that she was used goods, that no one would want to marry a whore.

(Survivor: "No one else will understand. Who wants to marry a prostitute?")

- I'd rape her.

(Survivor: "I kept wondering why he was doing this to me. I left for a while, but then he came to find me. No one knew I'd been raped.")

I made her afraid of leaving me:

- I told her that women's shelters were for women who needed it, not for women who wanted to give up on their family, not for whores and prostitutes. Only weak women live in those places.

(Survivor: "I believed him. I believed the shelter staff would not take me in, thinking that it was my choice. I didn't want to appear weak.")

- I made sure she knew she wouldn't get a dime from me if she left and that she'd be poor and homeless. I ruined her credit by putting things in her name and not paying for them.

(Survivor: "He told me, 'You leave with what you came with.' Even though I had lots of things and made lots of money, I couldn't take any of it with me.")

- I followed her without her knowing so I could make her believe I had people watching her.

  (Survivor: "I thought there were cameras in my car. I thought I was crazy as I searched for the camera." "He knew all my actions—what I'd done the day before. He said he'd dreamed it.")

- I threatened suicide.

  (Survivor: "I felt like he needed me.")

- I told her I would kill her.

  (Survivor: "I believed him.")

- I threatened to hurt people she loved.

  (Survivor: "I knew he was capable of this. I would do anything to protect them. The abuse was a 'small price to pay' to keep them safe.")

- I would lock up all her things, including the social security cards, birth certificates, and pictures. I'd take things that were important to her so she'd come back or reach out.

  (Survivor: "I thought, How am I going to start again? I feel hopeless.")

- I broke things and told her that it was her fault for upsetting me.

  (Survivor: "I knew better than to do what made him mad. I should get my mind right.")

- I reminded her of the last time she left me, that it only made things worse.

  (Survivor: "I thought, He's right; it did get worse last time I tried to leave.")

- I told her I'd never let her go, no matter what it took.

  (Survivor: "I thought, He loves me that much that nothing can separate our love.")

- I convinced her that I'd find her wherever she went.

  (Survivor: "He had.")

- I laughed and told her about men who had violently hurt (or murdered) their whores when they tried to leave.

  (Survivor: "He threatened to take me to his friend's house to have them burn me or douse me with gasoline. I knew they had done it to others, so I was afraid."

- I always kept one of the kids with me so that she'd always come back.

  (Survivor: "How could I leave my stepson to take all my pimp's anger? The children couldn't handle it.")

I convinced her that I deserved another chance:

- I convinced her that I was sorry for what I'd done.

  (Survivor: "He said he knew he had problems and he wanted to change.")

- I cried to her.

  (Survivor: "I believed him.")

- I promised to change my ways.

  (Survivor: "It got better for a while.")

- I promised to go to drug and alcohol treatment.

  (Survivor: "He looked up class times online and they all conflicted with his schedule. Well, he tried.")

- I promised to go to counseling.

  (Survivor: "But how could a square doctor understand our lifestyle? I didn't want him to subject himself to that kind of judgment, so I insisted he didn't.")

- I blamed the abuse on stress.

  (Survivor: "I thought, We are going through a lot right now. It will get better soon.")

- I romanced her with flowers, took her shopping, talking about all the good times and how much she meant to me.

  (Survivor: "I thought, This is how things are supposed to be . . . if only I'd start acting right.")

- I arranged for us to take a romantic trip together to get back on track.

  (Survivor: "We went to Mexico on a week's vacation." "He took me and the kids to Disneyland.")

- I made her think she needed to stick with me because of all I gave up to be with her.

  (Survivor: "I reminded myself, People in love stick it out through rough times. You don't just give up.")

- I made her feel sorry for me and convinced her that her love could change me.

  (Survivor: "I believed our love was that strong.")

- If she didn't have children, I'd introduce her to mine and tell her I wanted a family with *only* her because she was special.

(Survivor: "I believed our situation was different. I am different from other girls.")

- I'd give her a night off and rent movies and spend quality time to convince her that I cared.

(Survivor: "I thought, This is how life will be when we finally have enough money.")

ABOUT THE BENDERS

Today, Rebecca, with the support of her husband, Matt, dedicates her life to help women go after the call of God regardless of their past. She founded the Rebecca Bender Initiative (RBI), using trainings, speeches, books, curricula, films, and other media to change the culture's view of sex for sale. RBI also is the founder of Elevate Academy, the largest online school in the world for survivors of the commercial sex industry, helping these women to explore new careers and professional development. The RBI speaking team has trained over one hundred thousand first responders and community professionals, including the FBI, Homeland Security, undercover police officers, local police departments, medical professionals, lawyers, judges, and district attorneys, as well as leaders in faith communities, domestic-violence services, and homeless-youth shelters across America. Elevate Academy has empowered over six hundred survivors to go after their dreams and is coming alongside to equip and empower them along the way. It continues to grow monthly and is now helping all women go after the call of God, regardless of their past.

Deshae Wise, Rebecca's daughter, is now attending UC Berkeley on a track scholarship. She was named one of Oregon's all-time greatest athletes, breaking over twenty-five records during her high school career and solidifying herself as the second fastest female hurdler in Oregon's history. She has been accepted into Haas, Berkeley's business school, and is interested in social justice issues, including prison reform and combatting gender and racial inequality. She has been featured in *Sports Illustrated*.

Rebecca has worked or consulted on some of the largest legal cases across America, including the Sherri Papini case in Redding, California, the Long Island Serial Killer case, *State of Oregon v. Javeion Drum, State of Oregon v. Ahmanda Parke, State of Oregon v. Virgil Rucker, State of California v. Herbert Goodwin, Jr.,* and *State of California v. Jonathan Boyd.* Rebecca received a special-operations, all-access pass to assist police in Minneapolis during Super Bowl 2018, working both on the undercover locations as a victims' advocate and participating at command post as an advisor. She also assisted *Dateline* in an undercover operation in Houston during Super Bowl 2017.

Rebecca serves on the United States National Advisory Committee to Health and Human Services, the Presidential Advisory Council, and is also on Oregon's Department of Justice Human Trafficking Advisory Committee. She is the recipient of the Unlikely Hero Award, Female Overcomer Award, Equiano Award, and Hero to Our Generation Award, and has received special FBI recognition and congressional recognition.

Rebecca is now focusing on preaching and writing more Bible studies with her degree in Christian Thought, so she can bring humor, edge, and biblical truth to today's issues. She is thankful to have moved beyond simply sharing her story to embracing the talents and gifts that had been dormant for far too long. Learn more about Rebecca at www.rebeccabender.org.

NOTES

Chapter 1: Vice Night

15 "Then I passed by": Ezekiel 16:6

Chapter 2: The Romeo Effect

30 "But the serpent said": Genesis 3:4 ESV

Chapter 3: The Slammer

45 "Stand firm": Galatians 5:1

Chapter 4: No Easy Exits

61 "Be alert and of sober mind": 1 Peter 5:8

Chapter 5: Home from Jail

72 "So let God work": James 4:7–10 MSG

Chapter 6: Rock Bottom

79 "Truly I tell you": Matthew 21:31

Chapter 7: Delivered

87 "Charm is deceptive": Proverbs 31:30

YOU'VE READ THE BOOK.
NOW, JOIN THE PURSUIT.

Fight trafficking by changing culture in areas of **government**, **social impact**, and **faith**.

Connect with us today!
rebeccabender.org/donate-learn-more